At the turn of the century, Main Street, Chelsea could double as the Main Street for any small village in the USA. This photo was taken sometime before 1910. The first house on the left served as the town's first hospital. The post office, built during the Depression, now sits on the site.

Courtesy Chelsea Area Historical Society

Sleeping Bear Press
310 North Main Street
P.O. Box 20
Chelsea, MI 48118
www.sleepingbearpress.com

Printed and bound in Canada.

10 9 8 7 6 5 4 3 2 1

Library of Congress Cataloging-in-Publication Data on file
ISBN: 1-58536-000-7

Our Hometown

America's History, As Seen through the Eyes of a Midwestern Village

Cynthia Furlong Reynolds

*Portions of the proceeds from the sale of this book will benefit
the Chelsea Community Foundation and the Purple Rose Theatre Company.*

Sleeping Bear Press

This book is dedicated

to the people of Chelsea, Michigan,
who opened their hearts and shared their stories...

to the people of a thousand villages, hamlets, towns and
farms throughout the Midwest, whose stories are very similar...

to everyone, everywhere, who ever lived in a Hometown...

and especially, to those who have wished for their own Hometown.

Chelsea, Michigan, is just a small dot on an Interstate map until you get out of your car, take off your headphones, shed your baggage, pull up a chair in Pierce's Pastries Plus and share a cup of hot chocolate and memories with the people who live here.

Chelsea is proud of its four-star generals, resident movie star, former advisor to the World Bank, missionary to China, ambassador to Czechoslovakia, ill-fated *Titanic* passenger, entrepreneurs, sire to the Lone Ranger's Silver!, and the village's connections to a pizza mogul. But it is equally proud of the people whose names haven't graced history books or newspaper headlines. If you change the names in this book and then look closely at cherished tintypes and graying photographs, you might see your face or the face of your father, or your grandmother, or a friend. If you walk through the mossy aisles of the local cemeteries or the spic-and-span aisles of the Chelsea Market, you'll find people you know—or wish you knew.

This book tells the story of an ordinary, and very extraordinary, Hometown.

From the Author

The best journalists serve not as interpreters or commentators, but as mirrors, reflecting in word pictures the faces and events they encounter. To do that well, the pictures must be painted with true colors and with all the beauty, blemishes, comedy, pathos, joys, sorrows, and details accurately portrayed. That can be a daunting job, but it brings great rewards if the writer can bring herself—or himself—to stand outside the frame of that mirror and observe without intrusion or participation.

I did my best to serve as a mirror to this town, whose story was captured at an extraordinary moment in its history. Chelsea is one of the few quintessential Midwestern towns still intact, with a flourishing downtown, fifth- and sixth-generation shopkeepers, a relatively prosperous farm community and a strong history of self-sufficiency. It lies close enough to cities to give it contact with urban amenities, but far enough away to remain relatively untainted by suburban sprawl—yet.

Although Chelsea's date of settlement has officially been pinpointed as 1834, its origins are actually far more ancient. New England served as the launching pad for many of the earliest pioneers, but Chelsea also shares strong ties to post-Revolutionary New York State, nineteenth century Germany, Alsace-Lorraine, and Celtic Ireland. Within Chelsea's cemeteries are buried hundreds of World War I and II veterans, more than 100 Civil War veterans, dozens of War of 1812 veterans, and even a handful of Revolutionary War patriots. Through the memories and stories captured by the people of this town, Chelsea tells its own version of America's history, as it affected the village and was enacted within its boundaries.

Life in this Michigan village is still vibrant, which is surprising in an age of sprawling bedroom communities and suburban spread, megamalls and computer-based sales. Customers who walk over the thresholds of the town's nineteenth century Italianate storefronts are served by a surprising number of fourth-, fifth-, and sixth-generation shopkeepers. Many of their best customers are farmers whose roots extend back more than a century and a half in southeast Michigan's soil. But change is banging on Chelsea's door. Just as the names and faces are beginning to change on school rolls and tax rolls, so too are the traditional ways of life in a small Victorian village. "We're on the brink of a future that is very different—and very threatening—to people who have lived here all their lives," observes Kathleen Clark, president of the Chelsea Area Historical Society and a major contributor to this book. She's right.

When I was asked to write this book, I was given one name as a starting point: attorney John Keusch, who was born in the first decade of the twentieth century and who retains memories sharper and more detailed than most people half his age can claim. His remembrances gave this book its backbone and I am more grateful to him than I can say.

After studying the fine histories that had been written by native-born Chelsea residents for the 125th and 150th anniversary of the town's founding, I realized that a new history of Chelsea couldn't and shouldn't compete with the facts, figures, and dates offered in those detailed chronologies. What I needed to do was paint the portrait of the people themselves: why they came here, what they did here, what life is—and especially was—like, how Chelsea's people had influenced and had been influenced by world events. I wanted to know what made Chelsea different from any other place in America and what made Chelsea representative of every other small town in America.

When I left the first of many interviews with Mr. Keusch, I turned to Sue Starkey at the Chamber of Commerce for my initial list of contacts, all of whom would prove invaluable. Ann Feeney, director of the Downtown Development Authority, loaned me my first armful of historical sources and Jackie Frank offered me my first tour of an historical Chelsea home, and names of additional people I should contact. One cool and rainy autumn afternoon I discovered three treasures within the Historical Society headquarters at the Depot: Kathleen Clark, president of the society and a fine writer herself; Marjorie Hepburn, long-time sustaining member; and Kim Myles, president of Preservation Chelsea. Sandy Shultz of the Chelsea Milling Company went far out of her way to assist me in acquiring information and photographs. So did Donna Lane of Lane Animal Hospital and Katie Wagner and her daughter Sis, who introduced me to the archives of the Chelsea Library.

In the course of researching this book, I spoke with or read the memoirs of more than 80 residents and past residents—and I wish that time and space had been available to interview many more. Each had a unique and intriguing story to tell.

Every word of my multitude of manuscripts and rewrites has been read and reread countless times by both John Keusch and Kathleen Clark, who enriched the story of Chelsea every time they offered a comment. Marjorie Hepburn also put in long hours studying my first official draft.

And Claude Sears Rogers, a Chelsea native born in 1912, served as one of my finest editors. But that isn't to say that any errors, either of omission or commission, are their responsibility. The strengths of this book are all due to them. The mistakes are all unintentional, but all mine. And, I hope, they are few and far between.

Others outside Chelsea contributed substantially to this book. My family endured long months watching my hands fly over computer keys, listening to me mumble to myself about chapter organization, or climbing over enormous stacks of papers. Poet and novelist Laura Kasischke, who lives in Chelsea, edited my copy and encouraged me on my way, as did a friend, Anne Vollbrecht. They helped answer my questions of "Should I?" or "Shouldn't I?," dotted some I's and crossed some T's. I am very grateful to them.

Most of all, I am extremely grateful to Sleeping Bear Press for offering me the chance to fulfill a long-time dream.

Contents

The Silhouette Against the Landscape

Clang! Clang! Clang!

The sound of the bell ringing from the tower of the Sylvan Town Hall cut into the cold, clear night on March 25, 1895. The Frank P. Glazier family—Frank and Henrietta, their four young children and Grandmother Emily Glazier—were comfortably gathered in their grand Victorian mansion on South Street, leisurely making their way toward bed when they heard the alarm. Almost immediately, the clamor of the bell was joined by the squeal of the Electric Light Company's whistle, alerting Chelsea's citizens to the danger posed at their doorsteps.

Fire!

Not an unusual occurrence in the days of wooden buildings, wooden shake roofs, wood-burning stoves, soot-clogged chimneys, and coal-burning trains that routinely belched smoke and cinders as they charged through town. Still, the joint alarm was a sound that caused every citizen, from babies snoozing in cradles to elderly men and women dozing in their beds, to gasp, sit up, listen, and sniff the air before dashing to their front doors.

A year ago, the chorus of whistle and bell had sounded a wake-up call for Frank Porter Glazier, owner of the Glazier Stove Works, manufacturers of the "Brightest and Best" oil- and kerosene-burning stoves. That fire had destroyed the Glazier office building, two stores used for mounting and storing stoves, and the nearby Congregational Church and parsonage. The smoke and flames from the "nightmarish conflagration" had billowed into the sky and could be seen for miles around the sleepy Midwestern village, past cultivated fields, through wooded copses and over barns. Farmers living miles away had jumped onto their horses, urging them into full gallop to dash to the scene of

One of several fires suffered by the Glazier Stove Works took place February 18, 1894. The following day, Chelsea residents turned out to survey the smoldering ruins on Main Street; this is now the site of Johnson's How-To Hardware.
Courtesy Chelsea Area Historical Society

the fire, fearful that the entire town would disappear in the flames.

But certainly not this time…

Still, as his family looked at him anxiously, Frank P. Glazier began pulling on his overcoat, hat, and gloves. He could hear slamming doors, the shouts of neighbors, the sucking sounds of men running through the thick, gelatinous mud that was South Street. He would join them. Just to be sure.

Bam! Bam! Bam!

As Glazier reached for the doorknob, feet pounded up the wide front steps and onto the porch.

"Mr. Glazier! Mr. Glazier! It's the factory again!" shouted a familiar voice with an Irish lilt.

～

The fire had started in the tin shop on the corner of Main and North streets. That building, along with the stove-testing plant and a large warehouse, burned right down to the ground. No one was injured, although several of the town's volunteer firemen suffered from the effects of smoke inhalation the next morning.

As soon as night became morning, an army of men went to work clearing away the smoldering debris. Meanwhile, a crew of carpenters was ordered to haul lumber to an open space on Glazier's industrial ground, then swing hammers, pound nails and erect a temporary frame building. Quickly.

"We have a large number of orders which must be filled and it is expected that this factory will be turning out stoves again within 10 days," Frank P. Glazier announced to the town.

～

Three days after the fire, the *Chelsea Herald* published a front-page article revealing that Mr. Glazier estimated the losses from this fire at $50,000, "on which there is $31,000 insurance," the newspaper reported, meticulously listing all the insurance carriers involved: North British, $3,300; Commercial Union, $2,500; Aetna, $8,000; Manchester, $1,000; Orient, $2,500; Liverpool, London & Globe, $3,300; Home, $2,500; German, $2,275; Germania, $2,550; Continental, $2,000; Rockford, $1,500; Northwest, $2,000; Grand Rapids, $1,000; Fireman's Fund, $1,500.

No issue exists indicating that Glazier's own *Chelsea Standard* went to press that week to supply additional details.

≈

Young children and old men had cast furtive glances at the elegantly attired gentleman silhouetted against the cold night sky on Monday, March 25, 1895, watching soot-faced men wave fire hoses at the gigantic flames engulfing his buildings and seeing others tossing buckets of water on nearby roofs. The townspeople had wondered what the square, self-contained Frank Porter Glazier was thinking as he watched his financial empire, the largest manufacturing plant in Chelsea—and one of the largest in the state of Michigan—go up in smoke.

Unbeknownst to them, he was already planning how the phoenix would rise from the flames.

It was time to bring his imprint to bear on this sleepy old village.

Forever.

PRESIDENTS
Andrew Jackson, 1829-37 • Martin Van Buren, 1837-41
William Henry Harrison, 1841 • John Tyler, 1841-45
James K. Polk, 1845-49 • Zachary Taylor, 1849-50
Millard Fillmore, 1850-53 • Franklin Pierce, 1853-57
James Buchanan, 1857-61

James Monroe, framer of the U.S. Constitution and 5th President, dies, 1831 • Charles Carroll, last surviving signer of the Declaration of Independence, dies, 1832 • The word "Socialism" appears in French and English circles • General Lafayette dies, 1834 • Abraham Lincoln enters politics, 1834 • Mark Twain is born, 1835 • Battle of The Alamo, 1836 • Michigan becomes a state, 1837 • James Fenimore Cooper's The *Pathfinder* is bestseller, 1841 • Revolts break out in Poland, 1846 • Austrian, Russian troops enter Cracow, 1846 • Irish Potato Famine, 1846 • Revolt in Paris, 1848 • Revolutions in Vienna, Venice, Berlin, Milan, Parma, 1848 • Serfdom abolished in Austria, 1848 • California Gold Rush, 1848 • Revolts in Dresden and Baden, 1849 • Hungarian Diet proclaims independence, 1849 • Harriet Beecher Stowe's *Uncle Tom's Cabin* published, 1852 • Samuel Colt revolutionizes manufacture of small firearms, 1853 • War of "Bleeding Kansas" between slave and free staters, 1854 • Walt Whitman writes *Leaves Of Grass*, Henry Wadsworth Longfellow writes *Song of Hiawatha*, 1855 • Financial and economic crises rage throughout Europe, 1857 • France declares war on Austria, 1859 • Abraham Lincoln elected 16th president and South Carolina secedes in protest, 1860

U.S. POPULATION
1830: 12.8 million • 1840: 17 million
1850: 23 million including 3.2 million slaves

The Beginning

In the beginning was the land.
And the land was rich and fertile and beautiful.
The relentless advance and retreat of continental glaciers over millions of years had worked the soil until it was fine, and then shaped and molded the land, forming gently rolling hills, broad flat plains, and deep spring-fed lakes.

Within the area that would one day become Chelsea and its necklace of townships were fields of sandy loam, marl deposits, wet and rich bog lands, as well as fertile clays that retained water, ensuring that crops might survive in times of drought. Scattered over the land were vast trees, some of them four feet in diameter. The combination of hickory, white oak, sugar maple, tamarack, elm, beech, white ash, black walnut, and black cherry trees created almost a park-like setting. This was a beautiful, civilized-looking country long before settlers with European last names came to claim and break the land.

Later, agronomists estimated that one-third of this land was tillable clay; one-quarter was fertile, sandy soil; one-third was a gravelly loam. "The rest doesn't lend itself to agriculture," they concluded, referring to the swamps and lakes. Over and over again, newspapers throughout the years would acknowledge the community's dependence on the land. On July 31, 1879, for instance, the *Chelsea Standard* noted, "The wheat crop this year will go a long ways toward deciding the financial problem. After all, the money must come out of the ground."

Deer, wild turkeys, prairie chickens, and geese prospered on this ground, thanks to the abundant grass that offered pasture. Wolves prowled in packs. Healthy populations of red and gray foxes, rabbits, opossums, ducks, raccoons, and otters dug their burrows here. The waters held abundant schools of fish. Maples brimmed with a sugary sap in late winter. Wild strawberry plants covering entire fields yielded effortless crops in the spring. Berry bushes offered lavish harvests in summer and fall. Trees buzzed with bees, signaling hidden stores of honeycomb.

The first European to investigate the area was the French explorer Sieur de La Salle, who arrived in 1680 and followed a well-used Indian trail that started near present-day Island Lake in Lyndon Township and ended eight or nine miles later at the Huron River, where Mill Creek joins the river in what would become the village of Dexter.

Countless other Indian trails crisscrossed the area. For 10,000 years, the Algonquin-speaking Ottawa, Chippewa, and Potawatomi had camped along the streams, hunted in the forests, and planted cornfields in the meadows. But, by the 1820s, they were restless, searching for lands farther from white settlers. The remnants of their cornfields remained for another half century, the only monuments to the Native American's presence.

A few other adventurers and fur traders may have followed in La Salle's footsteps, but the area wasn't officially opened to settlement until 1805, when Congress organized the Michigan Territory. At first, there was little activity or interest in southern Michigan because of the difficulty of crossing the Great Lakes and the extensive swamplands here. Then, in 1818, *Walk-on-the-Water* was launched on Lake Erie. The first steamboat to make the voyage between Buffalo and Detroit opened up the new frontier by providing a highway for New Englanders and farmers from New York State who wanted a fresh start, more land, and better land. Pioneers began venturing into the Michigan Territory.

~

All of America seemed to be on the move in the 1820s, 1830s, and 1840s. Young families, individual fortune seekers and older couples left the banks of the Penobscot, Kennebec and Merrimac rivers in Maine and Massachusetts, the hill towns of New Hampshire and Vermont, the industrial centers of New England, and the less fertile fields of Connecticut and western New York State for the West.

At one time, 3,000 boats operated on Lake Erie between Albany and Buffalo, offering passage to pioneers, who could then transfer to steamboats bound for Detroit. The steamers left Buffalo morning and evening, charging $8 for individual fares, 38 cents per hundredweight of goods, and 50 cents for barrels, bulk goods, or furniture. The other option was the land route from Buffalo to Detroit via Cleveland and Sandusky. The stagecoach charged $35 for the trip, but could carry few possessions.

After disembarking in Detroit, some of those early pioneers walked west alongside ox-drawn wagons, often following the Huron River. Others paddled their way inland up the Huron River's waters. The first to arrive in southeast Michigan were natives of New England villages or New York State farms. A few were aging Revolutionary War veterans. Many had fought for their country during the War of 1812. Almost without exception, they were Americans, born and bred, who were making a second—or third—start in life.

Governor Lewis Cass christened and mapped Washtenaw County in 1822, dividing the area into 40 townships, but he left no explanation for the name. Some legends suggest that "Washtenaw" was the name of a wise, elderly Indian who lived here. Others believe it is a Potawatomi corruption of "Washington." Still others insist that it means "large stream or river" in the Algonquin language, although nineteenth-century historian Emerson Greenman insisted that "Washtenaw" means "far country" in Algonquin.

By 1825, the entire population in the county amounted to 1,500 souls; nine years later, it had mushroomed to 4,000. Ypsilanti was established in 1822, Ann Arbor in 1823. Dexter was settled in 1824 and platted in 1830. Saline was platted in 1830, but not incorporated until after the Civil War. Manchester too would wait until after the Civil War for official status.

∼

According to tradition, Cyrus Beckwith was the first settler in the Chelsea area. He set up camp in what would later become Sylvan Township on October 18, 1830, with "an employee" named William BeGole, who helped him erect a hasty log cabin. Both men immediately began clearing fields for farms.

A year later, Jesse Smith and Elias H. Kelly settled nearby. In 1832, Charles Henry Depew became the fifth white man to arrive in the area, settling on the north side of what would become Territorial Road (Old U.S. 12), west of what is now M-52 and across from the Chelsea Fairgrounds.

Depew built a substantial—even grand, by standards of the day—log cabin on 120 acres. No doubt the rooms were often filled

A log cabin built on 120 acres of land by early Chelsea pioneer Charles Henry Depew was captured on canvas by Phoebe McMillen, a descendent of Depew.

Courtesy Chelsea Area Historical Society

with tired travelers, but they also served as a community center for the new area. A Jacksonian Democrat, Depew had been active in politics in New York State and he maintained his interest in the new territory. Because of his fluency in the Algonquin language, he was appointed to a commission regulating Indian affairs and his cabin became a courthouse where he settled disputes between Native Americans and white settlers. Decades later, one of Depew's nine children, Mrs. Robert Foster, told tales of hosting as many as 200 Indians at a time in the yard of the old homestead.

One of the most visible and frequent of the Native Americans living in the area at that time was Okemos, nephew of Pontiac, chief of the Potawatomis. Early settlers remarked on his "cloven skull" (cracked by a tomahawk in battle), his fine horsemanship, and the long train of women and ponies that followed him in single file, laden with mocock, Indian sugar, when he went trading for traps and "edibles." According to the *History of Washtenaw County, Michigan, Illustrated*, printed in 1881, "Even the females of the early settlers were quite willing to allow the old Chief, with his numerous progeny, a quiet smoke by the fireside, or a wabunk upon the kitchen floor, as an offset for the convenience of this traveling market of suceasee and pokamin (venison and cranberries)…for the Chief was merchant, as well as governor, judge, jury, and the general depository of the secrets of his tribe."

Minor Rose and his family became fast friends with Okemos and his son, John. These New York State natives had settled on land in Lyndon Township at what would later become known as "Cheese Factory Corners," an area that had once been the hunting grounds for Chief Okemos. One year, shortly after the Roses established their farm, the band of Potawatomis camped on the grounds to tend to one of the chief's daughters, who was fatally ill. She died and was buried there, attended by the Roses. They erected a fence around the grave, and planted lilacs beside the fence.

According to a 1932 newspaper clipping, the last time the Roses saw the Potawatomis, in 1840, the Indians were being escorted out of the state by soldiers. The men were bound by ropes and riding in wagons, the teary-eyed women and children walked on foot or rode ponies. Minor Rose often told of how his mother ordered the officers to release the Indians so she could feed them her family's "warm biscuits and butter and a good boiled dinner." Her own family went hungry until she could cook another meal.

Over the years, the story of the Indian princess faded into legend. And then the original Rose home was demolished and another built nearby. When men dug the foundation, they discovered the bones of the young woman.

≈

Depew's neighbors and close friends were Nathan and Darius Pierce, who left Ontario County, New York, to settle in Michigan on 640 acres. Nathan established a hamlet named Pierceville on the land where Old U.S. 12 now intersects Manchester Road. At the other end of the future village of Chelsea, in the area that now comprises Veterans' Park and Weber Fields, Darius Pierce founded a settlement he named Kedron.

The name Kedron is based on the Biblical story that tells how Christ crossed the stream in the valley of Kedron outside Jerusalem on the evening of Maundy Thursday. In the nearby Garden of Gethsemane, he rested and prayed and later was betrayed there. Explains attorney Peter Flintoft, "The place on Letts Creek (North Main Street at the site of the Donna Lane residence) was named Kedron by teamsters who drove oxen on the trail between Adrian and Unadilla (believe it or not), which were the two transit points before the railroad arrived. The pull up the big sand hill (South Main) would tire the oxen, so the teamsters would water their animals in the stream and rest on the north side. Thus came the name of the place—crossing over a stream to rest. The name Kedron remained for postal purposes until the 1850s."

The oldest known house in Sylvan Township is the Hiram Pierce House, built in 1831 by the area's first settler. Located on Old U.S. 12, near M-52, this was the centerpiece of Pierceville, the earliest settlement in the area to boast a post office. Courtesy Chelsea Area Historical Society

Meanwhile, a cluster of families from Addison County, Vermont brought their weary oxen and children to rest on lands just south of the Pierce and Depew holdings. Very little is known of the settlers' backgrounds, but conditions in that section of Vermont must have encouraged a major exodus to the west in the early 1830s. William A. Davis, Truman Lawrence, and Orlo H. Fenn were the first to arrive. They were soon joined by former neighbors Daniel and Tully Fenn, Amos Davis, Dennis Warner, Mahlon Wines, Ira Spaulding, his son Ira, and their families. Local histories make no mention of the names of their wives, who also suffered the hardships of the journey and the early pioneering years. In time, the cluster of farmsteads they estab-

An enterprising photographer climbed the Clock Tower to capture Main Street as it meandered north of town, past the spot where the village of Kedron was established on Letts Creek. Courtesy of Larry Chapman

lished became known as the Vermont Colony. A small cemetery was consecrated in 1832 for the small band of friends and neighbors who committed their futures together. It still rests in peace, but now it faces M-52, south of Chelsea.

In 1837, the year that Michigan became a state, Martin Keusch, great-grandfather of George Staffan and John Keusch, acquired 160 acres in Freedom Township on the south shores of Pleasant Lake. The remains of his log house were visible as late as the 1920s, when both George and John were boys.

An early account of the frontier life these settlers faced, published in the *Lakota Journal,* explains how pioneering families survived miles away from stores, shops, or mills:

The family ate onions, plums, strawberries, blackberries and cranberries, honey and nuts. There were no matches, so they obtained fire from flint stones and for light burned cloths soaked in deer tallow.

They made maple sugar, mined honey bee trees for their sugary wealth, burned corn cobs to get soda, drank sage tea and used partridges rather than chickens for meat pies. Animals they hunted were deer and wild turkey. Also around were wolves and bears. The bears loved little pigs and they had to be protected in high, fenced places. One reason pigs were raised was that they were immune to the bites of the many snakes in Michigan. To get flour, the pioneers went to the large cities like Detroit to buy it. They took their sheep wool and traded for groceries.

The pioneers not only faced dangers from bears, but also from wolves, who roamed in packs, threatening the larger livestock. In one night a wolf pack could—and too often did—wipe out a farmer's entire herd of livestock, often his entire livelihood.

But despite the hardships, in 1834 there were enough settlers in this part of the county to hold an election and form a local government. The township was named Sylvan at the suggestion of a well-read pioneer's wife who explained that "sylvan" means woodland. Three years later, Lyndon was organized into a township and its settlers built the first licensed schoolhouse in western Washtenaw County.

The pioneers' reasons for coming to the area were as varied as their backgrounds.

Three young brothers, Selah, Josiah, and Harrison Collins, came to put down roots and establish farms and families. They arrived in 1833 and became Lyndon's first settlers. According to the *History of Washtenaw County, Michigan, Illustrated*, the Collins brothers "cut a stack of hay that summer, and in November following built the first house…Although but a simple log house, its construction was no little of an undertaking, as brick, lime and boards—everything needed for it except the logs—had to be hauled from Ann Arbor." As soon as his house was complete, Selah Collins was married and the newlyweds moved into the house. "Thus was effected the first settlement."

Samuel Boyce must have had a bit of wanderlust. He and his wife Sarah Cutter Boyce moved from Woburn, Massachusetts to Steuben County, New York, where he established a farm on 50 acres. Their first seven children were born there, but something made the Boyces decide to move westward once again. They settled in Lyndon Township, where their last two children were born. According to family tradition, Samuel Boyce was a huge man, standing six-foot-eight-inches tall and weighing 300 pounds "without being fat" when he settled on 160 acres of land. Michigan must have suited him; at the time of his death in 1875, he weighed 350 pounds.

Charles Glenn was a pioneer in search of a new start. A farmer living in north-central New York State, he left the farm one day in 1831 for a few hours with his young son Benjamin and returned to discover that his farmhouse had burned to the ground and his young wife and two babies had died when a candle's flame ignited the flax that his wife had been spinning. A nephew, William Burkhardt, had narrowly escaped by leaping from an upper-story window. The next year, Charles Glenn convinced his two brothers and their families, as well as his Burkhardt and Bignall relatives, to join him in starting all over again. They, like the Vermont Colony settlers, formed a wagon train and headed west.

The Winans—whose name was originally spelled "Winant" —moved from the Finger Lakes of New York in search of richer land than what they were farming. They arrived in 1834, about the time Joel B. Boyington, John M. Cummings, Arnold Bell, Thomas and Isaac Godfrey, Adonijah Godfrey, M. Mecalf, John Jewett, Samuel Dunham, Ashael Backus and two brothers, James and Elisha Congdon, also purchased land in the Sylvan Township area.

Elisha and James Congdon, founders of Chelsea.

Courtesy Chelsea Area Historical Society

Elisha and James Congdon were the men who would be most intimately connected with the early days of Chelsea. Connecticut natives, they came in pursuit of a more prosperous life than the one they had known in the relatively ancient and industrial town of Norwich. Heading west together in 1833, they followed the route that many Michigan pioneers had taken and would continue to take. They crossed New York State on the Erie Canal, then boarded a boat bound for Detroit, where they purchased a team of oxen and a wagon and headed west.

The *History of Washtenaw County, Michigan, Illustrated,* published several years after Elisha's death, mentions only James Congdon, but the background pertains to both brothers:

Hon. James M. Congdon, one of the owners of the original plat of Chelsea village, was born in New London County, Conn., March 23, 1805, and is a son of Elisha and Abigail (Miner) Congdon. James was seven years old when his father was killed by a falling building, and the bereaved widow was left with 8 small children to provide for. The family were poor, and were obliged to seek employment in a cotton mill. At 16 years of age Mr. Congdon learned the carpenter's trade, and subsequently that of a machinist, being employed in the latter business until his twenty-eighth year. In 1833 he came to Michigan…

Elisha, the older and apparently more strong-willed brother, bought 160 acres of government lands that ranged between the tiny settlements of Pierceville and Kedron. James bought 300 acres adjacent to his brother's, directly to the west. "They must have come with some money, because they purchased large chunks of land," Merle Barr, a Congdon descendent, speculates.

The Congdons had a lot of country to choose from in 1834, so at first glance, their choice wasn't necessarily the best if they came intending to plant a village as well as a farm. The soil was rich and marshy enough for future onion fields and sandy enough for fine wheat crops, but the most essential element for a successful early settlement was missing. There was no river or lake to power a mill that would saw logs for new homes or grind grain for sustenance.

At first glance, nothing indicated that the Congdon holdings would be suited to nurturing a healthy, flourishing village. Nothing except Elisha Congdon's firm determination to make this place work.

"Chelsea exists because of the Congdons' commitment and because of surrounding swamps," Peter Flintoft says, explaining, "Early settlers called western Washtenaw County the 'land of the black swamps.' It was hard to pull a wagon through. Chelsea is a higher elevation and an easy place to cross the stream and get on to hard ground, south and north. The same is evident today. Look at the roads. All roads funnel into Main Street. Why? East and west are areas of swamp. All roads north of Chelsea parallel the east-west water and swamp courses—producing the twenty-first century traffic jams we have. When the railroad came to town, it took advantage of the same high ground. So you add the teamsters' route to the railroad and you get 'commerce.'"

≈

The Congdons had neighbors and passersby soon enough. By the 1840s, waves of newcomers were heading their way.

At this time, Europe was undergoing a tragic, tumultuous series of wars, revolts, epidemics, and upheavals. A terrifying cholera pandemic began in India in 1826, spread from Russia into Central Europe and reached Scotland in 1832. Whole villages were wiped out by the devastating illness. The resulting economic devastation encouraged those who survived to consider emigrating. The Kinsey family left Scotland in the mid-1830s and settled outside Chelsea on a farm.

In the mid-1840s, the Potato Famine hit Ireland and whole villages starved to death. Desperate to leave the horrors behind and start a new life, a staggering 924,000 people left Ireland between 1850 and 1860, bound for the United States. The Savages, Quigleys, Gormans, Flemings, Kennedys, Geraghtys, O'Connors, Cassidys, Burnses, Hagans, McIntees, Walshes, O'Neils, Marrianes, Morrisseys, Moans, Mullens, and McKunes all headed for Washtenaw County, Michigan.

In the early 1840s, Irish immigrants cleared and settled much of the land north and west of the Congdons' territory. "They passed over the lower areas in the south and east, which were not well drained, choosing instead the higher, more picturesque ground" John Keusch explains, adding, "However, with the passage of time, those lands to the south and east proved more fertile. The Germans settled in that direction."

The Irish organized a Catholic church in Sylvan Township at Mill Lake, three miles northwest of Chelsea. Once a month the priest from

Dexter arrived to serve mass. This church was abandoned when a Catholic parish was organized in Chelsea. Keusch recalls that the frame structure was destroyed by a fire of unknown origin, but the church yard is now the site of a large cemetery that boasts many Irish names. Among those buried there are the ancestors of Herbert J. McKune. John Looney's tombstone is decorated with an engraved locomotive, indicating that he was killed while serving as an engineer in a railroad wreck. "Many of the tombstones hold poetic descriptions, perhaps evidencing the poetic flair and literary bent for which the Irish are acclaimed," Keusch says. (He recalls his mother telling him that during her childhood after a burial men would stand guard over the grave site for several nights, in an effort to prevent robberies by men interested in providing cadavers for the University of Michigan Medical School.)

While Ireland was starving, Europe burst into flames—literally and figuratively—and the repercussions were felt as far away as the newly established state of Michigan.

Problems on the continent had been smoldering for years, but they began igniting in 1844, when an assassination attempt was made on the life of the Prussian King Frederick William IV. Catholics suffered from violent attacks in Switzerland. Revolts broke out in Poland. Austrian and Russian troops invaded Cracow. Vienna suffered through three revolutions in one year until Austrian statesman Klemens Metternich resigned and the emperor abdicated the throne in favor of his nephew. Revolts in Rome led to the assassination of the papal premier and the flight of Pope Pius IX from the Vatican. The Pan-Slav congress in Prague incited the Czechs to revolt. Sardinia declared war on Austria. Venice, Berlin, Milan, Parma, Dresden, and Baden all erupted in revolts.

As family members were killed, staggering taxes were imposed, crops were confiscated or destroyed by marching armies, and men were conscripted to fight in wars they knew nothing about, people from Germany, Austria, France, and Switzerland began a massive exodus to the nineteenth century's Promised Land.

Between 1820 and 1830, 15,000 Germans immigrated to the United States. Between 1830 and 1840, another 43,000 left their homeland. Between 1850 and 1860, the numbers swelled to an astounding 424,000. Among the emigrants were the Schenks, Eschelbachs, Blackwadles, Wiedemeyers, Wackers, Liebecks, Heims, Hellers, Keusches, and Kaerchers.

"The first Germans were mainly from Schwaben," Peter Flintoft says. "In that part of Germany, the local dialect ignores the gender declension of High German in the possessive sense, with the gender endings of *-es, -er, -en(-es)*, rather than *-le* attached to everything. This in time affected proper names. Therefore, you will find throughout this county a concentration of Aupprele, Bristle, Beuerle, Dietle, Dieterle, Diuble, Eisele, Fingerle, Jedele, Schaible, Schnearle, Schnierle, Stierle, Trinkle, etc."

According to Alton Grau, his great-great-grandparents fled from Prussia with their family in order to avoid military conscription. The Keusches and Staffans left Alsace-Lorraine, headed for Michigan. George Staffan, who was born in 1910, remembers that his grandfather could speak both French and German and that once he told his grandson his reason for leaving: "My homeland was torn between two countries and there would never be peace."

≈

By the 1850s, the Irish were beginning to cluster to the north and west of Chelsea. The *New Historical Atlas of Washtenaw County, Michigan*, published in 1874, notes that "Lyndon is populated by a mixed people, of whom about one-half are American; of the foreign population, the "sons of Eire" predominate. West of the Congdon holdings was a small settlement called Davidson Station, and later Gunntown, after a notorious local celebrity. Farther west was Grass Lake and Waterloo. Just to the north, Kedron was holding its own and Lyndon was flourishing. Down south, Sylvan was organized, Pierceville had a post office, and the Vermont colony had established a prosperous community. Farther south, the Germans were breaking land for farms around Rogers' Corners. To the east, clusters of New England families were forming tiny villages in Dexter and Scio, particularly along the Huron River.

At first, it looked as though the individual settlements dotting the countryside in western Washtenaw County would exist independently, separate and pretty much equal. Then along came the railroad.

One of the earliest photographs capturing life in Chelsea was taken at the time of the Civil War. Note the dress, substantial trees, and neatly painted picket fence.

Courtesy Chelsea Area Historical Society

A combination home, post office, and shop, this four-square building was the first structure Elisha Congdon erected in what would become the Village of Chelsea. He moved this structure into Chelsea's business section. Years later, the house was once again mounted on a wagon and transported south of town.

Courtesy Chelsea Area Historical Society

Imitation is the highest form of flattery, as Chelsea's founder realized. Elisha Congdon modeled his grand brick Georgian mansion after a house he greatly admired in Ann Arbor.

Courtesy Chelsea Area Historical Society

The railroad made location a critical issue, as Elisha Congdon instantly understood.

In 1836, 24 chartered railroads took on the task of laying 1,011 miles of track in Michigan, some of which would run through Washtenaw County. Land along projected railroad paths soared in value as settlers realized that the railroad would be the future lifeline for farmers and merchants. Elisha Congdon was determined that the railroad would come to him.

Congdon was a visionary and an entrepreneur with a very practical streak. He worried that the railroad wasn't accessible enough to his property because it stopped at the small, hastily constructed depot two miles away, at Davidson Station. The station burned down in 1848—historians would later speculate about what role Congdon played in this. They do know that he immediately offered the railroad a chunk of his land if a station were erected on his holdings and the railroad accepted.

By the early 1850s, James and Elisha Congdon must have been hard at work dividing their lands, at least on paper, into future streets and town lots. Unlike its neighbors—Stockbridge to the north, Dexter to the east, Manchester to the south, and Jackson to the west—this village has a narrow thoroughfare through town. The Congdons weren't concerned with designing broad avenues and incorporating parks. They were interested in getting down to business. And fast. The people who would move to Chelsea were people who were coming for economic opportunities and a fresh start in life. They would need to set up shop or establish a farm quickly and trade. To ensure the success of their big venture, the Congdons wanted to make sure that their village would be ready to welcome them.

The New Historical Atlas of Washtenaw County, Michigan, Illustrated, states that John C. Winans was the first person to join the Congdons within the town limits and then "the place settled up very rapidly." Shortly afterward, tinsmiths Reuben and C.H. Kempf joined the Congdons and Winans as principal landowners.

In 1850, Elisha's first home, a log cabin, burned to the ground and he built a frame house on the same knoll overlooking Main Street. At that time, the downtown businesses consisted of Winans' store, Congdon's store and a post office (Congdon served as post-master), doctor's office, blacksmith shop, and a sash and blind factory. When Congdon decided he didn't like the name Kedron, he convinced his neighbors to agree to change the name of their village from Kedron to Chelsea, after a pretty river landing outside the Congdons' home town of Norwich, Connecticut. By 1853, the population of the newly christened Chelsea numbered 63.

Shortly afterward, the town's founding father was doing well enough to build himself the house of his dreams. Known today by the name of its second owner, Timothy McKune, Congdon's home eventually became another resource for his village. A century after Congdon built his home, Mrs. McKune gave it to the town to house the library.

As time went on, Congdon offered acreage for public use to lure settlers to his village. He provided the land for the churches and for the school, or, perhaps, schools. No official records exist establishing the date of Chelsea's earliest school, but a family history written by Lois Palmer Moore states that in 1861, Elisha Congdon donated land for a "new" school to be built on the corner of what is now East and Park streets.

This photograph of Main Street, looking north, was taken before Frank Glazier began to put his architectural imprint on the town. Note the hitching posts, industrial smoke stack, windmill, and thriving business climate. Chances are good that the photographer

captured Main Street on a Wednesday or Saturday, when farmers and their families traditionally came into town.

Courtesy Chelsea Area Historical Society

"The school was first graded in 1868–69 under the supervision of Professor W. Cary Hill," according to Mrs. Moore. "He was a cultured, scholarly man who brought into this school, then on a level with schools in the county districts, a great deal of his own culture, and raised it to a higher plane."

≈

While all this was happening, the boundary that separated James' and Elisha's lands was becoming a major north-south thoroughfare and the Chelsea stretch offered special challenges to wagoners and travelers. Congdon's home sat on the largest sand mound in the region. Drivers of freight wagons, which ran regularly from Manchester to Stockbridge and back, had to unload half their freight at the foot of the hill, haul the remaining load up the hill, unload that at the top while their horses rested, and then return to the bottom for the first half. Over the years, shovelful by shovelful, the hill would be leveled.

Once the railroad moved its stop from Davidson Station to Chelsea and built a depot, settlers who had clustered around Davidson Station and Pierceville gradually began moving into town, to be nearer the post office, shops, railroad, and grist mill. "Eventually, every deed in the town of Chelsea would carry the Congdon name," Congdon descendent Merle Barr points out.

Elisha Congdon died in 1867. In the fall of 1870 and again in 1872, James Congdon was elected Representative to the State Legislature. After his service, according to the *History of Washtenaw County, Michigan, Illustrated*, printed in 1881, "he has devoted his time to the management of his estate, which comprises 300 acres of valuable land." James built a Queen Anne Victorian home on the south side of West Middle Street, one of his descendents, the late Larry Walz, told Chelsea Area Historical Society President Kathleen Clark.

Recently, while Merle Barr and his sister Virginia Visel were paging through family records, they discovered something they didn't know existed: a large fading photograph of an elderly and fierce-looking pioneer with a mane of white hair and a luxuriant white mustache who closely resembles the identified photograph of Elisha's son Arthur. On the back of the pioneer's picture, in spidery handwriting, is the inscription, "Property of Sarah Congdon." Sarah was Elisha's daughter. "This must be Elisha himself," the brother and sister now believe.

When they were children, an elderly great-aunt told them what she remembered about staying with her grandparents, Mr. and Mrs. Elisha Congdon, in the big brick house during the 1860s. The old school grounds (now the site of the School House Apartments) were part of Elisha's wheat fields, she said. And she also gave them one intriguing glimpse into the character of Chelsea's founding father.

Elisha remarried later in life in Chelsea and insisted that his grown children, evidently against their wills, attend his marriage to Elouisa Standish in the Congregational Church. "They did—but when the service began, they stood up and faced the back of the church in protest! Must have been quite a group!" Barr says in appreciation.

Elisha Congdon fathered 15 children as well as a town.

1861: Washington peace conference tries to preserve the Union, but congress of Montgomery forms Confederate States of America • Abraham Lincoln inaugurated as 16th president • Firing on Fort Sumter • Call to arms

1862: Union forces capture Fort Henry, Roanoke Island, Fort Donelson, Jacksonville, and New Orleans • Union armies defeated at second Battle of Bull Run, Fredericksburg • Emancipation Proclamation frees all slaves held in rebelling territories

1863: West Virginia splits from Virginia and becomes a U.S. State • Confederate victory at Chancellorsville, VA • Robert E. Lee defeated at Gettysburg, PA • Vicksburg, MS falls to Ulysses S. Grant • Confederate defeat at Chattanooga, TN• Confederate Victory at Chickamauga, GA • Lincoln's "Gettysburg Address" at dedication of the military cemetery

1864: Gen. Ulysses S. Grant succeeds Gen. Halleck as Union Army Commander-In-Chief • Gen. Wm. Tecumseh Sherman marches his army through Georgia, defeats Confederate Army at Atlanta, recaptures Savannah • President Lincoln re-elected

1865: Union Fleet captures Charleston, SC • Richmond, the confederate capital, surrenders to Grant • Jefferson Davis appoints Robert E. Lee General-In-Chief of Confederate Army • Confederate States of America surrender at Appomattox Apr. 9 • Abraham Lincoln assassinated Apr. 14, succeeded by Andrew Johnson • Jefferson Davis captured and imprisoned • U.S. Civil War ends May 26 with the surrender of the last Confederate Army at Shreveport, LA

U.S. POPULATION
32 million

The Civil War

In Search of History

On a bitterly cold January day, George Till pulls his winter coat close around him, stamps his feet in the snow to keep the circulation going, and sets off on his campaign to locate gravestones marking the final resting place of some of Chelsea's unsung Civil War heroes.

Brushing the snow off the surface of a granite stone in the Grass Lake cemetery, he says with satisfaction, "I knew he was here somewhere. This is the grave of John Powell, who is on the roster of the original 800 who enlisted in the 24th Michigan—the 24th was part of the famous Iron Brigade, you know."

Till has to lean close to the stone and trace some of its letters with his fingers to read:

John Powell
24th Michigan Infantry
Co. H.
Killed in the Battle of Gettysburg
July 4, 1863
Aged 27 years, 2 months, 2 days

This grave site particularly intrigues Till because Powell was killed in the first day's fighting at Gettysburg, and Till has stood beside his grave in the Gettysburg National Cemetery. "I haven't been able to discover whether his body was exhumed and moved here, or if the grieving family just erected a monument in his honor that they could visit," he says, reflectively.

Till pauses for a moment, then swings his arm in a northerly direction and adds, "Over there is a member of the Iron Brigade's cavalry. I need to do more research about him." Till estimates that there are more than 100 Civil War veterans buried in Chelsea or in cemeteries around Chelsea's outskirts. "A fair number of people who live here are related to those men."

George Till is a Civil War reenactor who serves in the reconstituted and renowned 24th Michigan. Some of his fellow reenactors assume the character and life of actual men who belonged to the brigade. "I don't. I'm not a fanatic—but even so, sometimes I feel as though I'm in a time warp," Till concedes. He serves as a private because, he explains, the 24th Michigan suffered 85 percent casualties, so there weren't many original officers left at the end of the war. And, as a private, he has served during the filming of two motion pictures dealing with the Civil War, *Glory* and *Gettysburg*, in which another Chelsea resident, Jeff Daniels, starred as Union officer Joshua Chamberlain. "I've heard a rumor that the sequel to *Gettysburg* will be filmed. I imagine we'll get a call about that, if it's true," he adds, as he continues his quest for fallen heroes in Chelsea cemeteries on this bleak winter day.

A preschool teacher by vocation and an historian by education and avocation, George Till moved to Chelsea 16 years ago and joined the 24th Michigan seven years later. Although most nineteenth century recruits from Chelsea joined Co. K, 20th Michigan, four native sons joined the 24th Michigan and countless others were scattered among other units. Local reenactors have focused their attention on

Chelsea's veterans who had served with Company K, 20th Michigan Infantry, during the Civil War gathered for a reunion in front of the Michigan Central Railroad Depot in 1900. Company K served as part of General Burnside's Ninth Corps early in the war.

Ann Arbor Federal Savings Village Book

the 24th because of the tremendous renown those soldiers acquired during the war, thanks to their participation in the famous Iron Brigade.

"Members of that brigade wore a very distinctive black hat and Confederates at the Battle of Fredericksburg were heard to remark, 'Here are those damned black-hat fellers again…'Tain't no militia—they're the Army of the Potomac,'" Till says. "The Iron Brigade was the Civil War's equivalent to the Green Berets."

One hundred other Civil War enthusiasts in this area join Till in the 24th Michigan's reenactments, one of them his neighbor, Bob MacLeod. Some purists use antique weapons, but most choose to shoot reproduction weapons because of safety issues. They all, however, dress authentically and camp on battlefields using nineteenth century equipment (authentic or reproduction) and foods.

The reenactors' movements are better scripted than some of the original battles and they will demonstrate historic moments (sometimes posing as members of other units), perform tactical movements, salute fallen soldiers in cemetery ceremonies, march in parades, and

Members of the illustrious 24th Michigan, which formed part of the famous Iron Brigade, gathered for a reunion during the commemoration of the Iron Brigade statue at Gettysburg. During the first day of fighting at Seminary Ridge, the Michigan 24th sent 496 men into battle; 399 were killed, wounded or missing by nightfall, among them some Chelsea residents. Their casualty list was the longest of any Union regiment that fought at Gettysburg.
Courtesy of Merle Barr

show a crowd something of what life was like in the Civil War, both in camp and on the battlefield.

One of the highlights every year for these part-time soldiers is the reenactment of the Battle of Gettysburg on the actual battlefield. The 24th Michigan reenactors join with Southern comrades, often members of the reconstituted 26th North Carolina, in staging one of the Civil War's many poignant moments that took place at Gettysburg—although the 24th wasn't there to see it. "The 26th North Carolina advanced farther than any other Confederate unit on the day of Pickett's Charge and a Union man held out his hand and said, 'Come to the side of the Lord, boys.' The Union troops didn't want to shoot such brave men and they took them prisoners," Till explains. "We play that scene for the crowd."

~

According to history books, the first Michigan regiments to leave for combat joined General Irvin McDowell's army in and around Washington, D.C., in the late spring of 1861. Michigan men—and several Michigan women dressed like men—participated in every major engagement of the Civil War.

Soon after Abraham Lincoln issued his call for soldiers, brothers, fathers, cousins, neighbors, and business associates living in Chelsea formed Co. K of the 20th Michigan Infantry. Elijah Hammond was elected captain. Elisha Congdon, son of Chelsea's founding father, was the company bugler. Nearly half the family names on the 1861 roll of the 20th can still be found in Chelsea: Ackley, Beeman, Bott, Brooks, Brownell, Canfield, Dancer, Doan, Franklin, Gorton, Hall, Hartigan, Horn, King, Leach, Lehman, McKenzie, McNally, Morton, Newton, Pierce, Prosser, Richards, Smith, Spencer, Swartout, Sweet, Thomas, Townsend, Tucker, Turnbull, Wallace, Ward, West, Widmayer (Wiedmier), and Williams.

Early in the war, the 20th Michigan served as part of General Burnside's Ninth Corps. In the summer of 1864, they fought at the Battle of Cold Harbor in Virginia and several weeks later helped besiege the city of Petersburg, Virginia, scene of the Battle of the Crater.

Pennsylvania coal miners dug a tunnel directly below the Confederate position at Petersburg and, on July 30, 1864, exploded four tons of powder, which sent earth, guns, carriages, earthworks, and men hurtling into the air, leaving an enormous crater, 170 feet long, 60 feet wide, and 30 feet deep. The Ninth Corps belatedly advanced and its soldiers were mired in the crater. The 20th Michigan was caught in terrible cross fire. A general's report later described what the Chelsea men faced:

The enemy had recovered from their surprise, and now concentrated so heavy a fire upon the point that our troops, in seeking temporary shelter, became still more mixed with each other and with the First Division, and lost their ranks and much of their regimental organization, in spite of the efforts of many of the officers, and every new regiment that marched into the breach only increased the huddle and confusion, and interfered (sic) with the officers in reforming for another advance.

This debacle cost Michigan 250 men, some of them from Chelsea.

Some time after Co. K, 20th Michigan was formed, the 24th Michigan Infantry was mustered into service. According to historian Frederick Williams, the 24th "was recruited in a hurry, drew most of its men from Wayne County and was honored by one of those florid ceremonies that usually attended a regiment's departure from Michigan." The 24th joined the Iron Brigade just after the Battle of Antietam in September 1862, and "the green Michigan soldiers had the awesome experience of marching across the battlefield, where shell-torn earth, charred buildings, splintered trees, a huge pile of amputated arms and legs, and freshly filled graves silently bespoke an epic to which they themselves would contribute gloriously," Williams writes in his book *Michigan Soldiers in the Civil War.*

One Michigan soldier wrote home describing what he saw:

It was a terrible sight to see the wagons coming in last night loaded with dead, cut, torn and mangled in every possible manner and the wounded running or hobbling along with arms & legs dangling or hanging by shreds or crawling on the ground dragging their limbs slowly after them crushed, broken, or torn off entirely.

The Michigan men got a cold reception from Iron Brigade veterans, but proved their worth two months later, at the Battle of Fredericksburg. There they earned the right to wear the headdress that had made the brigade famous. During the first day of fighting at Gettysburg, on the heights of Seminary Ridge, the Michigan 24th sent 496 men into battle; 399 were killed, wounded or missing by nightfall. Their casualty list was the longest of any Union regiment that fought at Gettysburg.

An extraordinary account of a Civil War soldier's life was penned by Orange Noah, who was 18 years old when he enlisted.

Courtesy of Ellis Boyce

Duane Noah of North Lake possesses the Civil War journal written by his great-grandfather, Orange Noah, as well as copies of William Noah's recollections of the war. The Boyce family, which married into the Noah family, cherishes copies of the same journal.

At the start of the war, Orange and Joshua Noah had enlisted in the 8th Michigan Infantry when Orange was 18, Joshua, 22. Later, they transferred to Co. D, U.S. Engineers. Together, they served in Pennsylvania, Maryland, Virginia, North and South Carolina, and Georgia. They took part in 15 major battles, including Beaufort, Pocataliga, the second battle of Bull Run, Kelly's Ford, Antietam, and South Mountain. The Noahs witnessed the sinking of the iron-clad *Merrimac* by the *Monitor* from aboard the *Vanderbilt*, the largest sailing vessel in the world at that time. They had been given three days' rations when they boarded the ship, but driven by storms and naval engagements, the ship took 21 days to land its starving, seasick soldiers on shore. Orange Noah's accounts make no note of the hardships, however. Just the facts.

In his pocket diary, which covers several volumes, Orange kept exact accounts of his clothing allotments, pay, loans to fellow officers, and daily activities. Some, with their staccato rhythm and short entries, illustrate the dreariness of camp life:

Monday, April 11, 1864. Battalion worked at rebuilding Corduroy near Culpepper. Signed Pay Rolls in the evening.

Tuesday, April 12, 1864. Companies C & D went to the Rapahannock and drilled Pontoon Drill. Was paid off in the afternoon. I was on garrison police.

Wednesday, April 13, 1864. I was a company police. I helped to repair Captain Turnbull's tent. Had Dress Parade. I received a letter from Mrs. Emeline Noah. I wrote a letter to Mrs. R.A. VanNess.

Thursday, April 14, 1864. Had Dress Parade. I mounted guard, was no.12 of 3rd relief. Lieutenant Howell was Officer of the day and the countersign was Ireland. I wrote a letter to Mr. Wm. H. Noah...

Other entries show the exacting and matter-of-fact way in which Orange Noah approached the daily grind of war. When he was far enough from the battlefield, he checked his pocket watch for accuracy and he also must have had access to maps because he carefully notes times and places. Readers need some behind-the-scenes information to understand that this soldier was in the thick of the action when he tersely wrote, in August 1863:

Went to a camp near Fredericks Burg the 7th...

Arrived at Barnetts Ford the evening of the 19th and camped one mile from the ford until the evening of the 20th when we went to Kelley Ford where we arrived at 12 o' clock that night. The next day at 12 o' clock we Forded the Rappihannhock River had a skermish and recrossed at evening and camped on the same ground for the night. The next morning we went to the Rappihannhock Station about six miles.

Our Division in line of battle that Aug. 22, the 23d. We went about 8 miles and stopped about 9 o' clock at night and Slept in the road until morning.

Sunday the 24th we marched to Sulpher Springs. The 25th we marched until 12 o' clock and rested until morning two miles from Warenton Junction. The 26th we went and about faced and marched back to Warrinton Junction, and from there to Manassas, and encamped that night in a large field; and I was on picket in a corn field that night.

We marched all day the 28th and encamped at night near Centerville. The 29th we went to Bull Run and was engaged in battle with the enemy and camped on the battle field at night.

Fought the next day and retreated back to Centreville that night. the 31st was on the advance. September 1st was engaged in the battle near Centreville…

At the end of that season's campaign, on October 25, 1862, Orange Noah enlisted in the U.S. Engineer Corps. The next summer he describes his new line of work. On July 28, he writes:

Left camp near Warrenton at 1 P.M. Marched 15 miles and encamped 2 miles west of Middleburg. Marched 15 miles and encamped near Rappahannock Station at 8½ P.M. Companies C & D turned out at 11 o' clock and unloaded a train of Pontoon boats and the Battalion turned out at day break to unload another train…

the 31st. Rations were sent to the detachment via the river road the distance of 5 miles.

Aug. 1. Train started to the ford at 6 P.M. and proceeded to construct the bridge eight boats in length. After being fired on by the rebel pickets—without injury, the bridge was finished at 12 n…Private James Rowan of Co. B was drowned at Kelley's ford August the 1st at ten P.M. and his corps(e) was found at 6 P.M. of the 2nd 1863…

Orange's brother Elmus also made "the ultimate sacrifice." While serving with his infantry in Beaufort, South Carolina, he contracted pneumonia and died.

Three years after his brothers enlisted, on August 24, 1864, William

Noah mustered into Co. D., 21st Michigan Volunteers—Infantry, 2nd Brigade, 1st Division, 14th Army Corps. He was 33 years old and the father of five children. Years later, he wrote a fascinating account of his service. William Noah was introduced to the realities of war a month after he was mustered into service:

Joining my Regiment, then stationed on Lookout Mountain, Tenn., on Sept. 27th, leaving the Mountain with the Regiment to take part in the pursuit of the Rebel Gen. (Nathan Bedford) Forrest then making a raid into our lines, to a point on the Tennessee River beyond Florence, Alabama, where he succeeded in crossing the River, thus escaping a battle and a probable defeat.

On November 1, 1864, Noah's unit received orders to join the 14th Army Corps under General William Tecumseh Sherman and advance on Atlanta. He later wrote:

Destroying railroads and other property that might be of any value to the enemy, we reached Atlanta on the 15th. After the destruction of that beautiful city on the day following we joined Sherman's Army for the Grand March from Atlanta to the Sea, its destination then unknown to all but Sherman…

The 21st Michigan arrived at the Rebel fortifications in front of Savannah on December 10 and occupied a position on the south side of the canal—"the most exposed position on the whole line," he remembered, describing how the men suffered from cold and hunger. The city surrendered without a fight and Sherman refused to put a match to it.

Noah's unit stayed outside Savannah until January 20, 1865, when the soldiers began to wind their way north, stopping at Sister's Ferry for 10 days while they went about "bridging and clearing timber from the road on the low lands on the opposite side of the River which the enemy had promiscuously felled across to retard our march, which it did, together with the help of high water."

He watched the city of Columbia, South Carolina go up in flames, helped destroy the railroad at Winnsboro, took part in a "sharp but short battle" at Averysboro, and marched into what would become a three-day battle at Bentonville on March 19. The last large pitched battle of th0e war "resulted in our favor, though sustaining a heavy loss in killed and wounded," Noah wrote. Out of 230 members of its unit who went into battle, 6 officers were killed and 86 men killed or wounded. William Noah was among those wounded. Years later, he recalls:

Having received a gunshot wound in my right arm near the shoulder the first day, undergoing amputation the following day and two days later boarded an ambulance train for Goldsborough where we arrived the evening of the 3rd day; there with two others also wounded were given lodging on the second floor in a brick building with nothing but the floor for our bed...remaining there for two weeks.

He and other wounded Union soldiers were eventually loaded onto ships that set sail for New York. He spent three weeks in a New York hospital, then was loaded onto a train bound for Cleveland and Detroit, where he remained in Harper Hospital for nearly three months. He received his pay and discharge on July 18, 1865, and reached home the 22nd, "to enjoy the fruits of the result of the War." That November, he went through a second amputation because his arm had refused to heal.

"These are some of the trifling sacrifices necessary to be made that our country might live and remain one and inseparable," he observes as he ends his account.

$\approx$

By the end of the war, more than 90,000 Michigan men—85,000 of them volunteers—had responded to President Lincoln's call to arms. Fourteen thousand lost their lives, 9,900 of those from disease, 4,100 killed or mortally wounded on the battlefield. Countless numbers were decorated or cited for valor. Sixty-nine received the Congressional Medal of Honor.

Those who survived the battlefields and sick bays returned home to raise families, start businesses, plant crops, or nurse old wounds. A crumbling roster housed in the Chelsea Library lists all known Civil War veterans within the Chelsea area, their terms of enlistment, units, wounds and dates of service. An old-fashioned black spidery script inscribes 180 names—but there is no indication of who created the list or kept the list. Perhaps it was compiled for the local chapter of the Grand Army of the Republic or for an official responsible for veterans' war benefits claims.

Other than that roster, a few local family histories offer the only tidbits of additional information about Chelsea's Civil War past and what became of its soldiers.

Four years of combat were enough for Orange and Joshua Noah. They resisted efforts by recruiters and were mustered out of service September 26, 1864, in Washington, D.C., returning to Michigan soil October 15. From that point on, they lived the everyday lives of farmers, businessmen, husbands, fathers, and neighbors, relating war experiences at night to the family around the fire, or swapping stories with neighbors at the local store.

Joshua Noah established a farm after the war and lived to be 89.

Orange Noah bought 80 acres of farmland in Dexter Township and settled down on the farm with his family. One day, much later in his life, while sitting on his front porch, Orange Noah saw a tall, lean gentleman walk up his front yard. It was Henry Ford, who had seen Noah's unusual side-hill plow out in the field and had come to ask if he could buy it for his Greenfield Village Museum. Orange Noah agreed. After that, Henry Ford periodically came out to visit and talk about the old days. Orange Noah was 88 years old when he died.

William Noah, the oldest of the 17 Noah children, returned to his family in Michigan nine months after his brothers' homecoming, with a sleeve pinned up over the stump of his arm. He resumed his life as a family man, storekeeper, farmer, and postmaster and died at the age of 98.

Richard Whalien, a veteran of the Seventh Michigan Calvary, was captured and sent to Andersonville, the most infamous Confederate prison camp. He would tell younger generations about life in that horrible place, with thousands of men herded into an unsheltered muddy field without tents or adequate food. He also told of a ferocious thunderstorm that shook the earth one night. Lightning, he said, struck the ground in the camp, causing a spring to well up that saved some of the parched and starving Union prisoners.

"When my children were young, we stopped at Andersonville and asked the historian about this old family story, not really expecting him to know anything about it—or even believe it," Donna Lane says, adding, "To our surprise, they confirmed the story."

Although he survived Andersonville, Whalien couldn't survive the Michigan Central Railroad. In 1922, the automobile he was driving was struck by a train and he was killed.

According to notes in the possession of the Chelsea Area Historical Society written by Lois Palmer Moore, J.P. Wood served with the 24th Michigan Infantry for three years, after which "he returned to the business with his brother," as a dealer of wheat, oats, corn, and wood. He died in 1887.

Thomas Jefferson Stimson served with the 12th Michigan Infantry until he was shot above the knee during the battle of Shiloh. "He was discharged to heal his wounds as a result of the war," Mrs. Moore wrote, adding, "He was in business in Parma and later became junior partner with F.P. Glazier and Co. Bank-Drug Store." He died June 28, 1889.

The Hadley family genealogy notes simply, "Uncle Harrison Daniels was a Civil War vet."

George Turnbull, a native of Canada, settled in Chelsea in 1859—just in time to serve in the Union Army. After the war, he returned to his adopted village and passed the bar at the age of 40. An able lawyer, he was elected to two terms as village president and served as choirmaster at the Congregational Church for decades. According to an account Paul Hoffman wrote in 1977, Turnbull was a man with a "handsome countenance" who later in life suffered from gout so extensively that "he was compelled to hire a drayman with a team to transport him to and from his home on Congdon Street and his office, reclining all the way in a heavy overstuffed chair." He died in 1902.

Company K veteran Angus Steger bought a home at 609 West Middle Street in 1882. Hoffman reports that Steger used the house, barn, and outbuildings right in the middle of the downtown "as a poultry and produce establishment for the better part of two decades."

The Michigan Central Railroad's *Highlight* magazine, dated 1895, goes into detail about the war record of Chelsea businessman J.A. Palmer, who returned to Chelsea to become a cashier in Kempf Brothers' Bank. "He has resided in this city since 1858," the *Highlight* reads. "He was a member of the First Michigan Infantry and Fourth Michigan Cavalry, serving over three years in the late War of the Rebellion, taking part in many important engagements, including the first battle of Bull Run, Stone River, Chickamauga, all through the Atlanta Campaign, was with General Thomas in the Nashville fight and many others, serving with bravery and distinction."

Old copies of the *Chelsea Standard*, *Chelsea Tribune*, and *Chelsea Herald* offer hints about the fate of other veterans who returned from the war between the states. A *Chelsea Standard* clipping dated March 7, 1895, entitled "THE GRIM DESTROYER Has Been In Our Midst And Taken Two Of Our Citizens," presents a brief biography of the life of one Civil War soldier who had fought bravely, endured great physical suffering, and returned home to live for another 30 years. To modern-day readers, the article raises more questions than it answers about the old soldier's life, but apparently the *Standard's* readers knew the story behind the story:

Mr. Leman Erastus Sparks passed quietly away last Sunday morning at eleven o'clock. He had not been well for many months, and his strength gradually failed though he made a heroic struggle for life. Few men could have lived as long as he did with his disease...Mr. Sparks was born at Green, Trumbull Co., Ohio, August 7, 1844. He came to Michigan with his parents thirty-nine years ago next April, and settled at Leoni, Jackson Co. He entered the army in 1862 and fought in Burnside's division of the Army of the Potomac. With it he crossed Cumberland Gap five times. The last fourteen months of his service he was in the hospital. He returned to Leoni. He was married June 16, 1867 to Miss Delia E. Burchard at Sylvan, and resided there...He first came to Chelsea in September, 1879...Mr. Sparks was known as an upright man, a tireless worker and one whose influence always counted for every good cause. He united with the Methodist church when only about fourteen. During the war he drifted from his religious faith, but renewed his Christian vows by uniting with the Congregational church...

~

Handsome dark-haired, dark-eyed Arthur Standish Congdon sat for this photograph just before the 22-year-old son of Chelsea's founder left for war. A young drummer boy, perhaps another Chelsea native, leans on his shoulder.

Courtesy of Merle Barr and Virginia Barr Visel

Remembrances of the war still linger in Chelsea 140 years later. In cemeteries throughout the area, tiny American flags placed in bronze Grand Army of the Republic flagstaffs fly beside tombstones. In Oak Grove Cemetery at the end of East Middle Street, a statue of a Civil War soldier in winter dress surveys the burial place for soldiers of all wars and their families. Protecting the granite soldier are cannons that the war department donated to the village long after Robert E. Lee surrendered to Ulysses S. Grant.

Virginia Barr Visel, a descendent of Chelsea's founding father, Elisha Congdon, cherishes a tiny tintype portrait of a young woman that was made into a pin. Her great-great-grandfather, Arthur Standish Congdon, wore this picture of his wife on his uniform throughout the war.

Merle Barr owns a photograph of the soldier who wore that pin, probably taken when the 22-year-old Arthur enlisted. It shows a handsome dark-haired, dark-eyed man with a dashing mustache wearing a dark blue uniform and Union army forage cap. A young drummer boy, perhaps another Chelsea native, leans on his shoulder. Arthur survived the war and lived to the age of 57. He is buried near his father in the Oak Grove Cemetery. Barr owns an original print of the 20th Michigan reunion photo and speculates about which ancient veteran is Arthur.

As the war faded into memories, veterans began attending reunions of their old companies, regiments, and battalions, some of them on the battlegrounds where they fought. Just before the turn of the century, veterans of Co. K, 20th Michigan Infantry, posed in uniforms and decorations for a group portrait in front of Chelsea's Depot. Homes in Chelsea still display copies of this photograph. George Till owns a copy of a photograph taken of the survivors of the 24th Michigan who returned to Seminary Ridge in Gettysburg 50 years after the battle, in 1913. In 1920, Orange Noah attended his last reunion of the Eighth Michigan Infantry in Lansing. His descendent, Donna Noah Lane, has a photo of Michigan troops stationed behind a redoubt in Virginia during the war.

Some Civil war veterans survived well into the twentieth century. Dudley Holmes, Claude Sears Rogers and George Staffan remember seeing Grand Army of the Republic veterans marching in Memorial Day parades during the 1920s and 1930s. Staffan has a relative buried in Oak Grove Cemetery without a stone who served with the 24th Michigan Infantry for four years and his grandfather, J.P. Wood, was numbered among the veterans posing for the Company K reunion photograph. He had been the leader of the unit's band. "When he was 24 years old, his unit gave him a cornet with his name inscribed on it," Staffan recalls.

Staffan particularly remembers two colorful Civil War heroes who lived on into the twentieth century. "One, a man by the name of Strahle, lived on South Main Street. He had half his ear shot off," he says. "The other was a man named Captain Negus."

"Captain Negus lived on East Middle Street and always led the Decoration Day parade," Rogers recalls. "A Mr. Runciman lost an arm in the Civil War. He lived on Townsend Street. David N. Rogers, whose father was one of the founders of Stockbridge, was a Civil War veteran who lived on Summit Street for many years before his death in 1923, at the age of 86."

George Staffan's cousin, John Keusch, also remembers Civil War veteran Dr. Rolla Armstrong. "I heard him tell his stories, but I was too young and didn't pay enough attention," Keusch says. "I wish I'd listened better."

PRESIDENTS
Ulysses S. Grant, 1869-77 • Rutherford B. Hayes, 1877-81
James A. Garfield, 1881 • Chester Arthur, 1881-85
Grover Cleveland, 1885-89, 1893-97

Robert E. Lee dies • Thomas Edison and J.W. Swan independently devise the first practical electric lights • Mark Twain writes *The Adventures of Huckleberry Finn* • The Cincinnati Red Stockings become the first salaried baseball team • Robert Koch creates an inoculation against anthrax • Buffalo Bill Cody opens his "Wild West Show" • Nikola Tesla constructs electric motor • George Eastman perfects Kodak box camera • Alexander Graham Bell invents the telephone.

U.S. POPULATION
39 million

CHELSEA POPULATION
1870: 1,100

AND IN CHELSEA
"The wheat crop this year will go a long ways toward deciding the financial problem. After all, the money must come out of the ground."

—*Chelsea Herald,* July 31, 1879

VILLAGE ELECTION
Another battle of the ballots has been fought, another victory and another defeat is the record of Monday last. Victory to the one side, defeat to the other, and still the world wags on.

Two tickets were in the field—Citizens' and Workingman's. The entire Workingman's ticket was elected. The complete vote we give below.

PRESIDENT		TRUSTEES		TREASURER	
William Bacon, C.	131	Jacob Schumacher, C.	154	Louis T. Freeman, C.	155
George W. Beckwith, W.	228-77	Harmon S. Holmes, C.	149	John W. Beissl, W.	221-66
		Clarence W. Maroney, C.	148		
CLERK		August H. Mensing, W.	217	ASSESSOR	
John B. Cole, C.	151	George P. Glazier, W.	223	Albert E. Winans, C	143
Frederick R. Roedel, W.	226-75	John P. Foster, W.	221	Edgar A. Williams, W.	236-94

The vote on the Electric Light Plant question stood as follows: Yes, 85; No, 229.

Postwar America: The 1870s and 1880s

Home Sweet Home

Soldiers returning from war were anxious to reestablish their lives, to marry, build a home, start a family, settle into a career. Throughout the Midwest, the temporary, rough-and-ready homes, shops, and farm buildings were replaced by a new generation of architecture. In Chelsea, the small frame dwellings hastily erected as settlers first arrived were moved or torn down. On their sites appeared Victorian residences, some of them ornate, others more modest. The pace of life became more established, more leisurely, less hand-to-mouth. The quality of life improved, even mirroring the elegancies of refined city life.

On June 10, 1879, the *Chelsea Herald* ran a story contrasting home life in 1879 with Chelsea's earliest days. Under the title "The Good Old Times," the newspaper points out:

A half century ago, a large part of the people of the United States lived in houses unpainted, unplastered and utterly devoid of adornment. A well-fed fire in the yawning chasm of a huge chimney gave partial warmth to a single room, and it was a common remark that the inmates were roasting on one side while freezing the other; in contrast, a majority of the people of the older States now live in houses that are clapboarded, painted, blinded and comfortably warmed. Then the house-hold furniture consisted of a few plain chairs, a plain table, a bedstead made by the village carpenter. Carpets there were none. To-day, few are the homes in the city or the country that do not contain a carpet of some sort, while the average laborer by a week's work may earn enough to enable him to repose at night upon a spring bed.

Fifty years ago the kitchen "dressers" were set forth with a shining row of pewter plates. The farmer ate with a buck-handled knife, and an

What a catch! Frank P. Glazier (right) took his wife Henrietta (far left), his mother, Mrs. George Glazier, and his two youngest children on a vacation trip.

Courtesy of Geraldine Glazier Kraft

iron or pewter spoon, but the advancing civilization has sent the plates and spoons to the melting pot, while the knives and spoons have given place to nickel or silver-plated cutlery.

In those days, the utensils for cooking were dinner-pot, tea-kettle, skillet, Dutch oven and frying-pan; today there is no end of kitchen furniture.

The people of 1830 sat in the evening in the glowing light of a pitch-knot fire, or read their weekly newspaper by the flickering light of a "tallow-dip;" now, in city and village, their apartments are bright with the flame of the gas jet, or the softer radiance of kerosene. Then, if the fire went out upon the hearth, it was rekindled by a coal from a neighboring hearth, or by flint, steel and tinder. Those who indulged in pipes and cigars could light them only by some hearthstone. To-day we light fire and pipes by the dormant fireworks in the matchsafe, at a cost of one-hundredth of a cent.

In those days we guessed the hour by the creeping of the sunlight up the "noon-mark" drawn upon the floor. Only the well-to-do could afford a clock. To-day, who does not carry a watch?

Chelsea was a neat and orderly cluster of small farms, homes, and businesses in 1881. Many descendents of the business owners are still present in town.

Courtesy of Merle Barr

Times had changed, and the first to feel the change was the family. Here, on what had until recently been the frontier, the modern idea of comfort was introduced. Fireplaces were replaced with stoves, which kept rooms (at least downstairs) consistently warm. Chairs were padded and designed to conform to the human body, instead of vice versa. A piano or pump organ could be found in many middle-class parlors. Cooking stoves had a major impact on culinary arts. Cookbooks appeared in every kitchen and meals became larger, more varied and healthier. Beds were made with springs and mattresses rather than ropes topped with cornshuck pallets. Linens—on beds and on people—were changed more regularly. Housewives perfected the art of laundering, starching and ironing. Some men began shaving daily. Milliners and mantua-makers made their appearance on Main Street, improving the appearance of generations of women. For 25 cents a week, Chelsea's housewives could hire a farm girl or neighbor's daughter to help watch the children, make a meal, hang clothes on the line, or scrub floors.

In 1879, Chelsea had the amenities of civilized life: two newspapers, several cigar shops, tailors and barbershops as well as the necessary "merchantiles," blacksmith shops, mills and cooperages that had been established earlier.

Chelsea shops acquired all their fresh produce and dairy products from nearby farmers, whose wives churned butter, collected eggs and swapped them for groceries or fabric in the shops on Main Street on Wednesday or Saturday nights, when entire farm families climbed into wagons and went to town for shopping and socializing.

≈

John and Jacqueline Frank have renovated their elegant brick Victorian home on East Middle Street to mirror life in 1885, the year that George William Palmer, M.D. built the home for his wife, Ida Mae. The Franks painstakingly combined Victorian paint colors and wall coverings, and they chose furniture that an affluent midwestern family would have used in the home.

"The Victorians developed a philosophy behind decorating that followed a rigid set of rules. Everything in your public rooms had a place and a reason for being there," Jackie Frank says, as she surveys her home's reception room and front parlor.

In order to replicate a typical upper-middle-class Victorian deco-

After the Civil War, home life became more leisurely and luxurious. This family proudly displays their new upright piano and the trappings of a comfortable Victorian middle-class existence.

Courtesy Chelsea Area Historical Society

rating scheme, the Franks used 35 different wallpapers in their downstairs. They hung old family portraits, Victorian landscapes, and sentimental needlework ("Home Sweet Home") on their walls; displayed shells and travel souvenirs on knickknack shelves; and filled bookcases with nineteenth-century volumes, just as the home's original owners, the Palmer family, would have done.

"Homemakers strongly believed that the home was a statement of who the family was—and they wanted to present their best image," she explains.

Embroidery, tatting, and other handmade crafts, for instance, showed that the woman had leisure time and the refinement to pursue fine arts. The shells, postcards, and knickknacks demonstrated an interest in travel and a knowledge of distant places. Books provided the family's entertainment at night and the titles showed that the family had both the intention and the leisure time to be well read.

Not only the selection, but the placement of family heirlooms and treasures was critical. Jackie Frank points to the mantle in her hallway and explains, "Victorians believed that symmetry was important. The arrangement of objects could convey silent messages, just as the way a woman used her fan or fluttered her handkerchief would convey silent, but very well understood, messages. We've lost the art of silent communication, but the Victorians were masters of the art."

On the Franks' mantle, the tallest object sits in the center and the heights of other objects diminish until the smallest are at the outside edges of the mantle. "This arrangement conveyed a sense of optimism," she explains.

≈

Elisha Congdon's homes demonstrated Chelsea's progression in homebuilding. The first house erected at what would become 221 South Main Street was a temporary shelter, a log cabin, that was destroyed by fire. The second was a simple midwestern Victorian farmhouse; it made way for a square brick Georgian with Greek Revival elements. The third Congdon home provided an architectural standard that local businessmen and their wives would try to emulate or surpass in the coming decades. Congdon replicated the John Gott house on Jackson-Huron Road, which Elisha passed on his way to Ann Arbor when he went there on business.

Many people spent their entire lives in the same house. John Keusch was born on Christmas Day in 1909, in his family's home at 115 Van Buren Street. His father, who owned a grocery store on Main Street, had been born on an adjacent lot that faced Summit Street and he lived his entire life within a block of where he was born. Claude Sears Rogers was born on January 4, 1912, at 122 East Street, which George Beckwith built for his grandfather after the Civil War for $600.

Most townspeople still had connections to a farm. John Grau left his farm and moved into Chelsea when his son, Alton Sr., married and took over the agricultural responsibilities. John Keusch's grandfather owned 500 acres in what is now the Waterloo area and the town-dwelling family members routinely visited the farm, to help with the crops. William Schenk was born in 1858 on a 320-acre farm on Old u.s. 12. After operating a general store near home, in Sylvan Center, he came to Chelsea to work in 1877, leaving the management of the farm and its renowned orchards (the Schenks even raised a few prized "snow apple" trees) to his parents, Michael and Mary, and his 11 brothers and sisters. One of 14 children born on another Sylvan Township farm in 1850, attorney Michael Lehman moved to Chelsea when he began studying law.

Even when they lived in town, people weren't far from the land. Town families raised most of their own vegetables on their narrow town lots and bought or bartered for milk and butter from a neighbor who housed a cow in a shed out back. Youngsters would be sent to the neighbor's home after milking time, usually about 6:30 or 7:00 at night, with an enameled pail. Milk delivery didn't begin until the early 1920s.

During these years, farming was a labor-intensive business that required many hands. Generations of children—town and country—worked in the onion fields, picked and husked corn, raked hay, and helped with grain harvests and threshing. Farms of 120 acres or more required two or three farm hands throughout the year—and every able-bodied worker who could be recruited for harvesting. Beans were an important staple and an important cash crop.

Picking beans was a slow and tedious business that required many hands. Remembers John Keusch, "Beans were harvested by means of an implement drawn by a team of horses that uprooted the entire plant—and covered it with dirt. People armed with pitchforks followed behind and dug in the furrow, removing the plants with the pods on them. The vines were bundled and permitted to dry. Then they were gathered in wagons, placed in stacks, and threshed in the same manner that wheat and oats were threshed. If the weather was rainy, it affected the quality of the beans; they turned black. Once the beans were threshed, women and children removed all the small stones and black beans. Hand-picked beans, however, were harvested by hand in the fields, just as peas were picked."

Harvesting grains became community affairs, with teams of farmers, horses, and hired hands moving from farm to farm to offer assistance. Nearly every longtime Chelsea resident has vivid and happy memories of threshing times. Until the Depression, children were excused from school during harvests.

∼

Chelsea established its school system at the time when one-room schools began opening their doors throughout the country. Often the schoolhouses were built as a community effort on land donated by farmers with large broods or on public lands near churches or town halls at crossroads. Until the turn of the century, few of the local schoolmasters or mistresses had been educated much beyond the eighth grade themselves, but they taught as many as 75 students courses through the eighth grade level—or the level of the teacher's expertise.

St. Louis School, Sylvan Township School, Jerusalem Stone School, Rogers' Corners School, "Punkin College," Lima Township School, the Ira Spaulding School, Freedom School, Pleasant Lake School, Lyndon Township School, Freer School, the Red School, and a host of others taught children reading, writing, and arithmetic while reinforcing family values. Some, with enterprising scholars as teachers, even ventured into Greek and Latin. Several of the schools south of town were bilingual, with classes in German and English. In other cases, young children who could only speak German were sent home until they could master a rudimentary command of English.

Down through the generations have passed stories of early school days on the frontier here. An early Chelsea diarist stated that women were only allowed to teach during three seasons of the year because men feared that the big farm boys, who could only attend school in the winter months, might be too tough for a woman to handle, particularly when some of the teachers were as young as 16. Another story is told about a schoolmaster who packed a pistol to class, for times when the larger boys got rowdy. One schoolmaster taught himself to play the violin during school days when no children attended class—whether this was during harvest or whether the teacher was unpopular isn't remembered.

There were few occupations open to women other than home-making and teaching (and then, only if the women were unmarried), but in the course of Jackie Frank's research on old homes in Chelsea, she discovered that a surprising number of women owned property and bought and sold real estate without supervision from husbands or fathers—an exciting find for Frank, who is herself a Realtor.

"Ida Palmer, for instance, who lived in my house, was very active in local real estate," she says. "I've seen a number of deeds with her name. She bought and sold large amounts of farm land, as well as commercial properties and house lots." In fact, Ida Palmer even sold her own home, in 1890, six years after George Palmer signed the house at 138 East Middle Street over to his wife.

"Women may not have been visible in the business community, but they played a far more prominent role 50 and 100 years ago than we give them credit for," Jackie Frank suggests. "And they certainly had an important, and prominent role in the home, with all they had to do."

The Fellowship of Churches

For both town dwellers and farm families, in the early years, the churches offered direction, support, fellowship, a sense of community and shared heritage, and opportunities for socializing.

FIRST CONGREGATIONAL CHURCH

The Congregational Church was the first organized congregation in the area, brought by the colony of New England Congregationalists who emigrated to the territory of Michigan from Shoreham, Addison County, Vermont in 1830.

Until the Ira Spaulding School was built on Manchester Road in 1834, services were held in homes. Later, circuit-riding ministers would preach two-hour-long sermons while the congregation sat on long, wooden benches behind desks. Within a year, members began discussing an official church organization and agreed to unite with the Presbyterian Church, which had headquarters in Monroe, because there was no Congregational branch in the territory.

A step up in the world was offered to the Chelsea Congregational Church when the street was lowered by eight feet, allowing the church to excavate a full basement beneath the sanctuary. Courtesy of Marjorie Hepburn

A church history explains, "In the pioneer days of Michigan, relations between the Congregationalists and Presbyterians were unusually close and cordial. It was thought that the Congregational church belonged exclusively to New England and the Presbyterian church was especially adapted to new communities. Therefore, Congregational ministers advised their people moving west to become Presbyterians. The two churches were alike in many respects: each was free to formulate its own creed, arrange its own form of worship, elect its own officers, call its own pastor, and own its own property."

The Rev. Beach of Ann Arbor, the Rev. C.G. Clark of Webster and the Rev. Enoch Bouten of Lima headed a committee that adopted the Presbyterian Articles of Faith, Covenant and Practice in 1835. On the motion of Mahlon Wines and John C. Winans, it was voted to adopt the Presbyterian form of government. The Presbyterian Church of Sylvan was founded.

Seven men and eleven women joined as charter members. During the first church service, the Rev. Bouten administered the rites of communion and six children were presented for baptism.

In 1842, trouble developed among members of the school district and the school building was destroyed by a mob in the winter of 1843—though no details remain to explain why. With no place to meet and strong feelings of animosity within the community, the Presbyterian Church of Sylvan disbanded.

But not for long. Within five years, on February 21, 1849, the Congregational Church of Sylvan was formed with the same members. John Winans and Amos Davis were chosen deacons. C.H. Wines was named clerk. Sixteen members formed this church and the Rev. Josephus Morton was called to be first minister.

According to the church history, an intense religious revival swept Chelsea during the year 1850. "Under the leadership of Rev. Morton, the people showed an intense religious enthusiasm. Records show that thirty-two new members were added to the roll and no one was dismissed."

Before being admitted to church membership, the applicant signed a pledge of abstinence from the making, vending, or use of all intoxicating drinks. Frequently members were excommunicated for breaking the pledge or for laxity in church attendance.

Within a year, the congregation outgrew the Sylvan Center School and moved to a schoolhouse a half mile south of Chelsea, in the prospective village of Pierceville. At the same time, however, Elisha and James Congdon were laying out the town of Chelsea.

When Elisha Congdon offered land, farsighted men saw the advantages and moved the church to Chelsea. The Congregational Church of Chelsea started building in the fall of 1851, and by the summer of 1852, the church was dedicated, with 54 members and the Rev. Josephus Morton as traveling pastor.

For eight years, this pioneer church, with bare walls and floors, unshaded windows and low-backed pews, was the only church building in town. The congregation shared its sanctuary with the Methodists on alternate Sundays. The first full-time Congregational minister received his call in 1854, with a salary of $500 per year and the promise of an annual donation.

During the Civil War, "Work for the army through the Christian Commission was the leading employment of ladies' societies and church festivals," the church history says. By 1871, with veterans and their new families overflowing the pews, the congregation decided that the church should be enlarged. Several years earlier, Middle Street had been leveled, leaving the church in an elevated position. By excavating the ground to street level and then a few feet lower, a basement was created and a furnace installed—the second Chelsea building with a basement and the second furnace in town.

The heated basement was in great demand as a meeting place. Home talent shows, lectures, magicians, and bell-ringers all performed there. Because of its constant use, the village council erected the first street lamp outside the church door.

Starting in 1869, officials from the Lima church discussed uniting with the Chelsea congregation "because of the deficit in provision of the pastor's salary." In 1875, the Lima property was sold and the two congregations merged.

Another religious revival swept the town in the 1880s, and churches began strong outreach programs. Mrs. W.F. Hatch, Mrs. C.H. Kempf, and Mrs. H.G. Hoag established a Home Missionary Society in 1887. At first, collections at meetings were as small as 16 cents, but by 1891, the society was sending box loads of shoes and clothing to mission churches. At the same time, the church hired a chorister, G.W. Turnbull, and an organist, Sarah Van Tyne. A parsonage was built and a committee was formed to discuss whether the church should once again be enlarged.

When the Glazier Stove Works caught fire on February 18, 1894, the flames quickly spread to the Chelsea Congregational Church and parsonage. Courtesy of Marjorie Hepburn

The answer to that question came on February 18, 1894, when the church and parsonage were destroyed by a fire that started in the Glazier Stove Works buildings.

Zealous parishioners immediately started a fund-raising campaign and local builder John Foster began constructing the new church in June. The Rev. William Walker, "a man of remarkable ability," was pastor during this chaotic time and, the church history notes, "what at first appeared to be a catastrophe was found to have developed an increased determination to build for a greater future."

On January 31, 1895, the new—and present—sanctuary was dedicated. The inscription on its bell reads:

I praise the True God,
I announce the Sabbath;
I call the people,
I arouse the indolent.

ST. MARY'S CATHOLIC CHURCH

The Irish were among the earliest pioneers in Sylvan and Lyndon townships. As early as 1833, they gathered in the home of Thomas Carroll of Cedar Lake for services. Two years later, Chelsea pioneer Darius Pierce, by then a member of the Michigan State Legislature, offered two acres of land for the establishment of a Catholic church and cemetery. Irish settlers quickly built a plain, unpainted building with neither a bell nor a cross. Priests from St. Joseph's Parish in Dexter served masses for a short time, until the church was consumed by fire. Among the prominent parishioners here were the McKunes, McKanes, Savages, Cassidys, Burnses, Dorans, Hagans, McIntees, Walshes, Gormans, Duffeys, Walls, Ryans, Kennedys, Flemings, Geraghtys, O'Conners, O'Neils, Quigleys, Marrrianes, Morans, and Mullens.

In the 1840s, clusters of German Catholics began arriving in the Chelsea area. They joined with the earlier Irish settlers in services on the rare occasions when a missionary priest made visits to hold mass. The priest's arrival was always heralded by a horseback-riding messenger who notified parishioners of the time and place for the services.

In 1869, the cornerstone for the first Catholic Church, which became known as "Old St. Mary's" was laid. The building was constructed for $12,000 and the adjacent two-story wooden rectory for $4,000.

At first, the church was called Our Lady of the Sacred Heart, but eventually the name was changed to St. Mary's—no one remembers why. One local boy who became a priest, Monsignor James Savage, was buried where the main altar of that first church once stood. "He was not only an outstanding clergyman, but also an avid fisherman, who was responsible for stocking trout in the Waterloo trout ponds," John Keusch remembers. "He was beloved. The morning on which he was buried, all the shops in town closed in his honor."

Among generations of Chelsea's hoopsters were these eight women who formed the 1920 women's basketball team for St. Mary's.
Courtesy Chelsea Area Historical Society

Another prominent priest affiliated with the Mill Creek church was Reverend Dr. Reilly, who established a Dominican Order of Sisters in Adrian. According to Keusch, at least 30 young women from Chelsea joined the Dominican Order. One, Dorothy Weber, served as president of Berry College in Florida. Her sister, Genevieve, became Mother Superior for the Order.

Father William Considine was of Irish descent and during his long pastorate in Chelsea, St. Patrick's Day was celebrated in an elaborate manner, John Keusch remembers. "Every year a very formal banquet was held with prominent speakers and talented musical entertainers from out of town." The priest's pastorate was long enough to give him the opportunity to marry many of the children he had baptized—and then to baptize their children.

In 1925, when John Keusch (top, left) was a sophomore on the St. Mary's basketball team, they won the Class D championship.
Courtesy Chelsea Area Historical Society

During Father Considine's pastorate, in 1906, the parish elementary school was built. By World War I, the parish consisted of 180 families, half of them Irish, half German, and the school had expanded to offer a high school curriculum. St. Mary's developed a passion for sports. In 1925, when John Keusch was a sophomore player, St. Mary's basketball team gained fame throughout the state by winning the Class D championship. In 1926, the team just missed repeating the feat, by one point. According to Claude S. Rogers, who was 14 that year, "Two of the players had fouled out and the team had to finish the game with only three players. There were no more substitutes." Chelsea natives can still list the names of the players on that famous team.

Fire whistles shrieked in Chelsea on the morning of February 6, 1925 as St. Mary's School building burned to the ground. John Keusch and several teammates had been practicing their shots the night before and Keusch speculates that the cause of the blaze may

St. Mary's Catholic Church established a parochial school that served generations of Chelsea's German and Irish families. On February 6, 1925, fire consumed the school.

Courtesy Chelsea Area Historical Society

have been a faulty furnace. The parish carted the rubble away and began constructing the new school almost immediately. Classes were held in buildings and offices throughout town until the school was finished. Just a few years later, in 1934, the high school was discontinued.

In 1961, time caught up with St. Mary's Church. Section by section, the 92-year-old antique was dismantled. The roof, floor, and fixtures were moved and then the wrecking ball pounded the brick walls to the ground. The parish moved into the high school gymnasium while the problems involving the provision of a new church were discussed.

Groundbreaking for the present church took place in 1965. Three years later, the grade school merged with the public school and in 1971-72, St. Mary's School closed.

NORTH LAKE METHODIST CHURCH

Members of the Noah and Boyce families cherish genealogies that contain records of a church that their ancestors founded in 1836.

One year before Michigan was admitted to the Union, 12 families gathered in the home of John and Jane Glenn to form the Methodist Episcopal Society of North Lake. Unlike other local churches, the founders included women as well as men: Charles and Mary Ascena Glenn, John and Jane Glenn, Isaac Glenn, Aaron and Catherine Vedder, Joseph and Phoebe Hartsuff, Jasper and Martha Moore, Elijah and Clarissa Brown. Soon, Sarah Searles, Benjamin Glenn, James Crane, James Brown, Anna Johnson, and Joseph Whitcomb were added to the society.

Charles Glenn, who had led his family from New York State to Michigan in 1833, assumed the leadership of the early church. For 30 years, he served as pastor, performing weddings, burials, and services when circuit ministers were unavailable. His son, Hamlin Glenn, succeeded him in this role, and then William Wood took over the leadership; he served for 21 years.

The first class book for the North Lake Methodist Church is dated 1838, when the society was part of the Dexter circuit and the members came from miles around to hear Charles Glenn as well as circuit-riding ministers and missionaries preach the gospel. In 1942, Ruth Boyce wrote a history of the church that explains its longevity.

Charles Glenn directed the settlement of the (Lyndon Township) vicinity so that the Protestants were all in a group and the Catholics were in another group to the north and east...Because of his fore-thought, our small community church has been a lasting one.

Over the years, this church survived while many fellow congregations disappeared. Once, Methodist churches were situated in Williamsville, Lima Center, Unadilla, Pinckney, Dexter, Waterloo, and North Waterloo. Now, only Dexter and North Lake have Methodist services.

Throughout the 1830s, services were held in Charles Glenn's barn, often with the boys sitting on the beams during Sunday School. In 1846, John and Charles Glenn built a one-story clapboard building, 20 by 26 feet in size, to serve as a sanctuary and a school. Eleven years later, John and Jane Glenn deeded the land on which the church stands to the society.

As soon as the Civil War ended, the congregation met to consider building a new sanctuary. The small white, shuttered clapboard church was built in 1866, at a cost of $2,645.87. Charles Glenn presented the church with a pulpit Bible and a sexton was hired for eight dollars a year. Until an organ was installed—decades after the church was built—a tuning fork offered the pitch ("sometimes right, but more often wrong") before the congregation burst into song.

If the members had enough time, they attended a singing class held once a week during the winter months to teach them the words and tunes of the Sunday hymns. Once a week, the whole community gathered in homes for supper and prayer meetings. Church socials were frequent and full of fun. "Everyone turned out for these activities because they were the only social events the community had," Ruth Boyce wrote.

Revival meetings were held every year, the largest in 1876, when 33 newcomers pledged themselves to the church. One of the earliest revivals on record in Michigan was also one of the most important. In 1837, Judson Dwight Collins, a farm boy living near Unadilla, was converted. He went on to become a member of the first graduating class of the University of Michigan, studied theology, and then became a missionary in China, converting hundreds to Christianity. He return to his hometown in 1852, suffering from "ill health due to overwork, poor food and hardships in China." He died shortly afterward and was buried in Lyndon Township.

Early Methodist ministers didn't receive salaries. Instead, members of the congregation brought them anything they had in surplus. "Pound socials" were events in which members brought pounds of homegrown or homemade products which the minister could sell for money to live on.

On the Friday of the weekend prior to the circuit's quarterly meetings, the entire Methodist community would fast and pray. Then everyone in the circuit—which covered large geographic areas—would gather for the meeting at one member's farm. Homemakers packed enormous picnics to share and sheets were sewn together and stuffed with straw to make beds to accommodate them all.

Drunkenness, buying or selling of spirituous liquors, or "drinking them unless in case of extreme necessity" were banned by the Methodist Church General Rules. So too were slaveholding and slavetrading.

In 1919, electricity was installed in the little white clapboard church with green shutters. Six years later, the nearby Grange Hall was purchased for one dollar and the entire congregation helped move the hall to the south of the church for use as an educational building.

THE UNITED METHODIST CHURCH

In 1853, when the Rev. Ebeneezer Steele held the first Methodist Evangelical Church service in Chelsea, he became a busy man. He rode a circuit to congregations in Lima Center, East Lima, Sylvan Center, Rogers Corners, Irving, and Chelsea, meeting in churches or homes. The Boynton, Clements, Boyd, Warner, Raymond, Cushman, Hawks, Storms, Davidson, and Preston families agreed to provide $200 for the preacher's "quarterage" each year, $130 for table expense, $50 for travel expenses, and $20 for fuel.

The Chelsea services were first held in an old brick schoolhouse that was located between the homes of John Schenk and George P.

Glazier. Later, they met on alternate Sundays in the Congregational Church until the Mite Box Society raised enough money to build a church. To become a member of the society, ladies paid a nickel and gentlemen a dime.

By the end of the decade, Elisha Congdon had agreed to donate ground for the church and parsonage and plans were immediately launched to raise a New England-style clapboard church. According to a church history, "The members, though few in numbers, did a noble work in erecting so fine a building, finer than any in Ann Arbor at the time." The cost: $8,000.

The church was dedicated September 8, 1859 and it stood "forty years and four months to the day" when it burned to the ground from "unknown causes" on January 8, 1899. The church's history then became intimately connected with the history of Frank P. Glazier, who spearheaded the committee to rebuild the church and offered the services of his architect, Claire Allen, in its design. The Gothic-style stone sanctuary was dedicated in February 1900. An educational wing was built for $80,000 in 1959 and another was completed in 1999.

ST. PAUL EVANGELICAL AND REFORMED CHURCH

The same wave of German immigration that led to the formation of St. Mary's Catholic Church also brought German Protestants, who organized St. Paul Evangelical and Reformed Church (now the United Church of Christ) in 1854. That year, the Rev. Friedrich Schmidt, a pioneer German missionary who had founded 20 churches in Michigan, began riding his horse out to Chelsea to conduct occasional services in the homes of the original five member families.

In time, the reverend encouraged Christian Spring, who had arrived in Scio Township as a teacher, to study for the ministry "because of his broad knowledge." Spring followed his advice. In 1858, Spring was named pastor of St. Jacob's Church at Waterloo and he became an itinerant speaker who visited Chelsea for the next 15 years.

The congregation grew. In 1865, 16 families banded together to form St. Paul's congregation. The charter members included John Schaible, David Faist, John Scheffel, Fred Broesamle, Jacob Buehler, George Mast, George Wackenhut, Jacob Schumacher, August Boos, Joseph Schatz, George Haselschwardt, J. Fahrner, Michael Lehmann, Sr., Fred and Israel Vogel, and John Mohrlock. Three years later, they built a church on East Summit Street, and later a parsonage. Records state that on January 10, 1869, "forty-three persons partook of Holy Communion in the new place." Even today, on Christmas Eve, the first verse of *Silent Night* is sung by the congregation in German.

A Sunday School is first mentioned in church records in 1875. The Ladies' Aid Society was founded in the 1880s, at about the same time that other churches established societies to promote education and outreach. One of the more unusual church organizations was established by the late Mrs. Elizabeth Wackenhut in 1935; the Mission Club membership was restricted to women over the age of 70.

ZION LUTHERAN CHURCH

German Lutherans living in the tight-knit community of Freedom Township established Zion Lutheran Church at Rogers' Corners with the aim of preserving their native language and traditional form of worship. In the 1970s, longtime church members Edith and Ingrid Weber devoted countless hours to translating the church archives from "Old German" into "New German." Later, the New German was translated into English and the fruits of their labors were published in 1998. The minutes of the old German church tell their own story about the church history and its people.

The first entry, dated 1867, announces,

We, the signed members who have built a new ev. Lutheran Zion congregation, were the majority of the members of the old Thomas congregation, which was founded by the venerable Pastor Schmidt in Ann Arbor. The reason for the separation was partly due to the inconvenient time…To fulfill the need of the community, it was decided by us that in October 1865, we will build our own house of God.

During the building process, the congregation, led by Pastor Hildner of the Bethel congregation in Freedom, held services in the schoolhouse. At the end of November 1865, the first church was complete.

The congregation adopted the Bremzisch Catechism and the Lutheran Hymnal and agreed to share pastors with Ann Arbor's congregation. Then, in 1873, the Rev. John Baumann was called for full-time service. That year the sanctuary was built for $3,213.35 and the pastor was furnished with a parsonage.

In 1879, the church opened a German school, which was held for three months in the winter to teach Old World German to the children, grandchildren and great-grandchildren of Washtenaw's German-speaking immigrants. The following year, the congregation built a bakehouse for bread on the cemetery grounds and took a strong stand on the payment of pledges. According to the annual meeting notes,

A decision has been made to divide the congregation into classes according to each member's ability to pay for the church's support which affects everyone. The stated amount must be paid…Furthermore, it was decided that if Heinrich Daviedter does not take back what he said about the church council and if he doesn't pay the $30.00 for the pastor's salary, he then will be expelled from the congregation. He has one month to do this.

No record exists of Heinrich Daviedter's response, but in 1890, matters again became heated:

It was decided that we not let our pastor go. Also, wafers will be used, instead of bread, during the Communion services. It was decided that those members who will not have paid their arrears for the congregation by December 1890 will be expelled from the parish. Then, Mr. John Messner announced that he wants to be expelled.

Things got even more complicated in 1891:

The board, like the congregation, attests the fact that it is a lie that the pastor announced from the pulpit that no one who signed the paper that refers to the summoning of a special meeting on April 9, 1890 is allowed to take Holy Communion.

Two years later, the nationwide financial Panic of 1893 hit this little German congregation hard, as the records show. Its members struggled to pay $50 of their $101 debt. "Because times are bad," the records say, "the pastor told them that they do not have to pay the rest of the money (to him)."

In 1909, the congregation was growing and times were evidently better, because the church had collected $1,175 toward the construction of a new church chancel and the addition of art glass. Just before World War I, the pastor's salary was set at $500, with payments on May 1 and October 1.

A cyclone badly damaged the church, school, parsonage, and barn Wednesday, June 6, 1917, at two o'clock in the afternoon. The congregation decided that the tower "should be built from the bottom up and should be moved forward. The parsonage, the barn, and the schoolhouse are supposed to be rebuilt according to the original plans." The pastor's salary was raised to $700.

The first sign of modernity arrived in 1923, when the congregation discussed "electric plants:"

Zion Lutheran Church lost its roof and suffered serious damage during a cyclone that hit the church June 6, 1917.

Courtesy of the Grau family

It was decided that oil lamps will be temporarily used for the church's lighting…Special emphasis was put on the word "temporary" at that time. Then the church council purchased inexpensive oil lamps after the order of the congregation. At the time, they said when the electric plants are cheaper, then we will buy one for the church. In the meantime one has experienced that the current illumination does not fulfill its purpose and that it is unsightly. Above all, however, we noticed that we need a lot of electrical power for an organ blower. Now the time has come that electric plants are cheaper.

A committee was appointed to purchase the Delco plants and a one-kilowatt generator.

By 1926, the congregation confronted issues relating to the changing times. The congregation discussed at length whether to change services from German to English. The members decided to continue the main church service in German, but in "special situations" and youth classes, "the English language may also be spoken." Four years later, the congregation decided to use English in church services "as soon as it is feasible."

The church budget demonstrates just how hard the Depression hit this farming community. In 1930, the congregation was in arrears by $181 for the pastor's salary. The following year, they owed the sexton $25 and the organist $40, but somehow they mustered the money and agreed to donate an additional $25 to poor students. In 1933, the congregation owed the pastor $561, but he asked "that the amount of this money that can not be collected shall be crossed out of the cash-book."

The first English communion service was celebrated in 1936, and the financial picture began looking up—enough so that inquiries were to be made about installing a bathroom in the parsonage. The first indoor bathroom appeared there the following year.

In the midst of World War II, Zion Lutheran Church adopted a new constitution and bylaws and struggled once again to adjust to changing times. Church minutes note that it was impossible to find new copies of its catechism and hymnal, but they vowed to continue their use.

A two-story brick Parish Hall was built in 1949 across from the church, and in 1955 a modern parsonage, and later a new sanctuary, were constructed.

The meeting notes reveal not only glimpses of church history, but also the members' great generosity and strong sense of community. Clarence Koengeter donated all the roof tiles necessary for the old church in 1944 and the congregation agreed to put them in place. George Haist offered to lend the church the money it needed in 1948. Charlie Zahn was commended for maintaining the cemetery and church grounds meticulously. Arthur Wacker presented the church with the gift of its first oil burner in 1950.

The records note that the parish meetings always ended by singing the Doxology, "Praise God from whom all blessings flow." For nearly a century, the old song was sung in German.

Ready for Business

After the Civil War, a town was considered well established if it had four professional classes: a doctor, lawyer, minister, and jeweler. By 1865, Chelsea had all four.

Some Civil War veterans returned to family homesteads in the Chelsea area. Others veterans were newcomers who bought land and established farms, among them George Chapman, great-grandfather of a future village council president, and Orange Noah, founder of a large family and a farm on North Lake. Other veterans moved into town. J.A. Palmer, who had served with Sherman on his march through Georgia, went into the banking business, at Kempf Brothers' Bank. J.P. Wood opened a farmers' supply business in town. George Turnbull studied for the law and became a lawyer.

By 1865, the town had everything it needed to flourish: peace, the land, farms, mills, shops, entrepreneurs, street patterns, hitching posts, a watering trough, commercial and residential opportunities on Main Street and Middle Street, and the railroad. Chelsea, like a thousand other small towns in the Midwest, began to boom as the nation began healing from its war wounds.

As farms developed from self-sustaining homesteads to agricultural businesses, farm families in Freedom, Sylvan, Lyndon, Dexter, and Lima townships turned to Chelsea for trading, shopping, entertainment, professional services, church activities, and access to the railroad. Until the turn of the century, wheat was their leading cash crop, followed by wool.

"The grocery stores at the time did a thriving business selling wet goods as well as dry goods," wrote the daughter of pioneer Jacob Berry in 1870. "More whiskey was sold then than now."

At the same time, a tailor opened a shop and offered to sew suits of clothes and coats. Two boot makers, Thomas Breed and Thomas

Leach, made footwear. Lewis Winans sold groceries and later stocked a few drugs. Charles Kempf and his brother Reuben were tinsmiths. Newton Robinson shoed horses and made tools as the town's blacksmith. Tom Godfrey ran a restaurant. Elisha Congdon served as postmaster and ran a store. Ed Winters dispensed whiskey in the saloon. Asel Harris owned a hotel and Lewis Harlow kept a "bachelor hall." M.M. Boyd made wagons. L.L. Randall ran a store and a blacksmith shop.

In the fall of 1869, the townspeople of Chelsea had a great celebration to mark the opening of Orchard Street. Chelsea was growing, although anything south of present-day South Street was considered "out of town." The population numbered 1,100, a significant population jump; in 1853, the town had numbered 63.

"To compensate for the lack of water-power, (Chelsea) has railroad facilities and a large and fertile rural district tributary by the village, fostering its trade and manufactures," observed the *New Historical Atlas of Washtenaw County, Michigan* in 1874. The village also had Congregational, Methodist, Catholic, Lutheran, and Baptist churches, four of them brick; a fine "Union" schoolhouse, also brick; a bank; weekly newspaper, the *Chelsea Herald*; "and a fair proportion of stores, shops, etc."

"Should this County be divided, as has been proposed, this enterprising village would be likely to become the County seat," the *New Historical Atlas* speculated.

Nothing came of the move to make Chelsea a county seat, but the "fair proportion of stores, shops, etc." continued to grow.

Originally, the stores had been nothing more than a farmer's front parlor with a shelf or two of staples. Now, shops began lining Main Street, often with merchants living above or behind the store until their business was up and running. When a fire in 1870 destroyed the wooden structures housing businesses along the west side of Main Street, the businessmen rebuilt with brick and resumed trade. Six years later, another fire demolished the east side of Main Street. These businesses, too, were quickly rebuilt, this time in brick.

Two, and for a time three, weekly newspapers vied for readership and advertising dollars after the war. The earliest editions of the *Chelsea Herald* and *Chelsea Standard* preserved by the Chelsea Library on microfiche date back to 1879. A. Allison was editor and proprietor of the *Herald*, whose motto was "Of the People and For the People." O.T. Hoover ran the *Chelsea Standard*, which was printed on

Thursdays. When a third newspaper, the *Chelsea Tribune*, appeared, it was published on Tuesdays and Fridays. In time, the *Tribune* was sold to the *Standard*.

In Chelsea's early days, visitors had been welcomed into private homes, for the company and the news they would bring. Boyd's Hotel became the first public accommodation in town, built in part because of the heavy volume of traffic generated by the railroad. It advertised "superior accommodations" and a "genial, affable gentleman" who played the role of "mine host," Merritt Boyd. When Timothy McKune purchased the Congdon home in 1870, he opened a second fashionable inn, which he called the "McKune House."

By April of 1879, the *Chelsea Herald* was reporting that Chelsea "looks alive in a business point of view." Editor A. Allison noted that there are two brick stores on Main Street as well as "about twelve frame buildings scattered here and there" and two new hotels rising. There was talk of a new passenger depot in town and a lament that "OUR flouring mill has busted…The building will be left standing, for us to remember there was once a flour mill here." The editor notes, "We think there is a leak somewhere, either on the part of the proprietors, or the inhabitants to support it." The report was subsequently discovered to be unfounded. The mill was soon running under new management.

Chelsea raised a healthy crop of lawyers, who might—or might not—have had college credentials before they apprenticed with a practicing attorney.

One of the most influential of these early lawyers was Archie Wilkinson, a member of a pioneering family, whose public role in his hometown began in 1870, when he and his father, Thomas Wilkinson, rescued one of Chelsea's founders from financial ruin. James Congdon had mortgaged his properties and was on the brink of losing his 300 acres and holdings to a mortgage holder, University Regent Junius Beal of Ann Arbor. To prevent this, the Wilkinsons stepped in and assumed payment of the mortgage.

Andrew J. Sawyer, who would later become known as "the Dean of Washtenaw County Bar" by the time of his death in 1911, also practiced law in Chelsea after the war. In 1873, he moved to Ann Arbor and became affiliated with the University of Michigan School of Law.

George W. Turnbull was admitted to the practice of law in 1870, at the age of 40. According to John Keusch, himself an attorney, Turnbull came to Chelsea from Canada in 1859 to engage in the shoe and boot-making business. Despite his Canadian heritage, Turnbull enlisted in the Grand Army of the Republic during the Civil War and became active in pension procurement for Union Army veterans and their families after the war. When Turnbull died in 1902, the *Ann Arbor News* called him "one of the best counselors in Southern Michigan" and noted,

He was a man of modest means, retiring disposition, unassuming and never putting himself forward. Unselfish to a fault. Never used his profession or trust as a means of selfish gain. He was a peacemaker among those who quarreled and often sent away from his office as friends those who might have been enemies of one another.

Carpenter Frank Staffan Jr. was also well established as an undertaker by 1879, when his advertisement in the *Herald* announced, "he keeps constantly on hand, all styles and sizes of ready-made COFFINS and SHROUDS. Hearse in attendance on short notice."

Shops abounded in the last decades of the nineteenth century, offering everything the farmer, professional, or homemaker could want. In the January 2, 1879 issue of the *Chelsea Herald*, Holmes & Parker advertised "We are here first, with a full stock of goods, suitable for holiday presents—at first look at our FIVE CENT COUNTER, which is loaded with 'FIVE HUNDRED DOLLARS WORTH OF GOODS.'"

Kempf, Bacon & Co. advertised stoves, tinware, whips, axes, and crosscut saws.

Price was a firm consideration to local buyers. Durand & Tuttle advertised "Great Reduction in all kinds of Groceries, Provisions, Teas, Coffees, Spices." McKone & Heatley was "The Place To Buy Goods Cheap!" Wood Bros. & Co. announced they offered "A place to buy choice HOLIDAY presents!"

In January of 1879, the Chelsea Market advertised their grocery prices: Wheat, 83 cents a bushel; corn, 20 cents per bushel; beans, $1.25 per bushel; honey, 20 cents per pound; butter, 10 cents per pound; chickens, 6 cents per pound, ham, 7 cents per pound; hay, $10 per ton; salt, $1.25 per bushel; wool, 30 cents per pound; cranberries, $2.50 per bushel.

A few months later, the *Chelsea Standard* reported counting 25 wagons loaded with wool lined up downtown at one time. By the end of the day, more than 100,000 pounds of wool had been weighed, most harvested by farmers living east of Dexter—"which shows that our Chelsea buyers pay more for wool than any other market within 25 miles of this place," the editor crowed.

Wool dealers were paying farmers a respectable 30 to 34 cents a pound. By mid-July of 1879, Gilbert & Babcock had purchased 160,000 pounds of wool; R. Kempf & Bro., 150,000 pounds; Taylor Bros., 75,000 pounds; and William Judson, 80,000 pounds. Astute wool dealing established the fortunes of many local families.

Business made headlines on July 17, when the *Herald* noted, "The people of Chelsea talk about dull times among our merchants; that ain't so. Holmes & Parker, and Wood Bros. & Co., those two firms alone, done business on last Saturday to the amount of $300 each. How is that for business?" In another article, Allison pointed out, "Chelsea was full of business last Saturday, especially in the evening. We counted no less than 30 teams hitched, and what a throng of people you could see going to and fro."

Fun Times in the Young Town

With increasing amounts of leisure time, the town worked hard to offer entertainment to its citizens and guests. In July 1878, the Sylvan Township board accepted Frank Staffan's $240 bid to construct a Sylvan Town Hall. The building was to be 80 by 40 feet, made of brick, with walls 30 feet high in front and floors sloping slightly to the first-floor stage.

According to Kathleen Clark, president of the Chelsea Area Historical Society, Timothy McKune, H.G. Hoag, F. D. Cummings, and Mrs. Kathryn Winters all offered sites for the town hall. Mrs. Winters' offer was accepted, with an agreement that her home would be moved off her property on West Middle Street to land farther west for a sum of $1,000.

Operettas, card parties, comedians, minstrel shows, high school graduations, lectures, plays, and other forms of theatrical and musical entertainment took center stage in the town hall as soon as it opened. On Saturday nights during the winter, square dances were held and small boys hung over the gallery watching the "do-si-dos." Fred Gettner played the fiddle. Norman Klingler strummed the banjo.

Both Chelsea and St. Mary's high school basketball teams practiced and played at the Sylvan Town Hall before school gymnasiums were built. Local Golden Gloves boxing matches were staged there.

In 1878, Sylvan Township officials accepted Frank Staffan's $240 bid to construct the town hall.

Courtesy Chelsea Area Historical Society

architectural firm. Mason & Rice of Detroit created a classic Victorian wooden depot with elaborate gingerbread trim and separate accommodations for ladies and for gentlemen.

∽

Shabby, disreputable and unbecoming for an up-and-coming town was the way Chelsea residents viewed the Michigan Central Railroad's depot (shown here) after the Civil War.

Courtesy Chelsea Area Historical Society

Life wasn't all fun and games, however. There was a criminal element not often remembered in old-timers' reminiscences of the good old days. In a shed down the railroad tracks, close to the site of what would become the Methodist Retirement Home, lived a downtrodden wife and her alcoholic husband. One night, in despair, she shot him dead.

Burglars entered two dwellings and a store and robbed the store (unnamed in the *Chelsea Herald* article) of clothing in the spring of 1879. "The inhabitants ought to have their revolvers ready the next time they come, to give them a warm reception," editor A. Allison suggested.

A band of gypsies came to town with a pair of very attractive women one summer's day. As the women were reading palms and entertaining a crowd on Main Street, they encountered one of the town's leading citizens, who fancied himself a ladies' man. After exchanging pleasantries with the pretty girls, he proceeded on his way down the street, only to discover that his watch had been pilfered.

During the winter of 1879, the number of inmates in Washtenaw County's poorhouse hit record highs. "There are 160 persons maintained at the expense of tax payers," the *Herald* reported. That same year, a writer signing himself or herself "Spaniel" wrote a passionate letter to the editor lamenting the number of dogs poisoned within the community, town, and country.

In the nation's leading sheep-producing county, sheep-stealing was a serious problem. The *Chelsea Herald* reported in the spring of 1879 that "It seems every farmer in the county have had sheep stolen from time to time, and it is rumored that there is a gang of sheep thieves around. Four young men in the neighborhood of this village are supposed to be implicated and three of them have been arrested." No names were given.

Benjamin Harrison, 1889-93 • William Mckinley, 1897-1901
Theodore Roosevelt, 1891-09 • William H. Taft, 1909-13

Daughters of the American Revolution are founded • U.S. iron and steelworkers strike • "Remember the Maine" • Teddy Roosevelt leads the charge up San Juan Hill during the Spanish-American War • H.G. Wells writes *War of The Worlds* • Henry James Writes *The Buccaneers* • Queen Victoria's Diamond Jubilee • Zeppelin's first trial flight • Picasso's "Blue Period" • The 'Century of Electricity' begins • Albert Einstein develops Special Theory of Relativity • "Typhoid Mary" found and incarcerated • Wilbur Wright flies 30 miles in 40 minutes • Ford Motor Company produces the first Model T—15 million sold• The weekend becomes popular in U.S • Arizona, New Mexico become States

U.S. POPULATION
1900: 76 million

CHELSEA POPULATION
1895: 1,600

The Turn of the Century: 1890-1914

Business is Our Business

"The American Cathedral" is the title of an etching of a flour mill and grain elevators created by Ann Arbor native Jonathan A. Taylor. The original hangs in the Smithsonian Institute. A print hangs in the boardroom of the Chelsea Milling Company and the Holmes family believes that their Chelsea mill served as the artist's model.

Whether or not this is an apocryphal story, the artist's message is what is important: in the second half of the nineteenth century American Midwest, business supplanted the church as the center of America's focus. Making Chelsea grow and flourish was a community project, residents believed.

"All who lived here in the earlier years were deeply interested and dependent on local industry and business," John Keusch explains. "Buying out of town was frowned on."

As early as 1879, the *Chelsea Herald* notes, "If the inhabitants will only encourage 'home industry,' there will be no danger of losing the mill." An article published in the March 25, 1895 issue of the *Chelsea Herald* outlined how readers could do their part to "Help Chelsea Grow":

Patronize home industries.
Invest in something at home.
Welcome newcomers and visitors.
Encourage home institutions and enterprise.
Keep fraud and corruption out of public offices.
Never neglect to say a good word for Chelsea when you
*   are out of town.*
Advertise your business and our village honestly and constantly.
Insist upon neatness about your premises and don't tolerate
*   slovenly neighbors.*
Take your local newspapers and after reading them send them
*   to friends and relatives.*

The Chelsea Milling Company's silos and outbuildings probably served as the model for artist Jonathan Taylor's "American Cathedral".

Courtesy Chelsea Milling Company

Don't decry the unsuccessful efforts of our townsmen to start a new industry or public enterprise.
Make your home place—no matter if it is poor and cheap— beautiful by flowers and well kept walks.
Post yourselves as to the resources of the community and its progress and be ready to state facts—and facts only—to visitors and prospective settlers.

The Staffan family followed that advice. In 1883, more than 30 years after Frank Staffan left Alsace-Lorraine and emigrated to America, he managed to convince former neighbors to move to Chelsea. In a tintype photograph owned by descendents, Martin and Eva Eisele and their children Flo, Albert, George, Marie, and Martin are pictured on the front porch of their new home shortly after they arrived from Alsace-Lorraine. In 1978, Paul Hoffman wrote an account told him by his mother, Marie Eisele Hoffman, about the trials that faced the family on its trip to America:

As their destination became more imminent, their anxiety, apprehension and anticipation were heightened by the prospect of their impending meeting with their friends the Staffans and Joseph Eisele, a brother of Martin who preceded him here and with whom he was destined to work for many long years.

Running out of money as they reached Detroit, Marie and her brother Martin, then a boy of fourteen, were dispatched by their mother to beg food from nearby houses to sustain them until they reached Chelsea. Arriving in Chelsea in the early evening, they were met at the depot by Frank Staffan and his young son George, then a barefoot boy of eleven. With their meager belongings, which consisted of their luggage and their goose down mattresses which were used on the boat, and ten cents which Martin found on the floor of the Detroit depot, they were transported by the Staffan wagon to the home of Joseph Eisele on Taylor Street...The strange cargo with their European attire created quite a stir as it passed through town, much to the delight of young George, gleefully dancing and pointing so that all the onlookers should see.

The Eiseles were warmly welcomed into the growing community. Gifted stoneworkers, they were hired to craft much of the area's finest stonework.

Local residents weren't solely responsible for public relations efforts. The Michigan Central Railroad, which served as a lifeline between small villages and large cities, also promoted the municipalities along its route. Through the 1890s, the railroad issued a monthly publication called Headlight to promote locations along its Chicago to New York route. The November 1895 issue of the magazine features Chelsea, "one of the most pleasant and enterprising small towns along the line of the M.C.R.R.," the unknown writer enthused.

"The citizens are a happy, thrifty class of medium 'well-to-do' people, and are firm and staunch in their loyalty to Chelsea," the publication continued, adding that Chelsea "enjoys the reputation of being the largest produce market in the county, and the produce dealers of Chelsea are wide awake to this fact, and are enterprising enough to give the highest possible price that the market affords."

By that time, Chelsea families had strong connections to each other. Take the Bacon family, for instance. Donald Bacon's father and uncle, Jabez and William, were born in England in the 1850s and moved together to the village. William married the daughter of Chelsea cofounder James Congdon in 1876. Together they had seven children, two of whom married Palmer brothers, one of them Dr. A.A. Palmer. The Palmers were similarly well connected in the community.

Claude Sears Rogers, who was born January 4, 1912 in the front bedroom at 122 East Street, was related to Elisha Congdon through the family of his mother, Florence Martin Rogers, and her mother, a member of the Sears family. "Her great-uncle, Thomas Sears, owned what is now called the Merkel Farm at the east edge of town, on the road to the old cement plant," Rogers explains.

Headlight also provides biographical glimpses of the leading businessmen and professionals in Chelsea at the turn of the century.

The magazine starts with two prominent clergymen. At the head of the list is the Rev. Thomas Holmes, D.D., retired from the Congregational Church. "The gentleman is endowed with the highest order of intelligence, a close student and a Christian man." The Rev. William P. Considine, pastor of St. Mary's Catholic Church, is credited with having "largely increased the attendance of his church, and is highly esteemed and beloved."

Next in rank is American Express Agent William F. Hatch, the first clerk of the village, a justice of the peace and president of the Board of Village Trustees. "He has served…in an honest and capable way, and has the confidence and esteem of the entire community."

The two banks in town merited photographs of their personnel as well as their facilities. "No financial corporation in the State can point to a more satisfactory record of usefulness, conservative growth and prosperity than can this bank," the publication reports about the Chelsea Savings Bank, adding that Bank President George P. Glazier "is a thorough business man possessing executive ability, eminently fitting him for the highly important position he holds…No customer has had to wait for money during his long experience, not excepting the panics of 1873 and 1893."

Fellow banker Robert Kempf of R. Kempf & Bro., had served in the state senate and legislature by 1895. *Headlight* notes, "With such a capable and efficient business man in charge, ample capital at command, and the facilities they possess, the success of this bank is not surprising." Among Kempf's employees was J.A. Palmer, a Chelsea pioneer who served as for many years as president of the village and clerk of the township.

Merchants in town changed their business names and merchandise frequently, forming and dissolving partnerships and starting new ones. Many conducted several businesses at once. *Headlight* tried to detail all the financial implications.

Harmon Holmes, for instance, ran H.S. Holmes Merchantile, which sold "dry goods, carpets, cloaks, clothing, furnishing goods, boots, shoes and rubber boots." As the Holmes of Hoag & Holmes, he also dealt in hardware, furniture, and paints. He was a partner with W.J. Dancer in a store in Stockbridge and served as a director of the Chelsea Savings Bank. In 1904, Holmes became partners in Chelsea's milling operation with Enoch B. White. Several years later, Holmes' son Howard and White's daughter Mabel became partners for life.

Banker Robert Kempf also owned Kempf & Co., which sold lumber, salt, coal, lime, cement, and farm produce—"one of the most enterprising business houses in this section," according to *Headlight*.

R.S. Armstrong & Company, the ancestor of Fenn's Drug Store, dealt in drugs, groceries, and stationery. A half-dozen other drugstores would come and go over the years, one of them run by Larry Winans, who also sold jewelry.

Beissel & Staffan dealt in "staple and fancy groceries." W.J. Knapp sold general hardware and furniture. J.S. Cummings offered food for both men and animals—"groceries and provisions, hay, straw, feed, etc."

Attorney, state sator, and U.S. congressman J.S. Gorman ran a highly successful business manufacturing "Fine Havana and Domestic Cigars." *Headlight* notes, "He says very little about the cigars he manufactures, but offers his visitors a 'Royal Red Top' cigar, with the laconic remark that 'there is no better for the money.'"

JUST because a coat is a *raincoat* is no reason why it can't be a truly stylish light overcoat—as the Kuppenheimer Watershed *proves.*

Let us show you one—and demonstrate the difference.

SOLD EXCLUSIVELY BY

H. S. Holmes Mercantile Co.
CHELSEA, MICH.

Harmon Holmes ran H.S. Holmes Mercantile, was a partner in the hardware store Hoag & Holmes, had part interest in a Stockbridge store, served as director of the Chelsea Savings Bank, and later became owner of Chelsea's milling company.

Courtesy Chelsea Milling Company

Frank Kentlehner and Larry Winans sold jewelry. J.J. Raftrey and George Webster were merchant tailors. Miller and Son manufactured agricultural implements and patented a special plow geared to Washtenaw's landscape. L.T. Freeman offered to sell "Groceries, Crockery, Lamps, Wood and Willow Ware" to Chelsea's "genteel customers." J.P. Wood & Co. dealt in wheat, oats, corn, and wood. "Hand-picked Beans a Specialty," its advertisements promise. Charles Steinbach invented a new team harness pad which "for durability, cheapness, and beauty of design cannot be excelled," according to the *Herald*.

Two physicians and surgeons had shingles hanging in town. Dr. J.C. Twitchell had an office "equipped with the latest improved appliances" and R. McColgan paid "particular attention to diseases of the eye, ear, nose and throat." The town's dentist, H.H. Avery, also earned a ringing recommendation from the railroad's *Headlight*.

But Chelsea's most outstanding—and controversial—entrepreneur at the turn of the century was Frank Porter Glazier, son of the banker.

No one but Elisha Congdon had a greater impact on Chelsea than Frank Porter Glazier.
Courtesy Chelsea Area Historical Society

The Brightest and the Best

Frank Porter Glazier was a big man with a big presence in town. The industrialist and politician was responsible for Chelsea's golden age as well as for the greatest scandal to rock Chelsea and make statewide headlines.

"Frank Glazier was a fascinating character who made a major impact not only on Washtenaw County, but on the entire state of Michigan," believes historian Louis Doll, a Chelsea native who wrote *Less Than Immortal* about Glazier's life.

Square in build, with a booming voice and even stronger convictions, Glazier moved, governed, gifted, ruled, cajoled, coerced, built, rebuilt, invented and reinvented the once sleepy village of Chelsea. He assumed the role of visionary and community leader that had been abdicated when Elisha Congdon died in 1867. These two men were responsible for not only the physical appearance of the town, but also for its long-lasting prosperity. Glazier's impact is still felt on Chelsea, a century after his golden years here.

Frank Porter Glazier was born in Parma, a small hamlet outside Jackson, in 1862, but his family moved to Chelsea six years later, when George Glazier entered into a partnership to manage the "Bank-Drug Store."

In time, Frank followed in his father's footsteps, studying to be a druggist. After graduating from the University of Michigan in 1882

Straddling the railroad tracks in town at the turn of the century was the Glazier Stove Company. This photograph, looking south along Main Street, was taken before the fire of 1895.

Courtesy of Larry Chapman

and attending a business school in New York State, he returned home to take over his father's drugstore so that George Glazier could concentrate on other entrepreneurial opportunities, including what would become the Chelsea Savings Bank and a lumber, coal, and building company, the predecessor of Frank's enterprise.

The Glazier Stove Company, manufacturing the "Brightest and Best" oil and gas stoves, went into business in 1890. This was Chelsea's first interstate industry, Chelsea's largest employer and manufacturer, and one of the largest manufacturers in the state by the turn of the century. At its peak, 600 stoves were manufactured every day.

To produce electricity for his stove-making operations—and to cajole Chelsea into the "modern age"—Glazier established what would become the Chelsea Electric Light Company. Later, he created a waterworks. After a second disastrous fire at his plant, he built the Clock Tower to mask a giant water cistern which stored 35,000 gallons of water that could be utilized in case of fire.

Initially, Glazier sold electricity to the village and its residents for public and private use. In 1898, while president of the village council, he sold the light company and waterworks to the village, for $26,351 and $58,336, respectively.

That same year, Glazier was named chairman of the Chelsea Savings Bank. In 1901, when George Glazier died, Frank and his architect, Claire Allen of Jackson, embarked on a major era of construction, erecting the stone bank building on the corner of Main and South streets in honor of Glazier's father, a residence for his daughter and her family across from his Victorian mansion on South Street, the Clock Tower, Welfare Building, an office building adjacent to the railroad tracks, and other industrial buildings. Glazier built the first skyscraper in Ann Arbor, the Trustcorp Bank building on South Main and East Huron streets. He was also responsible for the design and a major portion of the funding for the new Methodist Church in Chelsea—and he may have been responsible for the incineration of the old church, people whispered at the time.

When Glazier didn't like what the newspapers were saying about him, he started a new newspaper—the *Ann Arbor News*—with the expressed intention of driving the *Ann Arbor Times* out of business.

When he quarreled with Frank Staffan, the local funeral director, he put a relative named Mapes into the mortuary business in Chelsea. When he didn't like his employees gambling in Chelsea's saloons, he organized a small army of men, marched into the saloons, confiscated the slot machines, and smashed and burned them in the village streets. When he was up for election, he commanded his employees to vote for him—and made sure they did.

A devout Methodist, Glazier was the first employer in the state of Michigan—and among the first in the Midwest—to care enough about his employees' welfare to build them a recreation and entertainment center. Most of his workers boarded in rooms throughout town during the week, then returned to their families in Detroit on Saturday's trains. One monument to Glazier's innovative and patriarchal intentions is the Welfare Building, which was designed to keep his men off the streets, out of the pool halls, and away from Chelsea's girls. The Welfare Building had a stage on which employees could perform theatricals, an indoor pool, a library, meeting rooms and game rooms.

At the turn of the century, Frank Glazier was elected state senator for Washtenaw and Jackson counties, then state treasurer. Still, while he was turning his attention to politics, his business was flourishing and he paid close attention to the progress of his building projects.

He erected monuments to his family on either end of Middle Street, hiring the Eiseles to construct the stone gates to Oak Grove Cemetery on East Middle Street and the stone gates to the Chelsea United Methodist Church Retirement Home on West Middle Street. He also was instrumental in establishing the "old folks' home."

In 1904, Glazier offered 18 acres of land in Chelsea and $5,000 toward the construction of the retirement home. He convinced his mother to offer another $5,000 contribution and together they agreed to provide $1,000 a year for 10 years to maintain the home—if it would cost at least $20,000 to build. In typical Glazier fashion, he also told the organizing committee of Methodist clergy that the Detroit/Ann Arbor/Jackson Railroad, which ran alongside the property, would donate an additional four acres.

On Halloween Day, 1907, the facility was completed and 10 residents were ready to move in. That was just about the time Glazier's troubles were mounting.

In 1901, the year George Glazier died, his son Frank commissioned architect Claire Allen of Jackson to design a monumental stone bank building on the corner of Main and South streets to honor his father.

Courtesy Chelsea Area Historical Society

Glazier's Welfare Building, built in the interest of his employees, offered recreational activities.

Courtesy Chelsea Area Historical Society

The Glazier empire came tumbling down at the end of 1907, when it was discovered that the state treasurer had put $500,000 of state funds into his own bank and then used the money in his many business enterprises.

Glazier proponents later insisted that the practices were not uncommon in the early days of banking and that he borrowed extensively in order to prevent the layoff of any of his employees during the financial Panic of 1907. But, although it was seldom enforced, the law placed a limit on the amount of state money that could be deposited in individual banks. Glazier's opponents used the law to prosecute the entrepreneur.

The late Harold Jones, a Chelsea historian who bought the old Glazier cottage on Cavanaugh Lake, always believed that Glazier could have weathered the political storm if the storm hadn't been unleashed during the financial Panic of 1907, if Glazier hadn't harbored ambitious plans to run for governor, and if his enemies—local as well as regional—had not been determined to ruin him.

Learning of his troubles, Detroit bankers called in the $250,000 in loans they had made to him. The Glazier Stove Company stock, which was used as collateral for the loans, plummeted in value, so Glazier couldn't meet the demands to pay the notes. He was arrested, tried, convicted, and sent to prison in Jackson. While serving time there, he also served as the prison druggist. Before his seven-year sentence was fulfilled, he was released for ill health.

Glazier's friends and business partners also suffered. When the bank failed and closed in December 1907, W.P. Schenk was hit with a

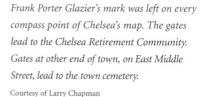

Frank Porter Glazier's mark was left on every compass point of Chelsea's map. The gates lead to the Chelsea Retirement Community. Gates at other end of town, on East Middle Street, lead to the town cemetery.

Courtesy of Larry Chapman

double "financial whammy." He had been Glazier's director and vice president in the stove works and he had been a stockholder and director for the Glazier-run Chelsea Savings Bank. Schenk not only lost his stock investment, he was also subject to the Bank Stock Double Liability Law. As attorney John Keusch explains it, "Under that law, if you have $1,000 invested as a stockholder, you are required to pay another $1,000 for depositors. After the Depression, in Michigan double liability was no longer imposed on bank stock. It is my information that losses to the bank's depositors were small."

Methodist Old Peoples Home, Chelsea, Mich.

As a tribute to his mother, Frank P. Glazier offered eighteen acres of land in Chelsea and $5,000 toward the construction of the Methodist Old People's Home, now known as the Chelsea Retirement Community.

Courtesy Chelsea Area Historical Society

Even a century after Glazier's empire came crashing down, townspeople remember who was pro- and who was anti-Glazier during the scandal. "Perhaps it's better if you don't mention that my father was an opponent," one elderly native requested.

"He might have made some unwise legal decisions, but the financial rules were different in those days. What you have to remember are the wonderful things he did for Chelsea. Frank Glazier put Chelsea on the map and engineered many of the modern systems that made Chelsea outstanding in its day—and in our day," points out Jackie Frank, former president of Preservation Chelsea. "Frank Glazier is responsible for some of Chelsea's most outstanding and lasting architectural features."

≈

The 1895 issue of *Headlight* called Glazier "prompt and honorable in his relations with mankind, affable, enterprising and liberal." His success, the writer concluded, "is a fitting monument to his industry, honesty, and integrity."

Historians since Glazier's fall in 1907 have argued about just how honest Glazier was, but Geraldine Glazier Kraft firmly, without question, believes in his innocence, honesty and integrity.

Although she lives on the second floor of the Chelsea United Methodist Retirement Home now—the home her grandfather helped establish—as a child she lived in the grandeur and opulence of the Glazier inner circles, which, by 1910 when she was born, extended from Detroit to Cavanaugh Lake. Blind and confined to a wheelchair now, her mind is still sharp, her voice is sweet, and her memories dance around what she calls her "best years," the years when she was the child of Henrietta and Frank P. Glazier.

She called Frank and Henrietta Glazier "Mama" and "Papa," because they raised her from infancy, but, in fact, Geraldine was the only child of the Glaziers' daughter Vera, who married Rice Howell of Howell at the home of her brother Harold, in Seattle. Vera died several weeks after Geraldine was born, and the grief-stricken young father allowed his in-laws to talk him into letting them bring the baby to their home and raising her as their own child. Several years later, Rice Howell remarried, moved back to Michigan, and eventually had two other daughters, but Geraldine continued to live with "Mama" and "Papa."

She was born shortly after Glazier was released from prison. The family spent winters in Detroit and summers at a palatial cottage on Cavanaugh Lake, until it burned in 1915. The Glaziers then moved to the older family cottage closer to the water.

Vera's two younger sisters, Dorothy and Edna, were still living near their parents at the time the new baby arrived, Dorothy at home and Edna married. The Glaziers' youngest son, Henry, was also at home, older than Geraldine, but closest to her in age. She loved all her family, but she adored her grandfather.

Henrietta Glazier was "very lovable, a wonderful Mama," Geraldine says, a tear rolling unobserved down her cheek. "She had brown hair and was about my height—and I am considered short. She had an 18-inch waist and when she dressed, a maid would tighten her corset by putting her knee at Mama's back, then pushing with her knee and pulling on the strings."

Geraldine's great-grandmother, Emily Glazier, also lived with them throughout Geraldine's childhood. "My grandfather was her only son and she was very proud of him," she says. "She was very, very proud. I remember her telling me, 'Straighten up! Straighten up!' For years when I was little, I never went to sleep without holding her hand. I always thought it was wonderful that she went to bed at the same time I did. It wasn't until I was an adult that I understood how much she loved me."

Geraldine particularly remembers festive holidays, when the entire family gathered together for old-fashioned celebrations, but she also cherishes pictures of everyday moments in her memory album: Papa shaving with an old-fashioned razor and strap, Papa telling her that he heard reindeer and Santa's sleigh bells on the roof

Christmas Eve, Mama's passion for making sure that her little girl wore immaculate and starched dresses, riding in Henry's pony cart around the lake, grand picnics on the lake shore and watching ice harvested during the winter, refusing to leave the ice even when the cutters came near her spot on the lake.

"I imagine that I ruled the roost," she admits with a faint smile.

Her grandfather died when she was 11. Her grandmother Henrietta died six years later. "Papa had a heart condition and was not a well man in his last years. He suffered from diabetes. His opponents didn't see him run for governor, which made them happy, but I think his ordeal broke his heart," she suggests. "Mama, Henry and I were with him when he died at the lake. He was awake until the end."

Frank Porter Glazier died at the age of 60, on New Year's Day, 1922. The 11-year-old sat holding her grandmother's hand as he breathed his last and also later, as mourners came to call. "I can remember Mama sitting beside his body in the little cottage. He was laid out on the couch, covered with a nice, warm blanket. She didn't want him in a casket. I remember her telling us, 'Kiss Grandpa goodbye.'"

After a moment where tears are shed from sightless eyes, Geraldine whispers, "It was very hard. I was very young and it was impossible to fathom what this meant—then, and to me in later years. But he had a marvelous history to leave his hometown. And I am very proud of that."

$\approx$

One of Frank Porter Glazier's closest friends and political allies was Archie Wilkinson who was, according to the 1895 issue of *Headlight*, "one of the younger members of the Bar of this county, and at the same time one of the best known."

Attorney John Keusch, who cherishes memories and mementos from Wilkinson's long and illustrious law career, believes that Archie Wilkinson stands second only to Frank Porter Glazier in the impact he had on the history and development of downtown Chelsea during the village's formative years. The 90-year-old attorney leans back in the leather armchair of his own office at Flintoft & Keusch, links his hands behind his head, and presents the case for Wilkinson's prominence among the village's most noteworthy movers and shakers.

"First," John Keusch says, "he and his father acquired James Congdon's property interest and assumed payment of the mortgage when Congdon was about to lose everything he owned in 1870. That rescued one of the town's founders from financial distress and possibly changed the course of the village's development."

Second, Keusch continues, "Archie Wilkinson was an entrepreneur with a vision." He served as editor of the *Chelsea Standard* during the Glazier era. He was responsible for bringing businesses to town, among them the Flanders Manufacturing Company, makers of the Flanders Motorcycle, which eventually set up shop in the Glazier plant facilities. Wilkinson was also one of the principal parties involved in establishing Chelsea's early telephone system.

Third, Wilkinson was a real estate magnate. He acquired the area around Flanders Street, much of the vacant land west of Chelsea, and the stone office building that had belonged to the Glazier Stove Company. He platted and developed the Flanders Street area in east Chelsea and the Wilkinson and Chandler Street area in west Chelsea.

Fourth, Wilkinson was a gifted attorney. He served as Frank P. Glazier's principal attorney and represented Glazier's interests during the receivership. He was the legal counsel principally involved in the disposition of Glazier's physical assets. And years later, during the Depression, he also effected the merger of the Farmers and Merchants Bank and the Kempf Commercial Savings Bank when they formed the Chelsea State Bank.

Later generations of some the names listed in this early 20th century advertisement as officers and directors of the Farmers and Merchants Bank are still involved in Chelsea's financial life.

Courtesy of Scott Otto

Fifth, he was a man with a taste for fun and for culture, and he shared his interests with his community. Wilkinson promoted lyceums in the Sylvan Town Hall with entertainers and lecturers who came all the way from Boston, New York, and other eastern cities to perform for Chelsea crowds. Playbills still exist of Wilkinson's promotional and cultural activities.

And, last, Wilkinson was civically minded, Keusch points out. "Archie Wilkinson was active in the office of the Michigan State Oil Inspection, which was at the time an office comparable to the State Highway Commissioner. Kerosene was used for cooking and lighting prior to electricity and gas, and his role was to ensure that all supplies of kerosene were free of explosive elements."

Getting a Start in Business

"My mother used to say that I exhausted all my ambition as a boy, concocting ways to earn money," John Keusch says with a grin. As a small boy prior to World War I, he trundled businessmen's heavy portmanteaus down to Main Street on his wagon, weeded his grandfather's fields, picked and shelled beans, packed wool ("A wool packer stands in a deep burlap bag using his hands to catch the fleeces, oily and weighing about ten pounds, then uses his feet to pack the fleece into the bag."), delivered ice, and stacked blocks of peat at the Morrisite Process Company, known locally as "the peat plant."

Keusch still has a pay envelope at home that he received while working for the peat plant. The boy was nine or ten years old at the time, and was paid the same rate as the old men working beside him.

A machine cut the raw peat, which came out in brickettes and workers lifted the wet brickettes onto drying racks. "Morrisite was never much of a production plant. It took too long to remove the water," Keusch says. "It was a stock venture thing and I was involved with the last promoter, who tried to sell the public on how much heat could be produced by burning peat and what a nice flame the brickettes made."

When the young entrepreneur was in the tenth grade, he farmed onions on his own for two years on land out on Trinkle Road. He also worked in the A&P Grocery Store during the summer for $5 a week, working noon to midnight on weekdays and all day Saturday, from opening until midnight. "That paid for my tuition at the university—it cost $100 a year," he says.

~

Among the seven children born to Chelsea pioneers Benjamin and Mary Winans were twin entrepreneurs who were born a generation before John Keusch. As teenagers, Albert and Elbert Winans worked in the "Chicken Pickin' Place," a shanty on Main Street where workers ran a machine with a brush to whip the feathers off butchered chickens. For twenty-five cents a day, the boys finished the plucking process and packed the chickens in barrels with ice. Local drayman Ed Chandler would cart them a block away to the town depot, where the barrels would be loaded on trains for Detroit.

Eventually, Elbert went to work for the railroad and Albert joined his Uncle Lewis in what would become the family jewelry business.

First located in the building that now belongs to Sam Johnson's How-To Shop, A.E. Winans started as a drugstore with a little jewelry department. "My Grandpa, Albert Winans, was a self-taught watch repairman and also an optometrist," George Winans says. "He and my father had a small office up over the store. They had little training, but evidently my Dad was a good optometrist."

One story about Albert and Elbert Winans became part of Chelsea folklore. Elbert was electrocuted while working on the tracks with a crew in Port Huron and somehow, in the mysterious connection that twins share, Albert sensed it immediately. "My grandparents were in the store working one afternoon," George Winans explains. "All of a sudden, my grandfather turned to his wife, very worried, and said, 'Alice, something's wrong with Elbert!' That was at 1:00. At 3:00 a telegram arrived saying he'd been killed."

One of Chelsea's oldest families, the Winans have operated a jewelry business in town since the Victorian era.

Courtesy Chelsea Area Historical Society

Albert's son, Elmer Winans, entered the family's jewelry business in the early years of the twentieth century, but left during World War I, to work in Detroit at the Henry Ford plant. "Henry Ford was the first manufacturer to pay $5-a-day wages and that was a big deal," George Winans explains. "A lot of country boys flocked to Detroit." When he returned, a new sign was painted above the shop, announcing a new generation of business: "A.E. Winans & Son."

∾

Attorney Archie Wilkinson at one time served as secretary of the Chelsea Telephone Company. In the 1920s, he wrote his memories of Chelsea's early telephone service, which dates back to the 1880s.

Local villages "whose residents could sling the local dirt over the back fence" were slow to recognize the value of a telephone service, Wilkinson points out in his article. "The demand came from farmers, who were the great developers of the phone system."

Farmers strung their own telephone lines between neighbors' properties and operated party-built systems without any station. Gradually, they saw the benefits of extending their connections farther afield—at about the time that George Glazier sensed a business opportunity. According to Wilkinson,

The forebear of the Michigan State Telephone Co., was induced to enter Chelsea about 1882, as I remember, or perhaps 1883, through the efforts of George P. Glazier. He induced the business men to buy coupon books containing coupons to pay for toll service and in five, ten and twenty-five dollar size. The purpose was to get enough money in advance to erect the line between Dexter and Chelsea. The office over the Glazier drug store was a toll station pure and simple. You went up the stairs, had the operator call the party you wanted by name and then a messenger would be sent out to locate the party and bring them to the central station.

The telephone station remained here until 1897 or 1898 and then moved over the Kempf bank. There was only one operator, and the office was closed at night, or at any time the operator was away. However, after hours, the switchboard was connected with the office of Dr. Smith…

The operators between 1882 and 1902, at which time toll lines were taken over by Chelsea Telephone Co., were, first, Hattie Robbins, then Mina Geddes and Fannie Warner…

About the only subscribers to Bell in Chelsea at the time lines were merged with the local company were Frank and George P. Glazier, W.W. Knapp, James P. Woods, Dr. Smith, John Farrell, who was lame and couldn't climb the stairs, C. J. Snyder the onion king, and five or six others. The interior of the boxes (telephones) furnished the subscribers were all the same, but some, instead of being on the wall, ran clear to the floor and were larger. There was an extra charge for the large ones…

In 1896, there were several farm independent lines centering in Waterloo where Lynn L. Gorton had a station, and to get access to Chelsea for those lines and connection between the merchants of Chelsea and Waterloo patrons, the Chelsea Telephone Company was born.

We started in with about 14 subscribers and the directory was printed on a 4x6 card and we had to use large print for the names to fill that space…Ours was a purely gossip line as we had no way to get out of town except, of course, at Waterloo…

A young lawyer, Nelson Freer, and his wife took care of the switchboard (in exchange) for rent of the room he used for his office…The gross income of the company at this time was under two hundred dollars a year but finally reached the sum of perhaps five hundred before we sold out to the Michigan Bell in 1904…

≈

Three years after Michigan Bell acquired the telephone company, the Chelsea Savings Bank closed in the wake of Glazier's scandal. That left the Kempf Commercial & Savings Bank as the only bank for miles around. In April 1908, the Farmers and Merchants Bank of Chelsea was chartered by the State of Michigan "with capital of $25,000, consisting of 250 shares of $100 par value," according to Paul Schaible. His father was one of the organizers and served as cashier until 1921, when he became president upon the death of President John Waltrous.

A new and exciting business opened on Main Street in 1908. Chelsea's first theater, the "Chicago Theatre," soon to become the Princess Theater, took up residence in the Merkel block of buildings.

The Princess Theater's first projectionist, Warren Geddes, was a local photographer who, by 1909, was also co-owner. An advertisement in the *Chelsea Standard/Herald* announces, "Westerland & Geddes, Proprietors of the Princess." In those early days of film, silent movies were the warm-up acts for vaudeville shows in town. Later, cylinder records and phonographs provided sound for silent films, and when the movies' reels were changed, a pianist entertained the audience.

A new and thrilling business opened on Main Street in 1908. The "Chicago Theatre," soon to be renamed the Princess Theater, took up residence in the Merkel block of buildings.

Courtesy of Jim Monahan

Two years before the theater's opening, Chelsea had been treated to some "trick photography" that was the precursor to motion pictures. Adelma Fisk Weber told Kathleen Clark about the first time she saw a moving picture in Chelsea. Her father paid a nickel for each family member to watch a five-minute silent film that illustrated an animation technique. "My dad was to town and he saw it, and thought it was just so unusual," she told the president of the Chelsea Area Historical Society. "He came all the way home (off Sylvan Rd.) and said, 'Everyone get ready to go. They're going to have that show in town.' Every one of us, even Grandma, had to go."

~

The origins of the Chelsea Milling Company are obscure, although records show a grist mill in town by 1853. In 1879, the *Chelsea Standard* reported a rumor that the company was about to be sold—unless local residents would agree to support the local business rather than "hauling their grain all over the county in search of the most favorable rates." Claude Rogers remembers hearing his mother say that there had been a fire at the White Milling Company sometime before the end of the nineteenth century, after Enoch B. White acquired the mill. According to White's great-grandson, Dudley Holmes, who was born in 1914, "Enoch White owned several mills in Illinois, Indiana and Michigan. He bought and sold them and loved to move around, apparently. At one time he owned five or six milling companies and Chelsea was just one stop in his career. He was a very well-informed man, enjoyed people and made friends easily."

Meanwhile, Harmon S. Holmes, a Dexter native and Chelsea transplant, was an entrepreneur always interested in listening to intriguing business propositions. He began eyeing the mill. A native of Scio Township in Dexter, where an early flour mill served a widely scattered community of pioneers, Holmes "was quite a versatile person business-wise. He was on the bank board here and ran a mercantile business, among other things," 87-year-old Dudley Holmes says of his grandfather.

In 1901, Harmon Holmes went into business with Enoch B. White and the Chelsea Milling Company was incorporated under the name of the William Bacon Holmes Company. In 1908, Holmes bought out White's share of the mill. Several years later, Harmon's son Howard married White's daughter Mabel.

According to an account written in 1987 by Howard Holmes, one of the twin sons born to that couple, "Chelsea Milling Company was originally, as the name would imply, strictly engaged in the milling of flour, which flour was sold to both the baking industry and the consumer field…Consumer items were packed in 100 lb., 50 lb., 25 lb., 10 lb., 5 lb., and 2 ½ lb. bags. The flour for bakers was packed in 140 lb. and 100 lb. bags."

Once Holmes and other local merchants and farmers weathered the nationwide financial Panic of 1907, as well as the Glazier crisis and resulting scandal, the town settled into a period of prosperity and optimism that led quietly to the First World War. With just a little bit of capital, entrepreneurs experimented with new cars, the newfangled airplane, better plows, mechanized tractors and trucks.

Harmon Holmes became a partner in the Chelsea Milling Company in 1901 and purchased Enoch B. White's share of the company in 1908. The milling operation, home of the "Jiffy" product line, is now run by the fourth generation of the Holmes family.

Courtesy Chelsea Milling Company

Planes, Trains, and Automobiles

The Congdons had been successful in situating a thriving village on their land because they had been successful in luring the railroad to build a depot on their land. The railroad dominated the town's life until after World War II. Trains provided a link to families and social trends back East, to new frontiers in the West, to manufacturers who would stock Chelsea's store shelves, and to Detroit and Chicago merchants who would buy Chelsea's vegetables, dairy products, chickens, lambs, wool, and wheat.

"Throughout its history, Chelsea relied on trains. The sound of the train whistle blowing was an important part of our lives," John Keusch says. "Remember, there were no trucks up until the twenties and horse power was slow and not always reliable. The train brought everything we needed: mail, store merchandise, farm equipment, newspapers. And farmers relied on the train to bring their produce to the cities. There was no refrigeration in those days. Dairy farmers and haulers would meet the trains with milk pails. Trains would bring the pails to the big dairies, then return the empty pails later that day."

THE INTERURBAN RAILROAD

Some people comb battlefields for relics. Others scour antique stores, flea markets, and old barns. George Sparrow, a retired history teacher, moved to Chelsea several years ago and began pursuing the ghost of the Detroit United Railroad, known locally as the Interurban. On a blustery fall day while sitting in the Big Boy restaurant, he pulls out a hand-lettered map of the town that pinpoints the discoveries he has made while walking through fields, scrambling through woods, driving slowly along roadways, and talking to old-timers.

"At the Methodist Home I found my first remnants of the roadbed, which crossed Wilkinson Street (to the left of the apartments there now)," he explains, tracing his route with his finger. "This is where Clio Loop was located, the turnaround for the Interurban. The trolley ran past the Prinzing property, beyond the stand of black walnut trees, then crossed just south of the priest's house for St. Mary's and across Congdon. The tracks ran right where the Federal Screw Works' double doors are situated and the station was across the street, where the Mobil Station now stands."

The tracks continued across the peat bog at Flanders Street, behind the present-day hospital, then continued past the site of Pierce Lake Elementary School, staying west of Freer Road before crossing it just north of Old U.S. 12. "As you drive down 12 East, you can see portions of the bed, if you look carefully," Sparrow says, still referring to his map. "The Interurban crossed the area that is now 94 at a point east of the bridge, and followed Jackson Road. The power station for the railroad is the brick home with the tower at Lima Center and it still has the big Delco storage batteries used by the train as it ran into Ann Arbor."

The trolley cars driven by "motormen" (often college boys) stopped in Chelsea every half hour. These cars would also stop at every road crossing or farmer's field to pick up and deposit passengers or freight. The Guthrie Farm on Pierce Road, three miles west of town, was a frequent stop. Neighbors would tether their horses in the Guthries' barn, do their business in town, then reclaim their horses for the ride home. On the hour, express trains passed through without stopping. "All the boys in town knew the schedules by heart. We went off on the trolley by ourselves, to Jackson or Ann Arbor, at quite a young age," John Keusch says.

As a boy, Keusch and his friends spent hours watching the trains and sometimes waiting for the trains, wagons at the ready, in order to assist salesmen with heavy sales cases. They pulled their wagon loads downtown to the shops and businesses on Main Street and earned a dime for their efforts.

Bert Conlan owned a livery stable on Jackson Street across from the railroad depot—the sign is still painted on the building. He also offered a taxi service that met all Interurban streetcars. His competitor was J. Edward Weber, owner of the Princess Theater and a local saloon. "Taxis in those days were not licensed, so anyone with an automobile could become a taxi operator," John Keusch explains.

As a regional transportation center, Chelsea boasted several livery stables and blacksmith shops, among them B.J. Conlan's Livery on Jackson Street across from the depot.

Courtesy of David C. Lixey

The Interurban once played a pivotal role in Chelsea's business environment and social life. And, occasionally, the Interurban made headlines in local newspapers with accidents and close encounters.

"Part of its route passed over the peat bog, which provided a spongy and not very satisfactory base for the tracks," John Keusch explains. "Occasionally the trolley would bounce off the tracks and land in the bog."

In the early days of motoring, there were a number of collisions between automobiles and trains on South Main Street. John Keusch remembers at least two deaths in separate accidents. Civil War veteran Richard Whalien was killed in 1922 when his car was struck by a train.

There were two major disasters on the Interurban in Chelsea. One occurred in the midst of World War I, the other took place in 1924, just beyond the Beach farm at Lima Center. But countless times, trolley cars flipped off the rails, with sometimes serious, sometimes humorous consequences.

"I was in a wreck on the Interurban," says Keusch's cousin, George Staffan. "We were on the sidetrack on Parker Road, waiting for another car to come, when the passing train jumped the sidetrack and hit our car. It hurt the motorman. I was five…six…maybe seven. My mother and I were sitting in front of the smoking room—the seats were like old school seats, wooden and bolted to the floor—but our seats became unbolted." Mrs. Staffan managed to reach the telegraph station and called her husband. "He had an old brass-rod Ford with gas headlights and when I saw those headlights in the distance, I knew it was him coming. We were some glad to see him."

THOSE NEW-FANGLED MACHINES

All kinds of new contraptions wheeled and reeled over Chelsea's streets and across the fields in the early years of the twentieth century. An early motorcycle called the Flanders Motorcycle was manufactured in the former Glazier industrial buildings, and up through the 1950s, the test track on North Main Street at the rear of the tower building, where the motorcycles were given a run for their money, could still be detected.

According to Claude S. Rogers, "When Flanders went into bankruptcy, my father, Dor L. Rogers, became the representative of a Detroit Trust Company, to wind up its affairs. I remember him driving a Flanders motorcycle home for lunch one day, which he had assembled from parts on hand. This must have been about 1916 or 1917."

In 1903, A.R. Welch established the Chelsea Manufacturing Company to build his Welch Automobile. The car was demonstrated at the Automobile Show of Chicago that year and Welch was greatly encouraged by the public response. He planned to produce 15 cars a month at a price of $2,000 f.o.b. Chelsea, but in 1904, he ran into financial problems, filed for bankruptcy, and moved to Pontiac, where he continued to produce automobiles under the name Welch-Pontiac. In 1911, he sold his company to William Durant of General Motors. The Oakland division was changed to the Pontiac division of General Motors, and is still operating today.

In 1915, Fred Lewis founded Lewis Spring & Axel Co., and became the second automobile manufacturer to start building cars in Chelsea. His two models, the Hollier Six and the Hollier Eight, were manufactured in Glazier's Tower Building, as well as other sites around town. The Hollier Eight was the first eight-cylinder car and it was priced to sell, at just under $1,000. An article in *Motor Mechanics*, printed just before the war, in 1917, commended Fred Lewis, the Hollier Six and Eight car manufacturer, for the company's "extreme care and practice in the design and construction of the power-plant," noted that "the rear axle is strong and sturdy," the front axle is "drop forged of high carbon steel, heat treated and pickled," and, "next to the dependability of the power plant and transmission and the sturdiness and proper design of such chassis units as the frame and axles, come the comfort and safety of the passengers."

The 1917 issue of *Motor Mechanics* continues, "Much adventuring capital and talent are flowing. Will it stay? The motor vehicle is the unit forming, so to speak, the cavalry of local goods carriage. A new public utility is rising to its strength. We may not be far from the day when long-term contracts for freight, or mail, or express may be entered into by motor vehicles between cities within a hundred miles of each other."

The December 8, 1921 issue of the *Chelsea Standard* announced, "A merchant of Fayette, West Virginia, who owns a Hollier Eight, which was made in this place, sent the engine here to have it overhauled. The work was done at Jones Garage, and last Saturday Mr. Jones shipped the engine by express to the owner." Not just Chelsea's farm products, but also its manufactured goods were going far beyond Chelsea's borders now.

"It was a classy-looking car," John Keusch says. "Some had fancy wheels, I remember. Mr. Lewis road-tested all the motors and he sold quite a few cars. He came right after the Flanders Motor Company went out of business and his cars were all hand-made—no assembly lines for him. The war (World War I) shut him down. After the war was over, bumpers for automobiles were made in the plant, but it wasn't run by Mr. Lewis then."

Some years after Fred Lewis left Chelsea, George Staffan, then a young boy, explored the old building where the Hollier Eight was made and learned more about the car than most of the town knew. "There was stuff strewn all over the floor," he remembers. "I read a letter from a man in Texas begging the company, 'Send me cars. I can

HOLLIER EIGHT—Large Five Passenger at $1185.

HOLLIER EIGHT—A Classy Four Passenger Roadster.

"High-class, modern in every way" was how Fred Lewis advertised his Chelsea-made automobile, the Hollier Eight.

From Ann Arbor Federal Savings Village Book

sell all you can send me.' Those were well made cars in great demand."

According to Staffan, Fred Lewis was a gifted machinist who built every part himself without any assembly line production methods. "He hired an efficiency expert to help him with the manufacturing and the expert rearranged all the machinery and told Mr. Lewis what to do. As soon as the expert left, Fred Lewis moved everything back to where it had been before and resumed his old ways. So, Mr. Lewis couldn't produce the cars fast enough to stay in business."

Later, in the easternmost part of the Glazier industrial buildings, another entrepreneur manufactured one airplane. "The plane sat in town for a long time, but someone finally fixed it up and got it going," Staffan remembers. "They flew her out of there, probably in 1920 or 1921."

At least one airplane was manufactured in Chelsea between the two World Wars. George Staffan remembers seeing the plane sit in town for a long time—"but someone finally fixed it up and got it going,… probably in 1920 or 1921."

From Ann Arbor Federal Savings Village Book

Automobile dealers appeared in town by 1910. The Leigh Palmer family launched Palmer Motor Sales in 1910 in a two-car garage at 130 East Middle Street, but moved to its present location on South Main Street the following year and acquired the Ford franchise in 1912. Michigan's oldest Ford dealership actually started out as a gas station and repair shop. Later, Palmer Motor Sales sold Dodges, Studebakers, and Fordson tractors. "For many farmers around here, Fordson was their first tractor," George Palmer says. "I remember seeing them as a kid. They were built before the days of balloon tires. They had big steel rims. You used to see signs on the highways saying, 'Tractors with lugs keep off' because they were deadly to asphalt."

George Palmer also remembers meeting Henry Ford in town. "I was only five or six, not old enough to realize who he was, but I saw him standing on the running board of a 1930s-era car and I recognized the name when someone told me who I was looking at. I ran home and told my folks and they didn't believe me. They just laughed. Who wouldn't?"

For many years director and vice-president of the Glazier Stove Works, W.P. Schenk was another early automobile dealer. He built the building that later housed the Purple Rose Theater Company, selling Buicks and Chevrolets from that location.

"Dealers in earlier days had perhaps one or two demonstrators at most," Keusch remembers. "Sales people would take prospective buyers for rides in the evening. If you purchased a car, it would be delivered in four or five weeks." The top floor of Schenk's building was used by local residents to store the cars—individual garages would not appear in Chelsea's backyards until decades later.

Warren Daniels began in the automobile business as a subdealer for Dodge Brothers automobiles. His first car arrived the day before Thanksgiving in 1917, but Daniels didn't make his first sale until March 1, 1918. On that day, he sold two cars, one to Jule Strieter, the other to Herb Paul. In 1925, he took over the Buick agency, and in 1933, the Oldsmobile agency. Daniels Motor Sales was incorporated on the 49th anniversary of the first sale: March 1, 1957.

Those dealers had other competition, among them Harold "Pappy" Spaulding, who in 1929 purchased a building on the spot where Charlie Kaercher's Wagon & Wood Working Shop once stood on North Main Street and launched Spaulding Chevrolet Sales.

Far-Away, Forgetton Battlefields

Max Hepburn has a photograph taken by Chelsea photographer E.F. Shaver in 1898 of his grandfather, James Hepburn, who was a member of the "Chelsea Rifles." "They were similar to the National Guard," explains Marjorie Hepburn. "Each town had their own 'guardians.'" Inspired by their fathers' patriotism during the Civil War, farm boys and town boys flocked to join up. Women formed their own military units, as members of the Auxiliary of the Grand Army of the Republic.

Before Frank Glazier began making statewide headlines during his battles with the banking industry, the Spanish-American War created some excitement in Chelsea. Conrad Lehman joined the Army after the *U.S.S. Maine* was sunk, in pursuit of the same adventure Teddy Roosevelt was seeking. After his stint in Cuba, the veteran returned from the war to open a saloon in downtown Chelsea.

At least one Chelsea man participated in the war in the Philippines, the turn-of-the-century's equivalent to the Vietnam War. Corporal Olvien Floyd, who would marry Allie Guthrie of Sylvan Township, was serving with Company "I" of the 26th Infantry when he wrote a letter that echoes the concerns of every homesick soldier in any war. From Cuartel de España, Manila, Philippine Islands on April 9, 1909 he writes:

Well, Uncle, I am sorry to hear that times are hard but it is no more

William James Hepburn, photographed in 1898, was a member of the Chelsea Rifles.
Courtesy of the Max Hepburn Family

The war in the Philippines directly affected at least one Chelsea family. Olvien Floyd of Sylvan Township (pictured on the left) served in the land that he described as filled with "heat and dust,... carabou (sic), small ponies, and bamboo and too much rain."

Courtesy of the Gallagher family

than I expected, for they say it has been the same way throughout the States for the last year or two but I hope they will improve before I come back…

We all have to go when our time comes and what bothers me is not being ready for I am one of the worst since I have been in the army, though I can proudly say that I do not drink and carouse around like some of the soldiers. Uncle, I am very glad that I can resist the temptation of drink for it has ruined lots of soldiers some of them stay drunk nearly all the time…

The heat and dust will kill me if I don't get away from here soon, Dear Uncle, you may want to hear me talk of the islands but I hope you will never have to come over here and stay as long as I have and two years is a short time here and there is nothing over here but half negroes, carabou (sic), small ponies and bamboo and too much rain in the wet season and too much heat in the dry season and it is summer here all the time which is more than I can stand much longer, but I am so glad that our time is getting short over here we leave here in June…

Puerto Rico and the Philippines were very far from rural Michigan. The two foreign wars were quickly relegated to history books and the few Chelsea veterans were quickly reabsorbed into peacetime pursuits.

Dear Old Golden Rule Days

By the turn of the century, Chelsea's public school system was well established and well regarded. After 1904, town residents could choose to have their children attend either St. Mary's parochial school west of Main Street or the public school east of Main Street, where all grades were at first housed in one large brick building, the Union School. Today, the only reminder of that school rests in the name "Schoolhouse Apartments," bestowed on the 1960s-era two-story apartment buildings that were erected on the former school grounds.

Prominent members of the board of education in 1895 included F.P. Glazier, who was largely responsible for coercing the village into building the high school, his business rival Harmon Holmes, W.J. Knapp, W.P. Schenk, and J.P. Wood.

The teachers in Chelsea, as well as in all other Michigan schools, were required to follow the "Rules For Teachers" established by Michigan's Board of Education in 1879:

1. Teachers each day will fill lamps, clean chimneys.
2. Each teacher will bring a bucket of water and a scuttle of coal for the day's session.
3. Make your pens carefully. You may whittle (goose quill) nibs to the individual taste of the pupils.
4. Men teachers may take one evening each week for courting purposes, or two evenings a week if they attend church regularly.
5. After ten hours in school, the teachers may spend the remaining time reading the Bible or other good books.
6. Women teachers who marry or engage in unseemly conduct will be dismissed.
7. Every teacher should lay aside from each pay a goodly sum of his earnings for his benefit during his declining years so that he will not become a burden on society.
8. Any teacher who smokes, uses liquor in any form, frequents pool rooms or public halls, or gets shaved in a barber shop will give good reasons to suspect his worth, intention, integrity, and honesty.
9. The teacher who performs his labor faithfully and without fault for five years will be given an increase of twenty-five cents per week in his pay, providing the Board of Education approves.

Only the name "Schoolhouse Apartments" remains on East Street to identify the location of the impressive brick Union School, which once housed all grades in Chelsea. Note the water pump for horses by the sidewalk in the foreground.

Courtesy of Larry Chapman

Throughout the farmlands surrounding Chelsea were one-room country schools attended by farmers' children. Typically, they went only to the eighth grade, so farmers who wanted their children to attend high school either moved into town, as was the case with the Beach family, or boarded their children in town if the children couldn't walk that far or find transportation.

When the Chelsea United Methodist Home decided to compile residents' memoirs in 1991, many of the old-timers' most vivid recollections revolved around their school days in one-room country schools.

Glen Wiseman remembered the most outstanding Halloween prank to hit Punkin College: revelers "tore the school up inside, took the stovepipe down and moved everything outside…We had quite a time putting it all back."

Every year the vacant land across from Punkin College would fill with gypsies, who tented and camped there, he reminisced. "Us kids, we were scared of them. They were tough-looking people. And they was always wandering around the neighborhood visiting people's houses. And the teacher always told us, 'Don't go out there! Don't go out there! They'll carry you off!' She scared the socks off us!"

When Don Drew attended the same school in the early years of the century, its attendance consisted of five children, two of them Fritzes, three of them Drews. One day, to generate a little excitement, he let two gophers loose in the schoolroom and howled with laughter as his teacher, screaming, scrambled to the top of her desk.

A Miss Savage, who taught at Savage School in the 1920s, had an even more harrowing adventure with wildlife. According to Myrtle Bidwell, "The teacher was always very, very upset because a neighbor's bull would escape the farm and come calling. The teacher would hide red coats for fear the bull would take after the children." One day she asked Myrtle and her sister to run as fast as possible to the farmer's house to get help. "There was no more bull calling on the school after that."

Myrtle later became one of those brave souls who faced budding young scholars in one-room settings. She taught in a North Lake school four miles from her home. After walking the four miles every morning, she built the fire before the children arrived, swept the floors, lugged buckets of water, washed windows, corrected papers, made lesson plans for each child—and "everything else," she explains. "Once in awhile there was an old man who would pick me up and take me home in his wagon. He always told me 'I had to go to Grass Lake.' It wasn't true. He was just being nice."

As the Roaring Twenties dawned and women began taking scissors to bob their long braids of hair, Winifred Cooley was teaching in a school closely supervised by the superintendent. "One day one of the lady teachers asked the superintendent if he cared if she had her hair cut. He told her, 'You know I won't like it, but you can.' The next week there were six of us got our hair cut."

During the last year of the Merkel School, Katie Chapman was one of only two students. To make sure that she received a good edu-

Dressed in their best and facing the future with an obvious steadfast purpose, the Chelsea High School Class of 1896 posed for a class photograph. The young man on the right already wears a wedding ring.

Courtesy Chelsea Area Historical Society

cation, her father decided to transport the two children to the Little Red School, which was farther down Manchester Road.

Before country-educated students were admitted to Chelsea High School, they had to prove their mettle by passing an admission test. "We were always proud of the fact that the country kids were smarter than the town kids—we knew we were, because we had to prove our aptitude," June Floyd Robinson, a graduate of the Sylvan Township School, says with a smile and a wink.

By the turn of the century, a few Chelsea High School students were continuing their education at the University of Michigan in Ann Arbor. Admission to college in those days only required a high school diploma.

The Town Was Jumping

Scott Otto, a man in his early forties with a passion for collecting, arrives at the Big Boy restaurant one sunny autumn day with a fraction of his collection of old Chelsea memorabilia. At home, he cherishes an ancient backdrop for a local play that was signed on the back by the community actors. He owns a chest full of World War I first aid supplies. Letters written from World War II battlefronts. Antique farm equipment. Signs and advertising pieces from bygone local businesses. Graying photographs of long-gone local celebrities and festivities. But the collection he carries in a suitcase today is something very different. Within the old leather suitcase is an intriguing—and probably forbidden—glimpse of the secrets of an extinct fraternal order called the Modern Woodmen of America ("The Giant of the Fraternal World").

"Opening this suitcase is like looking at strange relicts from another planet and trying to guess how—and why—they were used," he says, as he pulls out a box of black and white marbles ("They used these to vote on—or blackball—new members."), a roster containing 119 members' names (many of whom have children and grandchildren still living in Chelsea), a ritual book, some intriguing gizmos, and a catalogue with hundreds of pages of ritual accouterments and gags.

"Look at this: a fake branding iron (advertised "with wires to batteries to provide smoke"), goggles, wigs, fake beards and noses, buzzers, bells, blindfolds, bizarre costumes," he says, as he turns the catalogue pages. "I guess those men had some lively times when they got together!"

Fraternal orders and social groups abounded in Chelsea between the Civil War and the 1960s. The Temperance Society made its

Generations of Chelsea men belonged to at least one of the many fraternal orders in town.
Courtesy of Scott Otto

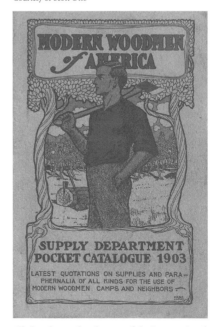

Chelsea boasted a chapter of the international organization known as the Modern Woodmen of America. Courtesy of Scott Otto

The Boy Scouts of America established a troop in Chelsea soon after its 1910 incorporation in the United States. This photograph was taken during or immediately following World War I; note the similarity in uniforms between the Chelsea Scouts and World War I soldiers.

Courtesy Chelsea Area Historical Society

appearance as soon as the village was founded. Its meetings, often held in the Congregational Church, drew big crowds well into the 1920s. The first fraternal order established in Chelsea arrived immediately after the Civil War, but the International Order of Odd Fellows was quickly succeeded by many others, both for men and women.

Most gentlemen in town appear to have participated in at least one fraternal organization over the years: the Grand Army of the Republic, Kiwanis Club, American Legion, Knights of Columbus, Knights of Pythias, International Order of Odd Fellows, Royal Arch Masons, Chelsea Volunteer Firemen, Maccabees, K.O.T.M., the Arbeiter Society, F.&A.M., and the Modern Woodmen of America. Ladies belonged to the Auxiliary to the Grand Army of the Republic; Olive Chapter No. 108, Order of the Eastern Star; Red Cross Auxiliary; Lady Maccabees; Woman's Club of Chelsea; Rebekah Lodge No. 130; Child Study Club; and a host of church groups.

"The Firemen had a hall on the second story of a building my father owned, above what is now the motorcycle shop, where they held meetings and suppers and dances," George Staffan says. "Some groups met above Merkel's and they would hold dances there, too."

A *Chelsea Herald* front-page article dated Thursday, March 21, 1895, reveals the fun that fraternal orders offered Chelsea residents. The newspaper reports:

On Friday night, March 14, Chelsea Tent No. 281 was busily engaged in its routine work, and was preparing to confer the Oriental degree upon some of its members who were anxiously waiting to enter into the mysteries of this solemn order. A shrill and blood-curdling war whoop came from the lonely picket, that strangers had entered the outpost of our camp; reinforcement were necessary or the whole camp would be captured.

The commander marshalled his whole available forces but to no purpose; the opposing forces were too strong and the smell of hot coffee too tempting to their stomachs. A consultation was held and all agreed to surrender the whole camp to the enemy, which was done. Commander Lady Boyd being absent, the emblem of authority was handed to Lady Martin who marshalled her forces with a masterly hand. The first in order was the initiating of a lady into the Oriental mysteries of the Lady Maccabees, which was well rendered and brought forth great applause from all present.

Next came the hot coffee, sandwiches and fried-cakes which vanished like frost in a noonday sun. The ladies then favored us with their grand march which was an honor to themselves, and to the order of which they belong. One of Carlton's poems was then recited by Sir Knight T.G. Speer which was well rendered. This concluded the evening's entertainment. All went from the lodge-room to their homes with pleasant thoughts of the evening, and wishing that more of the same would come in the near future.

Saturday nights were lively in Chelsea throughout the village's first century and a half. Saloons were open and full of convivial customers. Slot machines lured nickels, dimes, and quarters from hard-working factory workers and farm boys. Music spilled over onto the sidewalks and streets—and sometimes, so did brawls and fistfights. The stores were all open Wednesday and Saturday nights and full of shoppers.

They weren't the only ones in town in the evenings. On Saturday nights, farmers would finish their chores and drive their entire families into town, pull their wagons into the same spot every week, then shop, browse through the library's shelves for a week's supply of books, and visit with friends. On other warm evenings, the village residents would sit on each other's front porches and visit after supper dishes had been done.

Music—and local musicians—filled the streets, beer parlors, parks, and parades during the first 150 years of Chelsea's history. Roy Maier (middle) later played with Bing Crosby.

Courtesy of the Kaercher Family

Later, with the advent of the automobile, people would walk up and down the street and climb into the back of friends' cars to visit—"the cars served as front porches for country people coming into town," Marjorie Hepburn says. "They'd sit together for awhile and then move on to visit with other friends down the street."

For many years, a flagpole stood in the middle of Main Street and around the flagpole generations of town activities took place. On Saturday nights, a wagon would be pulled up to the flagpole, to serve as a stage for the community band. Every week throughout the summers, the band would entertain the crowd. "In my early days, Wesley Smith was the director and everyone who had an instrument would climb up there and play to the best of their abilities," Rolly Spaulding says, adding with a grin, "if you were bad, it didn't really matter. The noise was what was important."

Immaculate, well lit and well paved, Chelsea's Main Street and its businesses flourished during the 1920s. Note the flagpole in the middle of the street.

Courtesy of the Mitchell family

Conrad Lehman, who owned two Lincoln cars, drove one two blocks away to Main Street early on band concert days, so his wife and her sister would have front-row seats. Then he would walk home. He wasn't the only dutiful husband to do this. "The thrill of a band concert was more about people-watching than about listening to the pleasant tones of the band," John Keusch says.

Baseball was the all-American pastime by the turn of the century. Visiting teams toured the area, challenging locals to action on diamonds carved out of farmers' fields. In 1924, an old baseball was found in a drawer at Kempf Commercial & Savings Bank inscribed with the year 1902 and signed by players fielded by Chelsea in a showdown with the Ypsilanti Knights of Pythias. The local team won the game 10-8, with John Merrinan, catcher; Philip Steger, pitcher; A. Gulde at first base; George Staffan, second base; H.D. Witherell, third base; Frank Leach, right field; A.E. Winans, center field; L.P. Vogel, left field; J.S. Cummings, short stop. George BeGole and Hugh Van De Walker served as umpires during the game, and BeGole kept the ball as a memento. A 1924 *Chelsea Standard* article announcing the discovery noted, "The ball will be hung in Chelsea Knights of Pythius rooms, where it is expected it will attract considerable attention."

Once a year, Sharpstein's Medicine Show took up quarters in the Sylvan Township Hall. Magicians pulled rabbits out of hats, vaude-ville-type acts would sing and dance and give their pitch for the latest patent medicine. "The two pitch guys were pretty good," Spaulding says. "They'd run down the aisles getting the crowd excited and shouting, 'Here's another bottle sold!'" The medicines, which contained a high alcoholic content, offered to cure everything from "ladies' ailments" to arthritis and bunions, cost a dollar a bottle.

George Staffan remembers the show's "Popular Lady Contest" and learned the trick of making a soap look particularly effective. "Mr. Sharpstein would choose a lady and wash one of her hands with soap. Then he would hold her hand up to the audience, squeezing it at the wrist, which would drain the blood and make the hand look whiter than the unwashed hand!"

1914: Archduke Ferdinand assassinated • 10.5 million immigrants enter U.S. from southern and eastern Europe between 1905 and 1914 • Albert Schweitzer opens hospital in Congo • Chaplin stars in *Making a Living* • Germany declares war on Russia and France, invades Belgium • Britain declares war on Russia • France and Britain declare war on Turkey • Russians defeated at Masurian Lakes • Germans in Antwerp • First Battle of Ypres

1915: German Airships bomb East Anglian Ports • First German submarine attack • Second Battle of Ypres • German blockade of England • Germans sink *Lusitania* • Battles of Isonzo • Tetanus epidemics in the trenches

1916: Battle of Verdun • Allies attack Zeebrugge • Battle of Jutland • Italy declares war on Germany • Lloyd George becomes British Prime Minister • Briand becomes French War Minister • Germany sends peace note to Allies • Wilson sends peace note to all belligerents • Gen. Joffre named Marshal of France

1917: U.S. and Cuba declare war on Germany • Petain becomes Chief of French General Staff • Russian revolution • British Royal Family renounces German names and titles • General Pershing arrives in Paris to head American Forces • Food and fuel controls in U.S • China declares war on Germany and Austria • German aircraft attack London • Italian army routed at Caparetto • Balfour declaration on Palestine • October revolution in Russia • Clemenceau Premier of France • First tank battle • German-Russian armistice at Brest-Litovsk • U.S. declares war on Hungary and Austria • Starvation year in Germany • Allies execute Mata Hari as spy

1918: Wilson's 14 Points for World Peace • Gen. Foch takes over United Command on Western Front • 1,388 German Luftwaffe planes assemble for attack • Second Battle of Marne • Allied offensive on Western Front opens • Germany and Austria agree on Wilson's demand to retreat to their own territories • Allies sign armistice with Austria-Hungary • Allied Conference at Versailles agrees on peace terms for Germany • Armistice signed Nov. 11

WAR CASUALTIES
8.5 million killed, 21 million wounded, 7.5 million prisoners and missing

MOBILIZED FORCES
63 million

U.S. POPULATION
103.5 million

World War I: 1914-1918

We Remember

History books say that World War I had been too brief to have a deep and transforming effect on American society, but history books speak about social movements and economic reforms, not people's hearts and empty places around a family's supper table.

American Legion Post No. 31 is named for Herbert J. McKune, a 1914 graduate of St. Mary's High School who was born April 24, 1898. He was killed in action at Champagne, France, on October 4, 1918, when he was 20 years old. John Keusch remembers him as "a handsome man and one of the last men killed in the war." He died 38 days before the armistice was signed.

McKune didn't live to return home, to attend high school reunions, meet friends around the soda fountain at "John's," marry his sweetheart, plant crops or start a business. He would never raise a family of his own. Or have a chance to fulfill whatever dreams he had cherished as a boy. Singular losses of the war like these transformed small villages like Chelsea.

Herbert McKune was not the only Chelsea man who gave his life during the first World War. Arthur Boyd was also killed in action. Lester Hall, Ruben Fenner, Burt Snyder and Harold Carpenter died in service. The Purple Heart was awarded to Edmund J. Miller, John O'Hara, and C.J. Clinton for wounds received on the battlefield.

There was another side to the war story as well: the battles lost and won on the home front. Longtime Michigan residents with German names and accents—and there were many of them—were suddenly regarded with suspicion, and sometimes outright hostility. Alton Grau's great-grandparents emigrated to Michigan from Germany in the 1840s, but 70 years later, at the start of the war, they and their descendents were required to sign and carry Resident Alien cards noting their place of birth and nationality.

John Keusch, who was born in 1909, was a grade-school student at St. Mary's School when the war was declared April 1917.

He remembers the small, everyday changes the war made in Chelsea lives.

He and everyone else in town would comb the pages of the newspaper every evening for news about the war. ("The radio hadn't come to Chelsea yet."). Coal became so scarce during the war that St. Mary's students would crowd into the Sisters' Home and hold classes there, in order to conserve coal and keep everyone warm. Navy beans, a staple in battlefield messes, sold for a staggering $20 a bushel. The price of wool rose well over one dollar a pound because wool was used to make soldiers' uniforms. Washtenaw was the biggest wool producing county in the nation, and a number of wool dealers in Chelsea became rich in a very short period of time.

Everyone did their part for the war effort. John Keusch cherishes a photo of a line of local housewives dressed in Red Cross uniforms who were taught the fundamentals of first aid. They gathered lint for dressing wounds, rolled bandages, and knit socks and scarves for America's soldiers. Farmers plowed more fields and planted more crops to feed embattled European allies and American soldiers. The Hollier Eight, an automobile manufactured in Chelsea, had to cease production because steel and car parts were requisitioned by the War Department.

Even the schoolchildren contributed. They were enlisted to go work on local farms, helping with the bean and potato harvests. "Beans had to be picked by hand and shelled. It was a tough crop to harvest," Keusch says. George Staffan remembers making bean bags in school in second and third grade—"I don't know what the American military used them for, but we were told we were helping the war effort."

Propaganda was widespread and often aimed at schoolchildren, according to Keusch. Guest speakers would discuss the war in schools, on street corners or at meetings held in the township hall. "A Major Kressey came and talked about the excessive cruelty of the Germans in Serbia and how they cut off the hands of the Serbians. It was gruesome," recalls Keusch, whose family was of German-Irish descent. Local and national newspapers carried tales of alleged atrocities by the enemy.

Both St. Mary's Catholic School and the public schools held War Bond Drives. Once a week, students brought a dime or a quarter to

Every man, woman and child tried to do their part for the war effort during World War I. Local housewives underwent First Aid training and dressed in Red Cross uniforms for official duties. Chelsea attorney John Keusch remembers the day this photograph was taken.

Courtesy Chelsea Area Historical Society

school to invest in stamps. When they had accumulated enough stamps, they qualified for a U.S. War Bond.

Geraldine Glazier Kraft, who was born in 1910, remembers watching soldiers march past Grass Lake and down Michigan Avenue on their way to a fort outside Battle Creek. "I watched hundreds on foot or in trucks or the electric railroad." Chelsea hung a banner across the Welfare Building applauding the soldiers' courage. It could be seen by trainloads full of soldiers heading to Detroit and on to the battlefields of Europe.

Before the war ended, a tragedy that occurred on the Detroit United Railroad brought a sense of the war home to Chelsea residents. Dozens of civilians and soldiers were killed and wounded when a freight carrier and a passenger car collided near the site of the Chelsea Methodist Retirement Home. "I have always felt somewhat responsible for the accident because a friend and I distracted the crew," Keusch says.

"Lawrence Wackenhut and I were at the freight house talking with the crew while they were unloading freight," he explains. "The first section of the double header went through and gave a signal that there was another section of the passenger. Apparently, the signal was ignored or forgotten. Freight proceeded on west to a point beyond the Methodist Home, going by a sidetrack known as the Loop and the collision occurred across from Hafners' on a curve. The crew on the freight jumped and were not injured."

Eighteen passengers were killed, however, many of them soldiers from Camp Custer. This happened before there was a hospital closer than Jackson or Ann Arbor, so townspeople turned out to help. They offered emergency first aid to the injured and loaded the dead and wounded into their automobiles and drove them to the churches, the town hall, and schools. They carried in blankets, provisions, and first aid equipment and tended to the injured until doctors could reach town by train from Ann Arbor.

George Staffan remembers seeing the dead bodies lined up beside the tracks. His father, the local undertaker, had to work long hours to prepare them for funerals and shipment home.

Staffan and his cousin, John Keusch, also remember the ironies of the accident. "A fellow named George Alber was on that train. He rose to give his seat to a woman and went back to stand at the rear of the train. She was killed instantly, sitting in the seat that he vacated," Staffan recalls. "George lived to be almost 80 years of age," Keusch adds.

"I had a wonderful Mama to take care of me. She was as good as a trained nurse," remembers Geraldine Glazier Kraft, speaking of Henrietta Glazier. Like many local women, Mrs. Glazier was called upon to nurse family members and neighbors through the devastating influenza pandemic of 1918. The influenza killed as many people world-wide as the war did.

Courtesy Geraldine Glazier Kraft

While World War I raged on the battlefields of Europe and Asia, another devastating war began in 1918. A pandemic—a worldwide epidemic—slashed across every nation, mirroring the global impact of the first World War. The Spanish influenza left millions—soldiers and civilians—dead. Lenora Manore, a resident at the Methodist Retirement Home, told an historian in 1991, "During the flu epidemic, my mother and father were very busy helping people because some of them had lost so many family members they had no one to help them."

Geraldine Glazier Kraft was eight years old in 1918 and watched the influenza "take an awful lot of our people," among them her Aunt Nora's three children. She herself came down with the influenza and 83 years later she clearly remembers the weeks she spent in quarantine.

"I had a wonderful Mama to take care of me. She was as good as a trained nurse," Geraldine says. The little girl was kept in a darkened room in the family's winter home in Detroit, her eyes shielded from the light, her diet carefully monitored. Every morning she would have a cool bath and a fresh set of long underwear to don before returning to bed. "I survived, but Margaret, my Uncle Harold's daughter and my best friend, who was also eight, died. That was quite a shock to a small child…to have a cousin your age die."

For months after the influenza had run its course in Michigan, the Glazier family continued the ritual of fumigating everyone who entered the house. "We used fumigation candles and changed our clothes in the dining room as soon as we came home," Geraldine says. "Every piece of clothing we put on and took off was fumigated in the basement. By the time the influenza ended, millions of people had died, worldwide. It was a terrible time. A horrible time."

World War I officially ended with the surrender of the Central Powers on November 11, 1918. What few history books note, however, is the "false armistice" on November 7.

"Chelsea, like villages and towns and cities around the world, wildly celebrated the end of the war, only to be informed that the festivities were premature, that the armistice we celebrated was a fake," Dudley Holmes says. "So our boys had to get their noses in the mud again, until Germany finally did surrender. It was a cruel joke for many, many people."

John Keusch remembers being in school on November 7 and seeing as many as 200 people making their way through town, shouting that the war was over. "We jumped out of our seats and ran out of school to join them," he says. "All the school bells and church bells in town rang all day long—and then that evening we learned that it was a false alarm. But we were back on the streets on the 11th, lighting big bonfires."

A Chelsea man, Claire Fenn, had his photograph taken with Marshall Foch, Supreme Allied Commander, at the signing of the armistice. "That photograph got worldwide circulation," Keusch says.

Most of Chelsea's soldiers came home and returned to their occupations. But there were others who had been shell-shocked and gassed who came home to a sadly different life. Some of them never fully recovered, Keusch remembers.

World War I had a far-reaching effect on Michigan politics. After the close of the first World War, Washtenaw County voted Republican for five decades. "In part, it was because the German population held it against Woodrow Wilson that we were in the war," John Keusch suggests. "Franklin Delano Roosevelt never carried Washtenaw County once in four elections."

In 1912, Woodrow Wilson garnered 4,164 votes to William Howard Taft's 2,495. Wilson was the last Democrat to carry Washtenaw in a presidential election until 1964, when Lyndon B. Johnson won 42,089 votes to Barry Goldwater's 25,595.

Although Dudley Holmes was only four at the time of the armistice, he remembers watching young World War I veterans march with veterans of the Civil War through the streets of town in Memorial Day and Fourth of July parades soon after the war.

"Little towns seemed to thrive on that kind of activity. We would have ceremonies around the flagpole—which was in the center of Main Street at that time—and then we marched out to the cemetery, where a roll call of veterans was read, speeches were made, guns were fired. Then we marched back to the flag pole and were dismissed, ready for the village picnic."

Traditionally, every parade included a procession of prize farm animals that ambled far behind the veterans. Children would proudly march with their pet sheep, lambs, calves, and horses on parade day—"and everyone in town helped keep the animals from running around the town," Holmes says with a grin and a glint in his eye, acknowledging, "every once in awhile, one would get loose and then we'd see some fun!"

Food tables were set up in front of every store in town. "Nowhere but a small town could handle this kind of activity," Holmes says. "The food was plentiful and wonderful. Women worked for days ahead of time, making and baking their specialties. This was a German town and all those German women were good cooks. They thrived on their reputations for making the best pies or the best potato salads (the world here revolved around that stuff!). I remember huge slabs of roast beef, new potatoes, new peas, wonderful pies and everything else in the world that would tempt the appetite of ravenously hungry little boys."

Warren G. Harding, 1921-23 • Calvin Coolidge, 1923-29
Herbert Hoover, 1929-33

The Russian Civil War ends • Nicola Sacco and Bartolomeo Vanzetti arrested, tried, and executed for murder • Edith Wharton wins Pulitzer Prize for the *Age of Innocence* • Prohibition • First cross-country airmail flight • John T. Thompson patents his submachine gun (the "tommy gun") • Ku Klux Klan gains political power • Mrs. W.H. Felton becomes first woman U.S. senator • Le Corbusier espouses "Towards a New Architecture" • Americans sing *Yes! We Have No Bananas*, *Tea For Two*, and *Singin' In The Rain* • Ford Motor Company produces 10 millionth car • Knute Rockne coaches Notre Dame to win nine out of nine football games • 2.5 Million radios in U.S. homes • London Bible Society distributes 10.5 million Bibles in 566 languages • U.S. boasts 261,000 miles of railroads • Rudolph Valentino dies after filming *The Son Of The Sheik* • Babe Ruth hits 60 home runs for the Yankees • Republican Herbert Hoover elected president

U.S. POPULATION
1920: 117,823,165

The Roaring '20s

Relief, At Last!

The 1920s offered a decade of relief and prosperity wedged between the first World War and the Great Depression. Residences in town never looked neater, better painted, or more prosperous. Farmers' harvests were plentiful and brought good prices, even after prices dropped to more realistic levels following the war's inflationary period. Downtown businesses flourished. Radios invaded Chelsea's living rooms.

The world thrilled to the exploits of Charles Lindbergh. Girls bobbed their hair. College students wore beanies and raccoon coats. Teenagers danced the Lindy, Fandango and the Charleston. Ladies carried calling cards and families like the Glaziers would stop their carriages or automobiles when they reached the outskirts of town, so they could change their well-raised sons and daughters into spotless, perfectly ironed and starched clothes before visiting with friends or shopping on Main Street. Joseph Merkel and Joseph Weber of Sylvan delivered 2,821 sparrows and one woodchuck scalp to the township clerk and received $56.67 in payment.

This was also the era of Prohibition. In 1920, Congress signed the 18th Amendment forbidding the manufacture and sale of alcoholic beverages. The amendment stayed in effect for 13 years, effectively shutting down several local taverns. General Dwight Beach remembers the day that his father learned that the Prohibition bill had been passed. David Beach impounded his only bottle of whiskey, took it out back and smashed it, as a lesson to his three boys.

"Until Prohibition, some of the wealthiest men in town were the saloon owners. They all had nice houses. Obviously, Prohibition changed their lives," John Keusch says. "A pub in the same location as Cleary's became a restaurant run by a man named Kolb, for instance." J. Edward Weber, who owned a saloon as well as the Princess Theater, was forced into retirement because of Prohibition. So was Christopher Klein, who ran a tavern and saloon in the Seitz building.

Otherwise, Prohibition barely influenced the social life of Chelsea, despite enthusiastic efforts by local officials to prevent the sale and distribution of bootleg liquor, much of it smuggled across the nearby Canadian border.

"We didn't need stills in town," Rolly Spaulding says, explaining, "Every farmer had wine barrels and half the people in town made bathtub beer and homemade wine. We all had grape arbors and apple trees in our backyards, so it was easy to put our hands on homemade wine and hard cider."

Every once in awhile, Chelsea had a brush with fame and international headlines. That happened on April 15, 1912, when the unsinkable *S.S. Titanic* hit an iceberg and sank. In response to an inquiry about a Chelsea native, the White Star line responded:

Dear Sir,

A second class passenger named John Lingane booked here and sailed on the S.S. Titanic *11th last, and we regret to say that his name does not appear amongst the survivors of this disaster. We understand that he was spending a holiday in your district, and doubtless you will be familiar with the address of his relatives. We ask you to convey our deepest sympathy to them in their sad bereavement.*

Kindly furnish us with the name and address of his nearest relative, and his intended American address.

Awaiting the favor of your reply,
Yours truly,
James Scott

Chelsea buzzed with excitement and sorrow. John Lingane had been born on a potato farm in Ireland during the famine years and emigrated to Chelsea at the age of 24, marrying a local girl, Ellen Savage, and starting a farm in Sylvan Township. In the fall of 1911, after his wife's death, he returned to Ireland for the first time. A stone in the Mt. Olivet Cemetery was erected in his memory.

On the 75th anniversary of the ship's disaster, the *Ann Arbor News* dedicated a feature to John Lingane:

Sometimes death makes spectacular the lives of ordinary people.

That's what happened to an obscure Chelsea-area farmer 75 years ago last week.

Before April 12, 1912, no one but his family and friends had ever heard of John Lingane. But after that date his name gained a place on a list of international dead—the 1,500 people who lost their lives when the Titanic *struck an iceberg and sank in 10,000 feet of water off the Newfoundland coast.*

Lingane was an Irish immigrant, one of the faceless thousands who in the late 19th century fled the potato famines and the hard life of their native land for a chance at a fresh start in this country. He had come to Michigan as a young man in the 1870s, his only trade the good earth, his only asset a willingness to work.

He bought land on a lonely dirt road without a name, northwest of the hamlet of Chelsea. He hauled rocks out of the fields with a horse, planted, cultivated, harvested. He and his wife raised four sons...

Several years ago, one of Lingane's family members, Beth Easterwood, visited Chelsea with her son and showed Donna Lane pictures of the Linganes' barn raising in 1916. Then they left to put flowers on John Lingane's grave, April 15, 1998.

With a few exceptions like this one, life in Chelsea was as quiet and predictable as it would ever be. Rolly Spaulding's boyhood wasn't much different from the boyhood of children born 20 or 30 years before or after 1920.

Spaulding was born in 1920 on Brookes Farm, south of the village in the area of the Vermont Colony, but when his mother died shortly afterward, the boy moved into Chelsea to live with his grandparents, the Whitmers. He, like generations of other little boys, spent hours flipping over and twisting around the town's hitching rails on Main Street. Later, when he was a older, he spent as much time as he could in the peat marsh just outside town, on what is now the hospital grounds. "Every year a fire burned underneath the peat for weeks at a time and the grown-ups warned us not to go there—which is precisely why we headed there whenever we could get away," he says with a grin.

Occasionally there would be some excitement downtown. Spaulding used to visit Dr. Steger in his dentist office above the Kempf Commercial & Savings Bank, on the southwest corner of Main and West Middle streets, to study his collection of Indian arrowheads and marvel at the foot-long preserved baby alligator in the glass case. "One day I spotted the doctor's deer rifle in the corner and I asked him about it. He told me, 'If anybody robs the bank, the teller will push a button, which rings those two gong bells with clappers. I'll throw open the window, grab my deer rifle, and shoot any stranger on sight. So will Mr. Kantlehner (the jeweler whose business was across the street from the bank).'" Sixty years

"We were twin terrors," Dudley Holmes recalled proudly, speaking at the age of 87. Here Dudley and his twin brother Howard, who were born in 1914, stand with their grandfather, entrepreneur H.S. Holmes, in front of the family carriage house on East Middle Street. Courtesy of the Holmes family

later, Spaulding still remembers the fighting words.

In those days, young boys did all the things that boys have done throughout the ages: tease girls to distraction, drive their mothers to worry and keep a weather eye out for mischief. Dudley and Howard Holmes, who were born in 1914, were frequent participants in the boyhood ritual of tipping over outhouses. A decade later, Rolly Spaulding was initiated into the mysteries by a new generation of mischief-makers.

"There's a secret to overturning an outhouse—and every boy should know it," Holmes explains with a wink. "Time was limited—we had to be in by 7:30 every night. That meant that our victims would be awake, vigilant, and within yards of our destination. We had to line up at least three, four, or five boys—and preferably eight or ten—on one side. Someone would give a signal, and with a properly engineered shove, the outhouse tipped right over. Then you had to separate and run as fast as you could in different directions. I remember one old man came out with a whip and chased us farther than we ever thought possible. We had to be careful not to be seen—but even then, it was a small town and we couldn't wander far afield, so people could pretty accurately ascertain who had done the damage…Howard and I managed to acquire a fair number of spankings in those days.

"You got extra points if you managed to tip over an outhouse that had an occupant or two in it," Dudley Holmes adds with a grin, remembering the shrill screams of two feminine occupants who were unseated one evening. One elderly citizen who asks not to be quoted recalls transporting the constable's outhouse right onto his front porch—and then watching him open the front door early in the morning and walk right into The Necessary.

Halloween was a night when outhouse tipping became small potatoes and mischief took on more creative turns. Boys took the "trick" part of "trick-or-treating" seriously and occasionally suffered the consequences. "I remember writing 'A terrible cook lives here' on the doorpost of one house and we never harvested any treats from that woman again," Dudley Holmes admits, "but all the kids in town knew who would offer popcorn balls or who made the best candy in town—and we made it a point never to trick those houses."

Wintertime offered its own fun. The Holmes twins developed a sledding technique that guaranteed a smooth ride from a small rise in the center of West Middle Street, across Main Street and down East Middle Street all the way to the gates of the cemetery. Frozen ponds hosted skating parties. A friendly farmer might appear with a bobsled and offer the town kids a joyous ride.

But life wasn't all fun. Children began working at early ages. Girls would learn cooking and cleaning from their mothers and in time might work for neighbors as hired girls, earning 25 or even 50 cents a week. A few years later, Rolly Spaulding helped clean ashes out of furnaces in the spring, passed out handbills in front of the Princess Theater, and picked up "road apples," dried them and applied them to his grandmother's flower gardens as fertilizer. "Chelsea had the best petunias beds in the state," he boasts. Most boys in town headed out to the farms to help at harvest time and when silos needed filling. Their pay: $2 a week.

Men didn't have a total monopoly on the business world. Widows and single women ran farms—and married women were full-time partners in family farm businesses. There were also some early female entrepreneurs in business on Main Street. The Miller sisters ran a millinery enterprise. Several small shops were owned by ladies. Lida Guthrie received her pharmacist license during this decade, the first woman pharmacist in the area. A number of stores had memorable salesclerks who were women. And Nettie Irene Notten opened the Chelsea Private Hospital in 1926, on the site of the present-day post office. For a number of years, this was the only hospital in town and for the first time, women began having babies away from the home.

Both men and women had fraternal and community groups offering entertainment, civic projects, and camaraderie. The men also had billiard rooms and card rooms downtown, where they would meet neighbors for an hour or two. Conrad Lehman was an avid card player, particularly cribbage, and he played every noon at the downtown card room with his neighbor, Dr. A.L. Steger. The games were hotly contested and usually attracted spectators.

The area's first resort appeared at this time. Douglas A. Fraser sold the American Brass and Iron Company in 1916 and purchased 160 acres of land from Fred Glenn in Lyndon Township, the original

John Glenn homestead, which ran along North Territorial and included North Lake. After five years of farming, Fraser subdivided the property and built a golf course with the help of Detroit landscape engineer J. French Paddock and architects Conklin & Hampekin.

According to an article Kathleen Clark wrote, in 1925 Fraser first advertised his new enterprise, which he called Inverness, "The Lake Resort, Golf and Country Club of Most Unusual Features and Advantages." He offered moderately priced building lots fronting a nine-hole course, as well as beachfront lots on the lake, a few existing cottages, and more than 50 lots with lake access in the Park Lawn Subdivision. He dredged a lagoon and left the remaining settlers' cabin on the island he created.

People came from town and tourists came from the cities to play golf, enjoy chicken dinners in the clubhouse, ride horses and ponies, play tennis and swim.

Often, visitors to Inverness passed through Chelsea. In those days, every man, woman, and child knew the names of everyone else in town—and where they lived, the women's names prior to marriage, how townspeople were related, and how well they were doing. "We didn't have street signs for many years, so we might not know the name of the street, but we could get strangers anywhere they needed to go," Spaulding says. "People would stop me and give a street name and number. I might not recognize that address, but I'd ask who they were looking for and I could give them exact directions."

Thanks to Village President George Staffan, who ignored the voters' mandate, Main Street was paved in 1910. His daughter, Katharine Wagner, remembers that years later road contractors marveled at the quality of the paving work—which still exists, under the present-day macadam.

Like paved roads, street signs came as a response to the automobile, which brought increasing numbers of visitors and strangers to town. As if it were yesterday, Dudley Holmes remembers riding with his grandfather after he bought the family's first automobile. "You took your life in your hands when you rode in an automobile with my grandfather or his compatriots, people who were used to driving horses that did what you told them to do," he says, shaking his head. "It was a great

Main Street was paved in 1910. This photograph, which captures the east side of Main Street, looking south, was taken as the job was underway. Notice the hitching posts along the thoroughfare.

Courtesy of the Dan Maroney Family

good fortune to Chelsea that the early cars only went ten miles per hour—or there would have been many more casualties. When people saw those elderly men in their newfangled cars careening down the road, you can be sure they got out of the way—way out of the way. They could scare the hell out of you!"

Automobiles also launched the start of the exodus from the farms to the factories, from the country to the city. Henry Ford was the first manufacturer to offer $5 a day for workers, and farm boys flocked to the automobile plants. The electric motors that propelled the automobiles also ran farm tractors, trucks, and machinery. As farms became mechanized, fewer hired hands were needed. They, too, often headed to the cities.

In 1929, when George Staffan graduated, he was a member of Chelsea High School's largest graduating class in history—42 strong. Until the gymnasium was built ("against opposition from the farmers, who couldn't see the necessity—and money in those days was none too plentiful"), basketball games were played in the Sylvan Township Hall, where both John Keusch and George Staffan recall "almost standing with your back against the opposite wall to shoot a foul shot." Chelsea fielded strong basketball teams in those days, as did St. Mary's. Chelsea High School's football team participated in the state championships during Staffan's senior year, losing 6-0 to Vicksburg in a heartbreaking game.

Every once in awhile during the course of an ordinary day, an event would take place that would catch the attention of the family or the community. Like many children in the days before hospital births, young Ellis Boyce was at home when his sister was born. The cottage on North Lake where the family lived during the 1920s was small and had no interior doors. In the night, when his mother, Florence Boyce, went into labor, Ellis and his two sisters were moved to the back of the cottage and a temporary curtain was hung between the children and the birthing. "When the delivery was taking place, there was a lot of activity going on, so I peeked around the curtain to see what it was all about," he told his children a half century later. "I called to the girls, pretty loudly, 'Come quick! They're taking a baby out of Ma's leg!'"

Virginia Barr Visel remembers being told about an uncle who was born prematurely at a pound and a half—so small that their mother's wedding ring could fit around the baby's arm. "They wrapped the baby in cotton—there were no clothes small enough—and kept him in a shoe box on the back of the old wood stove's warming oven to keep warm!" she says. Her uncle actually survived infancy, but died at the age of 12 from pneumonia.

These were the days before antibiotics and people died tragic deaths that could easily be cured or avoided in later years. Alton Grau's grandfather died of appendicitis months after his first child was born. June Robinson's father died of "sleeping sickness" when she was a baby. Rolly Spaulding's mother died of complications from childbirth. So did Richard Kinsey's mother.

Influenza continued to add to the death toll over the years. Whooping cough, scarlet fever, mumps, and measles claimed countless children. "Children could be perfectly healthy and playing outside one day and two days later we would learn that they had died," Geraldine Glazier Kraft remembers.

Making his rounds by horse-drawn sleigh, Dr. Wilfred Lane provided the town's first veterinary services. Between calls, he worked for the livery stable, trading his labor for use of the phone and board for his horse.

Courtesy of Donna Lane

But there were just as many happy memories from childhood. Dr. Wilfred Lane, longtime veterinarian in town, was asked to speak to the Rotary Club in 1995 about Christmas in Chelsea. He smiled as he told his audience, "Things were indeed very different. Our village was much smaller and life was slower and much simpler. At Christmas, the churches had their family holiday programs. The children spoke their pieces or took part in a Christmas play. They sang the old familiar Christmas carols and were rewarded by a visit from the jolly old gentleman and each participant received a Christmas stocking filled with fruit and candy. In school, we had simple gift exchanges, a box of crayons or a pencil given with all the love of the holiday season."

Chelsea looked like a Currier & Ives Christmas card in those days, with sleighs dashing through town and the sound of sleigh bells tinkling in the cold and crystal air.

The Business Side of Town

The 1920s brought peace, prosperity, and dazzling business opportunities to area merchants and entrepreneurs. Nearly every businessman in town at one time or another tried his hand at dealing in wool, which was a valuable commodity. Many tried their hands at several businesses. The age of mechanization began to open broad new avenues of opportunity. Fewer hands were needed on the farm, so

farm boys could dabble at automobile repair or factory work. Automobile dealerships came—and most went—during this decade.

Harper Pontiac was established by Walter Harper in 1926, joining the ranks of local car dealers. The company was later purchased by the Oesterle family.

In response to the appearance of motor cars on city streets and back roads, Michigan and every other state in the Union started a massive road-building campaign. Roads needed cement and many public and private firms turned to the Chelsea Four Mile Lake Cement Plant for their supplies. The plant was located where the Honninger Grain Elevators now stand, where the railroad crosses the Dexter-Chelsea Road, four miles outside town.

"That cement plant had a strong impact on Michigan politics, especially the election of governors," John Keusch says.

According to Keusch, who worked at the plant during his college years, Governor Grosbeck in 1920 vowed to "take Michigan out of the mud" and instituted a massive road construction program. He quickly ran into rigged and fixed prices for cement, and he vowed to break what he called the Cement Trust. To do that, he had the state buy the Michigan Portland Cement Company, whose offices were in the former Glazier bank building on Main Street.

The plan was to use between 200 and 300 inmates of Jackson Prison as labor; they would be housed in dormitories on the plant site. Rolly Spaulding's grandfather, Frank Whitmer, was plant superintendent. Dave McLaughlin's grandfather came to Chelsea as a prison guard. Byford Speer operated a sewing machine to repair holes in cloth bags used to store cement.

After World War I, the automobile manufacturers sold cars as fast as they rolled off the assembly lines and both the industry and car owners began demanding better roads. As the nation's demand for cement to pave roads increased, the Chelsea Four Mile Lake Cement Plant opened. Business flourished until political concerns reared their ugly heads.

Courtesy of Larry Chapman

"That cement plant had a strong impact on Michigan politics, especially the election of governors," John Keusch believes. The Cement Trust mounted a strong campaign to corner the market on cement and to do this, they needed to eliminate Chelsea's flourishing cement business. Governor Brucker closed the facility in 1930 and the buildings were immediately demolished.

Courtesy of John Keusch

Limestone, gypsum, and marl mined from the ground around the plant were mixed with water to form a slurry, which was then mixed with ground coal dust and burned in three long metal kilns until small cinders, or "clinkers" were formed. After cooling, the clinkers were ground to form the cement, which was stored in those silos still on the site, then loaded into bags during construction season.

The plant area was covered with coal and cement dust. "It was like walking in snow," Keusch says.

The Cement Trust mounted a strong campaign to close this plant and corner the market on cement. When Grosbeck was defeated in the Republican primary by Fred Green, the death knell was sounded for the plant, although it took the Cement Trust two years to finalize legislation to shut the business down. Governor Brucker closed the facility in 1930 and the plant was quickly demolished. "The Cement Trust was taking no chance that the plant would be reopened," Keusch explains.

"Just as Chelsea was significant in Michigan politics during the Glazier era, 1900 to 1910, the Four Mile Lake Cement Plant, together with Prohibition, were the dominating factors in Michigan politics in the 1920s," he adds.

On a smaller scale, this decade was significant for other local businesses. In an effort to expand business, the Chelsea Elevator Company, which was housed in a large brick building on Main Street next to the railroad tracks facing its competitor, the Wm. Bacon Holmes Company, tried its hand—or, rather, many hands—in the chicken business, buying, selling, and even plucking chickens.

Just before the war, the elevator company had opened a dressed chicken operation on the second floor of a vacant building. Elbert and Albert Winans earned 25 cents for a long day of plucking, preparing, and packing chickens in what they always called "The Chicken Pluckin' Place." Within two weeks, the workers were shipping 500 dressed chickens a day packed in barrels to New York City. However, the success of the operation was short-lived. During the third week in business, the wooden floor caught fire under the kettles of hot water used to scald the chickens. The building burned and the chicken business died.

Several years later, in 1925, the Chelsea Lumber, Grain and Coal Company took over the interests of both the Chelsea Elevator

Company and the Chelsea Lumber and Coal Company. The *Chelsea Standard* on December 31, 1925, reported:

The new company, incorporated under the laws of Michigan, is capitalized at $600,000…In the transaction real estate as well as stocks and good will of the companies will come into possession of the new company and makes one of the biggest business transactions recorded here in recent years…

Consolidation of these two businesses brings together two of Chelsea's oldest enterprises. The Chelsea Elevator Co. came into being in 1908 and has continued in their present location since that time. Reorganization of the Wm. Bacon-Holmes interests about a year ago brought into being the Chelsea Lumber & Coal Co….However, fusion of the two interests into one will be received with gratification on the part of the public.

Frank Storms ran the business until 1939, when secretary/treasurer Warren Daniels took over the company, which in time evolved into the Chelsea Lumber Company.

While the elevator company was venturing into new fields, Dan McClaren owned and operated a bean and hay business along what is known as the "Bean Siding" of the railroad, employing as many as 25 local women to sort white beans there. Updyke & Harris bought Simon Hirth's blacksmith shop and started a sheet metal business. And, on the eve of the Depression, the local banking industry went through major changes.

In 1921, P.G. Schaible Sr. became president of Farmers & Merchants Bank and the bank flourished. Two years later, it declared a 100% stock dividend, increasing its common capital to $50,000, recalls Paul Schaible Jr. In 1927, the Farmers & Merchants Bank moved into the impressive—and vacant—stone bank building vacated by Glazier's bank after his financial distresses in 1907 and subsequently vacated by the Four Mile Lake Cement Plant officers. At this time, the F&M Bank had total assets of one million dollars and the Kempf Bank had assets of $810,000.

Spanish-American War veteran Conrad Lehman owned a saloon until Prohibition came to town and closed his business. In the early 1920s, he and M.J. Dunkle founded the Chelsea Screw Company. Dunkle supplied the industrial knowledge, and Lehman the financial backing. At the time the Federal Screw Works acquired the company,

At the close of World War I, businesses, including the F & M Bank, flourished. Note the newly minted cars and the watering trough for horses in the foreground on Main Street.

Courtesy the Dan Maroney Family

Lehman became an investor. He built a gas station on South Main Street where the Chelsea State Bank now stands, and acquired the L.P. Vogel Tower.

While the banking industry was flourishing, the Interurban was on its last run. In part, its demise was due to the advent of the automobile and improved roads. But, a series of disastrous accidents were also responsible. One of the worst took place on a rainy Saturday afternoon, June 18, 1921, at Lima Center, in front of Dwight Beach's home on Jackson Road. He and his brothers witnessed the crash and future historian Louis W. Doll was a small boy in town that day. Seventy-seven years later, Doll wrote about the disaster for the *Chelsea Standard*:

> *On the porch swing of the Edwin Keusch house, the second house east of Main, Nell Keusch was sitting with Aunt Delia Keusch, her mother-in-law, who was murmuring, "Poor Lizzie, poor Lizzie."*
>
> *I learned that there had been a terrible collision at Lima Center three miles east of Chelsea. A large number of people had been killed and injured, and among them was Elizabeth Keusch, a relative of Philip, Delia's husband.*
>
> *I hung around the corner across from the depot out of curiosity, which was soon rewarded when I saw one of those dirty, green steel interurban cars come into the station from the east. It was apparently bringing west-bound passengers on their way. A number of Chelsea residents got off, among them Doris Schumacher, who lived in the first house right across from the depot. She was weeping…*
>
> *There were two sections on the interurban that left Detroit on a regular run at about 3 P.M. The first section consisted of an older type frame car, while the second section consisted of one of the newer model's larger and heavier steel cars.*
>
> *They stopped at the Ann Arbor depot on Huron Street, where the first car filled up with standing-room-only and left. The large second section had lots of room.*
>
> *Later, the motorman of the second section reported having trouble with the brakes, all the way from Detroit…*
>
> *Both cars were on their way westward expecting to stop at the Warsaw siding at Lima Center to find out the location of the eastbound car they were expecting to pass at that point. The conductor of the first section pulled into the siding, leaving the switch open for the second section.*
>
> *It was 5 P.M. As he was telephoning, the second came rumbling on at a fast clip. The brakes failed, shutting off the power didn't slow the car,*

and it crashed into the first section, going halfway through it and driving it the length of the siding and down on the main line.

Four people were killed instantly, a fifth died later, within a few hours. Well over 20 people were injured, some seriously.

In addition to Elizabeth Keusch, two other Chelsea people were killed: Mr. and Mrs. Arthur Pierce, neighbors and family friends, for whom my parents grieved...

Later, I heard George Staffan, undertaker and first cousin of my mother, who conducted the burial services for the three Chelsea people, say that there wasn't a scratch or a bruise on their bodies, but every bone had been broken.

Perhaps in response to tragedies like these, the Interurban made its last run in 1927. No longer would the yellow and green cars rattle through Middle Street downtown. The motormen would no longer stop at farmers' platform—high steps to pick up milk cans. The ties were pulled up by a steam engine and all traces of the Interurban began to disappear.

Fun at the Lake

In the summer, it seemed that all of Chelsea emptied out and went to "The Lake"—mostly Cavanaugh Lake, although a loyal contingent headed to North Lake and a few independent thinkers had cottages on other nearby bodies of water.

On the Fourth of July, the entire town turned out to ride bicycles, walk or drive four miles west, to Cavanaugh Lake. Farm families for miles around dressed for fun, packed picnics early in the morning, piled into wagons and drove to the lake, greeting neighbors along the way. As early as July 2, 1879, the *Chelsea Standard* anticipated the holiday fun at Cavanaugh Lake:

At the Grand Fourth of July Celebration to be held at Cavanaugh Lake tomorrow (Friday), one and one-quarter miles north of Sylvan Center, there will be three bands in attendance, two cornet and one string, to furnish the music for the occasion. The following are the officers of the day: Hon. W.A. Holcomb, of Sylvan, President; J. Sweinforth, of Francisco, and C.J. Haselschwardt, of Sharon, Vice Presidents; E.L. Negus, of Chelsea, Chief Marshal; Frank Staffan, of Chelsea; George Ward of Sylvan, and G.W. Merkel of Sharon, Assistant Marshals. The orators of the day are Hon. W.E. Depew and M. Lehman, of Chelsea. There will be two immense processions. The Chelsea procession will form at 8:30 A.M., in the following order:

Chelsea Cornet Band, speakers, invited guests and citizens in carriages; Chief Marshal E.L. Negus. The Sylvan procession will form at 9 A.M., sharp, headed by the Helmet Cornet Band, of Francisco. There will be sports and games of all kinds, too numerous to mention. The exercises of the day will wind up with a grand balloon ascension from the Island at 5 P.M., and fire-works in the evening from the middle of the Lake, and parade of all nations at 6 P.M.

The speakers' names may have changed over the years, but for nearly a century bands still played, families and friends still picnicked together, children ran and played and swam, and the community thrilled to the sight of fireworks.

According to Chelsea Historical Society President Kathleen Clark, who lives at Cavanaugh Lake, the farmlands, woods, and marshlands surrounding the lake were owned by James Howe, Thomas Cassidy, Alice Sumner, and W.D. and James Ransom in the 1870s, when the lake first became a summertime destination. The Interurban Railroad brought cottage owners to the lake from Jackson, Detroit, and Ann Arbor until 1920, and families would remain all summer long, while businessmen commuted back and forth.

Civil War Captain Negus was one of the founders of the Cavanaugh Lake Club. A man of strong convictions, he once shared a cottage on the lake with another man and his family. A dispute so infuriated the two men that they sawed the home in half and moved one half to another lot, John Keusch remembers.

Ransom Armstrong and Freddie Bareis, a World War I veteran, owned the Cavanaugh Lake store, and Armstrong was employed by the Cavanaugh Lake Club to fill an icehouse in winter

The "Maid of the Mist" ferried passengers across Cavanaugh Lake to the island's dance pavillion, while amateur boaters enjoyed the water on a hot summer day.

Courtesy of Hazel Dittmar

and deliver ice to the cottagers in summer. A hotel was built a stone's throw away from the store, on the lake shore, by Eugene Smith. In the 1920s, the hotel was sold to the Ann Arbor YWCA, which later sold it when the YWCA moved to Clear Lake. The hotel was subsequently demolished.

The island mentioned in the newspaper account has long since disappeared, but memories and tales linger of the sunken island and the "*Maid of the Mist*" that ferried revelers out to the island, where they danced until late into the night.

An 1874 map of Sylvan Township shows an island between three and four acres in size that sat well above water level on the lake, which covers 199 acres.

"Neither the exact date the dance hall was built, nor its exact physical appearance is available," Kathleen Clark wrote in a *Chelsea Review* article in 1994. "By 1886, the Cavanaugh Lake Association began building cottages on the south end of the lake. It is very likely that the dance hall emerged at that time."

Folklore suggests that the dance hall was burned down by a jealous lover—but who the lovers were or why one was jealous is a mystery obscured by time. According to John Keusch, the dance hall had disappeared by 1900, but the island remained, though without foliage. "It was just a small sand pit—and wet," he says. Geraldine Kraft, granddaughter of Frank P. Glazier, remembers walking the sand bar to the island, waist-deep in water. "There were dances out there...A bridge went over the 'cut' on the east shore. It was a treacherous deal to get in a boat and ride to the island—and very few people could swim," she told Clark.

Charlie Winans and a friend camped on the island in the 1920s. "It didn't take us long to find that there were chiggers," he told Clark. "We burned off wood then spread it out to kill the chiggers, scraped off the ground, then put blankets down."

All that remains now of the Atlantis of Cavanaugh is enough space for a water volleyball net and anchorage for boats. The island seems to have disappeared in 1964. Bill Dittmar told Clark that University of Michigan students studied the sunken island when his family owned Cavanaugh Lake Store in the late 1960s. "Their instruments found a stream under the island," he remembered. "They told us the dirt was washed away and the island slowly settled into the lake." Others suggest that the sand and the bottom of the island was pulled out through the Spring Lake inlet as residents dug the drains or cleared blocked streams leading to the second lake.

Despite the fate of the island, the number and size of vacation cottages multiplied over time, and later would be renovated into, or replaced by, year-round homes.

The Keusch family built their cottage in 1921 and John Keusch may hold the record for the size of a fish caught in the lake. During the winter of 1924, he went ice fishing on the lake, but a late hour and cold winds convinced the boy to go home without pulling in his lines. The following weekend, he took the Interurban to a stop a mile and

The fish that didn't get away! John Keusch proudly displays his catch one frosty winter day in 1924. Courtesy of John Keusch

Frank Glazier's grand summer home at
Cavanaugh Lake at the turn of the century.
Courtesy Chelsea Area Historical Society

a half from the lake, trudged to his tip-ups, and began chopping the lines out of the ice. It was so cold that when his work was half done, he went into the Cavanaugh Lake Store to warm his hands and listen to stories. Late that afternoon, he returned to the ice, chopping around the last line, and to his amazement, pulled up a 16-pounder. The proud moment was caught on film and he still has the photograph hanging in his home.

The grandfather of all cottages was Frank Glazier's large two-story building encircled by a walnut verandah that had commanding views of the lake. It burned in 1915 and the family moved to the smaller cottage at the foot of the hill. The fire was yet another disappointment in the life of the great entrepreneur. A little over two years later, Frank P. Glazier died in the little cottage.

Geraldine Kraft remembers a wonderfully memorable birthday party given for her at the grand cottage at the lake when she was four or five. "I decided to make a grand entrance down the cottage's grand staircase and I fell head over applecart all the way down," she says with a faint smile. Few photographs remain of the place, but Geraldine remembers large rooms, two main floors and a full basement, six fireplaces, including two in the basement where cooking was done on hot summer days, and the hospitable porch that encircled the entire cottage. The fire took place the year she was five. Later, Geraldine and her first husband, Harlan Shelley, restored the smaller Glazier cottage. Eventually, it was replaced by actor Jeff Daniels' year-round home.

A small black-and-white photo of young twins Howard and Dudley Holmes shows them sitting on horses by their Cavanaugh Lake cottage sometime after World War I. "Every summer we rode the horses from our farm just north of town out to the lake. It was a grand total of four miles and we thought we were fine equestrians," Dudley Holmes remembers, explaining, "After all, it took my father's car—which ran 14 miles an hour at top speed—nearly an hour to get there."

The Holmes' cottage, like its neighbors, was informal, furnished with cast-off furnishings from the town house. Some cottages had fireplaces; many did not. George Winans, born a generation after Dudley Holmes, says that the cottages were all shells accommodated with old kerosene cookstoves and outhouses. He remembers riding his bicycle into town every day to peddle newspapers and stopping for a cool drink from a roadside spring. "One day my brother Charlie and I got the idea to see where that spring came from and we followed it to Mr. Laird's barnyard. We never drank from that spring again, I'll tell you!"

George and Charlie Winans helped their grandfather dust his apple orchard, which was near the lake, on very quiet summer nights. ("You could hear that machine for five miles around—the neighbors must have loved us.") Then, covered in dust, they would plunge into the chilly lake waters. "I can't remember a time when I couldn't swim," George Winans says, speaking for generations of Chelsea boys.

Originally, an informal road ran between the cottages and the lake shore, but when cars became larger, noisier, and more frequent, Jim Daniels and the Glazier Road Association convinced the county to run the road farther back, where it is today.

World War II changed life at Cavanaugh Lake entirely. As workers poured into Chelsea to man shifts at Central Fibre and the Federal Screw Works, an acute housing shortage developed. Many families who owned summer homes at the lake winterized the homes and moved out there, renting their village residences to factory workers. After the war, with a booming economy and plenty of automobiles, some of those who had moved to the lake decided to stay and others followed suit.

The same was true for North Lake and a dozen others in the area. Howard Brooks founded the Crescent Sporting Club at Blind Lake. "It was an organization well steeped in local lore," Keusch remembers, adding, "Many fine structures at Blind Lake are due to Mr. Brooks' activities in this club."

Patricia Paczkowski wrote a history of Pleasant Lake south of Chelsea in Freedom Township proving that the German settlement could have fun in the sun, too. She notes,

Pleasant Lake Road was a popular trail for travelers between Jackson and Ann Arbor, and Pleasant Lake was a natural half-way point to rest before continuing the long journey. You can imagine the thrill the Lutz children (Jacob Lutz, German settler here, was a fur trader and dealer in tin ware) would experience when one day each summer they would hear the clammering of wagon wheels and the loud trumpeting of elephants. They knew this announced that the circus was coming…The circus folks would be welcomed by Jacob and his family and would spend the night at the lake before continuing their journey…

In the early years, horses and buggies brought vacationers for the day to picnic, fish, and socialize with friends. The Pleasant Lake

"Every summer Howard and I rode the horses from our farm out to the lake," Dudley Holmes recalled, eight decades later.

Courtesy of the Holmes family

House was established in 1880 and when visitors stayed overnight, its dance hall would be partitioned off with folding screens and cots would be set in line for dormitory sleeping accommodations.

Many fish stories were pulled out of this lake. Helen Lutz Vogel loved to tell about a day when she was a little girl ice fishing with a spear. She dropped the small fish she was using as bait into the water, reached in to get it with her spear, and came up with a 12-pound pike. "Many fishermen, when they heard about her catch, offered money for it," Patricia Paczkowski remembers. "Helen refused. She proudly took the pike home with her to tell her tale."

When Manny Sodt purchased the hotel, his daughter Virginia, who later became Virginia Lutz, was tending bar one night when she overheard a man and woman plotting the murder of the woman's husband. "Ginny was quite young and couldn't believe her ears," the historian writes. She informed her father, who informed the police, but the tale was discounted—until the corpse appeared. "Ginny was a key witness," the historian notes.

Family and friends gathered together one lazy, hot, and hazy day of the summer of 1894, to enjoy the outdoors and the serenity of life at the lake. Courtesy Chelsea Area Historical Society

Dances would be held by the lake shore and the Fourth of July was the summer's highlight. At one time, everyone with a boat would form a parade, playing music. Prizes were offered for the outstanding entries—boats and humans. Fireworks were shot off from a small island in the center of the lake, bands played, families picnicked, young people danced and flirted and courted. In closing her reminiscences about the early days at the lake, Patricia Paczkowski writes, "Its future is for the dreamer."

A Stroll Down Main Street—and Memory Lane

Back in 1993, Dr. Wilfred C. Lane, beloved local veterinarian and frequent public speaker, escorted interested local residents on a tour of downtown that the historical society billed as "Memories of Saturday Nights in Chelsea." Dr. Lane's widow, Donna Lane, preserved his notes so that future generations could also share a stroll with the doctor down Main Street in the 1920s.

Put on your hat and gloves, pick up an umbrella that will double as a walking stick, and join the group as Dr. Lane starts his tour of Chelsea's downtown, circa 1920.

"I'd like to start at the corner of South Main Street and Van Buren," the doctor begins, explaining that anything south of this point was considered "out of town." As he surveys his audience, he explains, "In the 1920s, Chelsea's population was 2,080—while Brighton and Saline each had 750 residents. In those days, the people who lived here were dependent on local industry for employment. Buying anything out of town was frowned upon."

He points to the gas station on this corner, which looks deceptively modern, and explains that the building's framework was the former Interurban depot, but it was later turned at right angles. The Interurban, he says, "not only transported passengers, but also goods of all kinds from Detroit to Chicago on silent electrical cars."

At the corner of Orchard and Main streets, on the site of the future Chelsea State Bank, stands the Baptist Church in 1920. Later, it would be destroyed by fire. Unlike its contemporaries, the Methodist and Congregational churches, which also suffered devastating fires, the Baptist sanctuary would never be rebuilt. Its congregation disappeared, absorbed by the other churches in town. When Dr. Lane was a boy, a creamery operated here, until O.B. McLaughlin built a gas station on the spot for light automotive repairs, tires, lubrication, and car washing. Next door, to the east, the entrepreneur built a modern brick home so he could live close to his business. Later, McLaughlin started a Plymouth automobile agency.

Strolling north on Main Street, the veterinarian and his attentive tour group stop in front of the stately brick building that now houses the library. In the 1920s, it is the home of Mr. and Mrs. Ed McKune, who rent rooms to businessmen.

Katharine Wagner, a niece of Mrs. McKune, remembers many visits to her aunt's home throughout the years, until the house was donated to the library in 1958. "My aunt was a very loving and hospitable woman," she says. "This was an elegant house for most of its history, but by the 1950s, it was fraying a little around the edges." Mrs. Wagner and her brother, George Staffan, also remember the fire that destroyed the home's elaborate two-story carriage house during their childhood.

Moving north down the street, the doctor reaches the furniture store that in the 1920s houses Merkel Brothers Hardware—"one of Chelsea's oldest businesses," he points out. "Merkel's is one of three flourishing hardware stores in Chelsea serving farmers and craftsmen with tools, building supplies and—as I'll always remember—a

There is nothing so grand to a little boy as a summer day, a pull toy, a length of string, a piece of ground to dig in and some companions —even if they are feathered. Dressed in rompers, future Chelsea veterinarian Wilfred Lane was caught in the act of some summer fun by an intrepid photographer.

Courtesy of Donna Lane

beautiful display of hunting rifles and shotguns in a large case that can plainly be seen from the sidewalk."

In that same complex stands the Princess Theater, where children can see a double feature on Saturday afternoons for 10 cents admission ("25 cents for adults"). "This enterprise is operated by Mr. J. Edward Weber. Ed, as he was affectionately known, was a big, jovial man and I'll never forget that he usually wears a vest with a big chain leading to a watch in one pocket and a decoration on his lapel, perhaps a lodge emblem."

The projectionist at the Princess Theater is Warren Geddes, a little man who always wears a felt hat. He usually arrives at the theater early and gets his camera and films in order so the first show can commence precisely at 7 P.M. "Mr. Geddes is the grandfather of one of Chelsea's famous sons, Mr. Tom Monaghan of Domino's Pizza fame. Tom's mother was the valedictorian of the 1933 graduation class from Chelsea High School," the doctor says, resuming his stroll.

An ice cream parlor is conveniently located next to the Princess and next to that, Dillon and Tuttle's Barber Shop.

The corner shop in the Merkels' complex houses the Fred G. Loeffler & Son Meat Market. "I can remember seeing beef and pork carcasses hanging from rails in the store, which always had sawdust on the floor," Dr. Lane says. "The men wear coats and hats while they are working because it is always as cold as they can keep it."

In the early days of the century, shopping for meat offers a leisurely opportunity to visit with customers, who sit on round stools facing the meat counter and watch the father and son slice off the cuts they request.

"At this time, there are two butchers in Chelsea, Klingler and Loeffler, and both of the families come from farms south of town. You see, all farmers butchered their own meats and some of them went into the business—that was the case with Mr. Klingler and Fred Loeffler," explains Richard Kinsey.

When he was a schoolboy in the 1930s, Kinsey would make $7 a week working at Loefflers' butcher shop every afternoon from 3:30 to 6 P.M., and Saturdays from 7:30 A.M. to 10 P.M. His boss would one day become his father-in-law. "I remember watching him make sausage and hot dogs and I remember helping him kill chickens in the basement of the shop," Kinsey says.

In the 1920s, the Loefflers have an iron smokehouse behind the building where bacon and hams are cured with hickory fires and then stored. During the Depression, the butcher shop would expand its line of merchandise. Kinsey remembers their prices as though it were yesterday: 32 cents a pound for butter, 25 cents a pound for homemade baloney, 5 cents for link baloney ("kids bought them for snacks on the way home from school"), 5 cents for a box of wooden matches, 10 cents for a loaf of bread (or 25 cents for three loaves).

But that would happen later. Dr. Lane continues his stroll down the Main Street of the 1920s.

A grocery store has always stood on the northeast corner of Main and Park streets, he explains. "Schneiders has been there for over 50 years, but I can recall when it was operated by Mr. Chauncey Freeman. In the cool basement, a lady named Lizzie Mast holds forth and sells wallpaper, crocks, dishes and other household necessities. Next door is a men's store named Walworth & Strieter." Originally advertised as a "One Price Cash Store," it carries everything from custom clothing to boots, shoes, and furnishings.

Continuing to the north, the doctor points to the storefront and says, "This is where I remember the first post office. I even remember our box number—412. You have to know the combination to get your mail out." Later, when the post office moved, the building became Kroger's grocery store, situated next to the A&P. Wilfred Lane, like generations of Chelsea children, worked as a clerk in the A&P. He rose to the rank of produce manager before going to college.

"In these days, the provisions are on shelves behind the counter and the customers tell us what they want," he reminds his listeners. "We would grind coffee, cut the cheese from a big wheel (sometimes whittling off a chunk for ourselves), and figure up the amount owed on the back of a brown bag—if it is too much to add in our heads. The meat market here is operated by Fred Klingler, later by Adolph Duerr and R.B. Dexter, who did their own butchering and sausage-making."

Once again moving north, the doctor points his umbrella at the next shop front and announces, "This was the Chelsea Bakery, operated by Mr. Seyfried, his son Harold and daughter Viola. They are all big people and living examples of the power of the scrumptious cakes, pies, and pastries they produce." The three-story building hosts Boyd's Hotel, which was so glowingly described in the 1895 *Headlight*.

Cleary's Pub is the successor to Kolb's Restaurant. "Bill Kolb, a World War I mess sergeant, is a great cook," Dr. Lane says. "The coffee urns are big and shining and the hot beef sandwiches and mashed potatoes are the specialty of the house."

John Keusch remembers the names of nearly a dozen grocery stores that serviced Chelsea's shoppers over the years in various locations, but a grocery store has always stood on the northeast corner of Main and Park streets. Owned and operated by the Flintofts, Schneider's Grocery was a Chelsea institution.

Photograph from 1959 Chelsea High School Yearbook

Next door: Grove Brothers 5&10, where children and their mothers make annual pilgrimages in August to buy school supplies. "What I loved most is just inside the door," he reminisces with a smile, explaining, "The big glass case houses all kinds of candy treats, from sea-foam candy and dark chocolate to the jelly beans—which are about what I could generally afford."

Vogel & Wurster, a gentleman's clothing store, is the ancestor of Vogel's & Foster's. Helen Vogel, the daughter, runs the ladies' side of the business. "The thing I remember most about this joint venture is the big brass cage-type office that houses Ella Barber, a lady who kept the books and always made the change and gave you a receipt," the tour guide says, reminiscing. Miss Barber is also a correspondent for the *Chelsea Standard*. She sits on Schumacher's porch across from the Interurban station and jots down the names of arriving passengers, then telephones to learn where they had been. The next week, their names will appear in the newspaper.

Across the alley and up a few steps. You enter the Miller Sisters' Millinery Store. "These eccentric ladies are artists with ribbon and feathers," Dr. Lane says. "They can transform a piece of felt into an original creation."

The Miller Brothers (no relation) Barber Shop is situated next to the Miller Sisters. "This is the sports center of Chelsea. The Miller Brothers are great sandlot baseball players in their own right and this is Chelsea's answer to the Hot Stove League."

Mr. Kantlehner's Jewelry Store comes next, around the corner on East Middle Street, followed by Hindelang's Hardware (where the police station is now located), the office and print shop of the *Chelsea Standard*, another grocery store, and, on the end of the first building facing East Middle Street, the office of Dr. Faye Palmer, one of Chelsea's three dentists. ("The others are Dr. Brock and Dr. Steger.")

On the northeast corner of the 1920's Main and Middle Streets, another barber pole announces the shop manned by Billy Schantz, and later, his son. Conveniently located in the front parlor of the barber shop is a tobacco, magazine and newspaper store, then "The Candy Kitchen," which is more familiarly known as "John's." A favorite hangout for school children and courting couples, especially after dances, local theatrical productions, or football games, this shop is operated by a Greek family, Momma and John Panarites and their three sons, Jimmie, Nicki, and Charlie. "If you are anybody, you always take your date to John's for a coke after the movies," Dr. Lane explains with a smile.

Hinderer Brothers Grocery is the candy shop's neighbor, followed by Milton Baxter's Tailor Shop, where men's suits are handmade or altered. Several more shops, which tend to have rapid turnovers, lead to the Sylvan building, once the site of the old Crescent Hotel. "The Crescent was once a popular hotel, but eventually it becomes a haven for single men, some without jobs, until a tragic fire causes it to be closed," Dr. Lane says. "However, in the basement is what I believe to be Chelsea's first bowling alley." This, too, is a popular place for couples. Eventually, some of them will form the Chelsea bowling league. In the early days, high school boys are hired to set the pins—"a rather dangerous job," Dr. Lane says, reflectively.

The last building before Jackson Street is the Longworth building, once part of the Glazier complex where A.R. Welch built cars. This was also the original home of the Federal Screw Works, and then for upward of 40 years, W.R. Daniels Automobile Sales will be located there. "W.R. is one of the people active in the Chelsea Elevator Company with Frank Storms," John Keusch says. "He was a longtime president of the village and he sold Dodge, Plymouth, Buick and Oldsmobile cars."

Across from the Longworth Building in 1920 stands an elegant two-story gray stone building originally used as offices for the Glazier Stove Works until Frank Porter Glazier lost his assets in 1907. In Dr. Lane's boyhood, Dr. Thomas Woods, M.D., sees patients there. One of Chelsea's hottest fires would occur in this building many years later, when it housed the Frigid Products' frozen food lockers in the basement ("Housewives didn't have freezers at home, so they rented space here") and Heydlauff's Appliance & Television Store on the street level. The fire completely destroyed the building and the Heydlauffs rebuilt a one-story modern building with brick. That is what twenty-first century visitors see on Main Street.

Moving south, Dr. Lane mentions a succession of businesses: a laundress, dry goods store, and doctor's offices. "Doctors Papo and Botsford held offices here before the advent of the Chelsea Hospital."

The Farmers & Merchants Bank serves clients in the next storefront until 1927. Its president is P.G. Schaible, father of another bank president, Paul Schaible. After the bank moved, several businesses

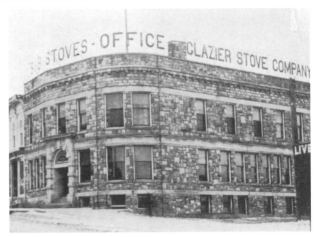

The "Brightest and Best" stoves were manufactured by Frank P. Glazier's stove company here in Chelsea.

Courtesy Chelsea Area Historical Society

succeeded the bank, including the Michigan Consolidated Gas Company and Gladys Doe's Restaurant.

The shop on the northwest corner of Main and West Middle streets, with its angled front door, is a drugstore first operated by the George and Frank Glazier, later by Louis P. Vogel. Eventually it would be acquired by Mr. Burg, whose daughters help him with the business. The Burgs would sell the drugstore to Charles Lancaster in 1948; he would rename it Chelsea Drug. "This store, like so many drugstores of the time, boasts a soda fountain with a marble-topped bar counter, stools, and a few small round tables with wire chairs. Lazy turning ceiling fans complete the picture and cool it in the summer before air conditioning."

Heading west on Middle Street sits Seitz's Tavern. "This watering hole is a family operation of three generations and a flagship of the Chelsea community," Dr. Lane tells his audience. "I can remember, however, when it housed a grocery store and the tavern was across the street." George Winans remembers seeing German farm wives served a glass of beer at the back door of the tavern while their husbands were inside—"women in those days would never go into a bar," he explains.

The Sylvan Township Hall is a Chelsea landmark which serves as the village's social center-and has, even long before the 1920s. Until the high school acquired a gymnasium in the late 1930s, all basketball games were played here. "People like John Keusch, Morry Hoffman, and Hooky Brooks became locally famous here," the guide says with a smile. The town hall also hosted Dr. Sharpstein's Medicine Show, the Chelsea Minstrels, golden gloves boxing matches and countless local talent shows, fashion shows, and theatrical productions.

In time, the Sylvan Town Hall would become so dilapidated that Maurice Hoffman, the longest-serving Sylvan Township Supervisor, would renovate and restore it. The sculptured wooden nameplate over the front door is the work of the late James K. Daniels.

Bill Wheeler operates a blacksmith shop next to the town hall. The large brick structure at one time also housed the Overland Sales & Service, an automobile repair service operated by Mr. Adam Faist, proprietor of a woodworking business. "I can still remember hearing the sound of saws and lathes coming from that building."

On the southwest corner of Main and Middle streets, the Kempf Commercial & Savings Bank stands like a sentinel, overseeing the town's watering trough and some of the hitching rails that run along both sides of Main Street—which, by the way, has only recently been paved. After the bank closes, the building will serve as the village's post office, then Grove's Variety Store and the Chelsea Public Library.

Winan's Jewelry Store remains in the same location throughout the decades, although its merchandise changes to suit the times.

W. P. Schenk's Department Store, a three-story flourishing enterprise, comes next, run at first by W.P. and John Schenk. John Keusch remembers W.P. Schenk in his later years closing shop and heading home with a new hat on his head, complete with price tag dangling on the side.

"William Schenk is a substantial contributor to Chelsea and has 15 employees and a machine that carries a customer's money to the cashier's cage at the back of the store," Dr. Lane says.

"William Schenk's first business was a general store at Sylvan Center," John Keusch says. "In 1877, he worked at H.S. Holmes' Mercantile (later Vogel's & Foster's) and in 1885 went into partnership with George Kempf. By 1889, he was a sole proprietor and in 1893 built the building which now houses the Common Grill…His merchandise ranged from groceries to carpets."

W.P. Schenk in the 1920s is serving on the Board of Education, the Chelsea State Bank board, and the Village Council. He is also one of the first automobile dealers in Chelsea.

Fenn's Drug Store, next door to Schenk's, is "a very proper apothecary carrying only drugs and medicines," Dr. Lane says. "Mr. Fenn's right-hand helper is a large and very proper maiden lady named Lida Guthrie, who greets all comers as 'Dearie.' Most children call her 'Auntie.'"

Frank Glazier built the strong and elegant stone building on the corner of Main and South streets as a bank and a memorial to his father in 1901. The Glazier name can still be seen above the entrance, but the building did not serve its original function long. In 1907, when Glazier is convicted of fraudulent money practices, the Chelsea Savings Bank closes its doors. In the future, in the late 1960s, this building would become home to the district court.

In 1901, noted Jackson architect Claire Allen designed and supervised the construction of the Chelsea Savings Bank. Frank P. Glazier had the building erected in memory of his father, George P. Glazier. Photos Courtesy of Larry Chapman & Ann Arbor Federal Savings Bank

Ice was stored in warehouses and underground icehouses until spring and summer, when icemen made their rounds from house to house.

Courtesy of Richard Kinsey

But to continue…

On the southwest corner of Main and South Street, a beautiful white house stands here in the 1920s, Dr. Lane says. "It was a small hospital operated by Mrs. Beatrice Notten. I had my tonsil and adenoids removed here, in the days when surgeries were done under local anesthesia. It's an experience that I hope you will never have to go through. In the 1930s, that lovely home would be replaced with the post office."

Besides the businesses ranging up and down Main Street, industrial and commercial warehouses and manufacturing plants line back streets and back roads. Four churches in town offer Sunday services. On side streets and alleys, icehouses store enormous blocks of ice that are packed in sawdust after being cut from local lakes—"in the hopes that enough could be stored to last through the long, hot summer."

In the 1920s, two livery stables serve Chelsea residents who drive to town or railroad passengers who need to rent horses, carriages, buggies, or sleighs. Martin's Livery Stable faces Park Street. Weiss' Livery Barn faces the railroad depot. It was here that Dr. Lane's father, Chandler Lane, Chelsea's first veterinarian, set up business in 1905. In exchange for stabling his horse here and receiving farmers' calls on the stable's telephone, the first Dr. Lane harnessed horses and delivered the horse and buggy to customers.

Chelsea also boasts of having three doctors, three dentists, one osteopath, two funeral homes, and seven or eight garages where cars could be purchased or repaired in the 1920s. "Chelsea is a vibrant, self-sufficient community," the tour guide says, meditatively.

Dr. Lane reaches the end of his tour and shakes hands with his appreciative audience before heading home.

Herbert Hoover, 1929-33 • Franklin Delano Roosevelt, 1933-45

Black Friday in New York • U.S. Stock Exchange collapses • St. Valentine's Day massacre • J.M. Keynes writes *Treatise on Money* • Sigmund Freud publishes *Civilization and Its Discontents* • Planet Pluto discovered • Pearl Buck writes *The Good Earth* • Al Capone jailed • Grant Wood paints "American Gothic" • Americans sing *When the Moon Comes Over the Mountain*; *Brother, Can You Spare a Dime?*, *April in Paris, Who's Afraid of The Big, Bad Wolf?* • The Lindbergh baby is kidnapped • Garbo stars in *Anna Karenina* • Orson Welles radio show, *War of the Worlds* causes panic • Clark Gable in *Gone With the Wind* • Jesse Owens wins four gold medals in Berlin Olympic Games • King Edward VIII abdicates the throne to marry Wallis Simpson • Johnstown floods • Stalin purges • Dirigible *Hindenberg* explodes • Roosevelt signs U.S. Neutrality Pact • Hitler appoints himself War Minister • Roosevelt asks Congress for $552 million in defense • Germany occupies Bohemia and Moravia • 500,000 Americans involved in sit-down strikes between 1936 and 1937 • Spanish rebels take Malaga • Mussolini and Hitler proclaim Rome-Berlin axis • Frank Lloyd Wright builds Taliesin West in Phoenix • Germany invades Poland • Women and children evacuated from London • Trotsky assassinated

U.S. POPULATION
1930: 132 million

The Depression: The 1930s

Brother, Can You Spare A Dime?

The Depression hit Chelsea much like it hit the rest of the country. Hard. Painfully, tearfully hard. But at least here, most people had the land or at least family connections to land. They could grow food to feed their families and they could hold onto something tangible.

Some people in town were affected more than others. Richard Kinsey, who was born in 1925, remembers hearing neighbors whisper about several sudden local deaths, suggesting they were suicides. "Everyone knew everyone else's business in those days and times were very, very hard," he says. "A number of people were wiped out financially. I remember that one man jumped in front of a train."

It was rumored that one of the owners of the Federal Screw Works, who had just recently built an impressive new home on Main Street and drove a brand new gleaming 16-cylinder Cadillac, lost millions at the time of the stock market crash. He suffered a mental collapse from which he never fully recovered.

"People who haven't lived through a national catastrophe like that can never fully understand what the times were like, how very desperate people felt," says Merle Barr.

Because everyone knew everyone else's business, a bag of vegetables or a few pieces of clothing might appear on a neighbor's doorstep in times of trouble. The town's shopkeepers would run a bill for long-time customers.

"Times were tough, so tough in the Depression, but people had too much pride to ask for help. So, we found ways to help each other out," Kinsey says. He remembers the Loefflers, who owned a local butcher shop, offering soup bones to housewives, "to take them off our hands." His father, the foreman of a sheet metal company, fixed the furnace for a neighbor with six young children. "They couldn't pay my father, but the next fall they gave us a bushel of potatoes," he says. "People helped their neighbors as much as they could and many of us went to a barter system of payment."

Katie Chapman was in high school during Black Friday and during a living history program at the Chelsea United Methodist Retirement Home, she recalled waking up one morning and hearing her parents talk about all the banks that had closed. "In some places, they were issuing scrip, which was paper money not backed by gold, because there was no money to be had…I remember a sinking feeling in my stomach thinking, 'What are we going to do now?' But we lived on a farm, so we had food."

Not long after the stock market crash, Chelsea native Floyd Boyce lost his job at a hardware store in Jackson. There was no such thing as unemployment pay, so Floyd and his wife Florence rolled up their sleeves and went to work. Explains their son, Ellis Boyce, who was born in 1920, "Mom made all kinds of baked goods and Dad went out and sold them. Actually, the entire family got into the production and selling. My sisters and I shared in delivering papers and that brought in a little money. However, it was not enough to make payments and in 1932 the bank foreclosed the mortgage on the house."

Like many other city dwellers, the Boyces moved back to the family farm, where they raised vegetables and lived without electricity, indoor plumbing or a telephone. "We didn't have much money, but we had good food to eat," Ellis Boyce remembers.

In the early 1930s, Marjorie Whipple Hepburn, the "tail end of 10 children," also moved to the outskirts of Chelsea, to a small rented farmhouse on what is now M-52, near Werkner Road, with one sister and her parents. Her father was an excellent carpenter, but he was a man who "couldn't handle finances" and the family hoped that Chelsea would provide a fresh start for them all. Throughout her childhood, even before the Depression, "money was hard to come by, but my mother never complained," Marjorie Hepburn remembers, explaining, "That's the way women were raised to be back then. My father was always proud of the fact that my mother never worked. I don't know how we lived—yet we knew that there were families worse off."

The mother and girls dug and planted a garden, harvested apples from an old orchard on the property, tended 50 chickens they had ordered by mail, canned vegetables.

"The Depression was a terrible time, but I was a pretty happy child," Mrs. Hepburn says. "As a tiny little girl, I knew we didn't have any money. I'd hear other children talking about Santa and somehow I knew that I wasn't going to be getting any gifts from him, even though I was a good girl. I just accepted it." When Marjorie's girl-friend invited her to join the Girl Scouts, the little girl asked, "Does it cost money?" When her friend told her about the dues, Marjorie didn't even bother to mention the invitation to her mother.

"Kids just knew and accepted how things were," she says. "Boys did odd jobs and they gave whatever they got to their family. I remember my husband telling me that he worked in the onion fields weeding until his fingers bled."

Still, her childhood was happy, she says. The family drove into town on Saturday nights and checked out a week's supply of books. ("I remember reading *True Stories* and *True Confessions*—that was the only sex education most girls received," she says, shaking her head.) During the summers, the family would drive to Chelsea, Stockbridge or Dexter to watch free movies that merchants rented and projected against a building's exterior. Edward Whipple had a beautiful singing voice and he would lead his family in song on nights at home. "You read stories about violence occurring in families when times are hard, but my father never drank, never did anything mean," she says. "We were very poor, but we had wonderful family times."

Mrs. Whipple, like most housewives in those days, was a good seamstress. People would offer the family clothes their children had worn and she would alter them for her daughters.

When Marjorie Whipple was 10, her parents gave her the first new dress she ever owned, a Shirley Temple dress that was breathtakingly beautiful to the little girl. Sixty-five years later, she can still describe its every detail: "It was plaid with red bands around the skirt, a round neck with red buttons running down the front. How I loved that dress! I wore it every Sunday to church," she says, with a far-away look. "I didn't think anything of that until one Sunday, when a little girl asked me, 'Don't you have any other dress?'"

To help pay her way through high school, Marjorie Whipple and dozens of other country children lived with a family in town and worked for room and board. "I never felt that people looked down upon me," she says. "I got good grades, and that's what mattered." Her one regret was that the woman she worked for didn't allow her much time away from her chores. She wanted desperately to be in the band, but cooking, cleaning, polishing, washing clothes, and watching the woman's little girl was what she had to do. Once, Marjorie was selected to direct a school play, an honor for the child, but the woman she worked for refused to let her go to the Saturday rehearsals.

When spring vacation came, Marjorie asked for several days off to visit a sister she hadn't seen in years. The lady wanted her spring cleaning done. Marjorie offered to work even harder in order to get all the work done in three days so she could have the rest of the week off. The woman refused. Marjorie quit and spent the rest of her high school months living with a sister in Dexter and hitching a ride with people who worked at Central Fibre in Chelsea.

Train cars carried cargoes of hobos who would roam the streets of Chelsea, hoping to find a sympathetic housewife who would give them a meal. Virginia Barr Visel remembers sitting in the window of her aunt's house, which overlooked the tracks, and counting as many as 20 men riding the open cars. "Hobos jumped off the trains and walked around town," Rolly Spaulding says. "One thing they always did was make some mark on the houses that were soft touches—housewives who would give them a meal. I never saw one, but it was probably on the road or curb or sidewalk."

Merle Barr and his sister, Virginia Visel, remember eating "a lot of watery bean soup and oatmeal" when times were hard. Others subsisted on soda crackers soaked in milk or potato soup with more broth than potatoes when times were especially tough.

The Chelsea Retirement Community came in for its share of hardships, as well. According to Kathleen Clark, during the Depression the Home sought to supplement its costs by supplying much of its own eggs, milk, and meat. Groundskeepers and anyone else who could help tended an orchard, planted vegetable gardens, collected eggs, and fed the chickens, cows, sheep, and hogs. Much of the hard work was done by an old horse named Jerry. "They cultivated only as much land as Jerry could plow," Clark says. "For 13 years, Jerry was one of the major factors in the production of food for the Home."

To save money, young couples would dispense with the formalities and expense of weddings. Geraldine Kraft and her first husband ran away to Bowling Green, Kentucky, to marry. "No one was climbing into a wedding gown in those days," she says. "It was quite the thing to do, to go away and come back and boomerang everyone with the announcement of your marriage." Several others eloped and kept their marriages secret, so working women could keep their jobs. Traditionally when a woman married, she was expected to quit her work and stay at home.

Chelsea's social life was one of the few things that wasn't sparse during those hard years. Fraternal organizations, women's organizations, church youth programs, lecture circuits, the movie theater and card-playing groups helped people take their minds off their worries. In 1936, the Chelsea Rod and Gun Club was formed. Two years later, as soon as he turned 18, Rolly Spaulding joined and faithfully attended the meetings on the second Tuesday of every month.

George Winans was eight years old when the Depression hit Chelsea, but he remembers how the lean, hard years affected the town. "There was nothing much for jobs. Industries shut down. Businesses would come and go from the industrial building by the railroad tracks."

Richard Kinsey delivered the *Jackson Citizen Patriot* on his bicycle to 106 customers. "If everyone paid, I made $6, but in those days someone always owed me. There were many who couldn't find the 18 cents for six papers a week," he says. Once, he asked his father for a dime to see a movie at the Princess Theater. "My father didn't have a dime, so I went to the dump and collected Roman Cleanser bottles. I could turn them in for a nickel apiece. That's the way I went to the theater."

John Keusch's father had to close his grocery store. "People had no money to spend," he says.

Elmer and Cora Winans had been given the elegant home on the corner of Adams and Madison Streets as a wedding present from Orrin Burkhardt, Mrs. Winans' father, who was a partner with Frank Storms and Warren Daniels in the Chelsea Lumber Company. Eventually, as their family expanded to make room for six boys and two girls, the Winans were forced to mortgage their property, which was a constant worry to the entire family.

Even the Chelsea landscape changed with the times. "You couldn't see a dead tree for miles around in those years. People went scavenging for firewood," John Keusch says. They also hunted and fished for food. Rabbits and squirrels became delicacies.

Rallying for Chelsea's Centennial

In the midst of some of the darkest days of the Depression, Chelsea rallied to celebrate the centennial of its founding on October 6 and 7, 1934. School children came pouring out of classroom doors at noon on Friday, October 6, happy for the several hours' reprieve. Thousands of former residents of Chelsea and surrounding townships returned to the village for the event, which was sponsored by the American Legion Post.

According to the *Ann Arbor Daily News*, "the centennial celebration has grown into a community-wide affair in which residents of surrounding townships are also joining. American Legion banners, and bright bunting will drape the streets and store windows will display historical relics. Indicative of the enthusiasm and support given the centennial is the repainting of Chelsea store fronts, and the co-operation of all Chelsea organizations."

Dr. A.L. Brock served as chairman of decorations. C.O. Bahnmiller headed the sports committee. Paul Maroney was assigned the task of issuing invitations to former residents. Henry Swickerath directed the poster advertising. Ed Eaton headed the program committee. Attorney William Rademacher, a World War I veteran and legionnaire, was responsible for the centennial editions of the *Chelsea Standard*.

Boxing exhibitions, mechanical rides, dances, theater programs and a few speeches, among them "Women's Place in the World," "State Affairs" and "Settlers' Hour" edified the crowd. A Children's Parade was led by the Original Flying German Band and American Legion members. Aerialists flew through the air. Soapbox derby contestants flew down the streets. Magicians pulled rabbits out of hats and coins from children's ears. The high school gymnasium hosted a homecoming dance and the festivities in town ended with a community sing and awarding of prizes at 10 P.M., Saturday night.

The Business Community Gets Hit on the Chin

Howard and Dudley Holmes were 17 years old and students at Phillips Exeter Academy in New Hampshire when the stock market crashed. They were among the fortunate few who could continue to go to college. But in 1931, tragedy hit their family, too. Their father fell to his death more than 70 feet from the top of one of the Chelsea Milling Company's grain elevators. Nineteen-year-old Dudley was at the milling company when the accident happened. After trying to comfort his mother, he brought her best friend to the Holmes' house, then drove to the University of Michigan to tell his twin brother the news.

The story is now a classic in the Holmes family, how Dudley went from office to office on campus, to discover where his brother was, then interrupted the engineering professor, dragged Howard out of class, and told him of the tragedy on their way home to Chelsea. The two teenage boys took over the business. And it flourished.

"We were smart enough to recognize the talent that my father had in place and we let them do what they did best," Dudley Holmes says. "A lot of the nuts-and-bolts companies in town went through the ringer during the Depression and took it on the chin for a few years. But we were a food company and people can't stop eating—fortunately—even in times of crisis, so we sailed through the Depression in pretty good shape."

In 1930, Mabel White Holmes, the twins' mother, concocted a baking mix in her kitchen on East Middle Street that helped launch a new generation of food products. She called the mix "Jiffy" because, the story goes, her family cook used to say "the biscuits will be done in a jiffy."

Other companies had to scramble to stay in business. When storefront rents jumped from $15 a month to $25 a month during the Depression, the Winans and Heydlauff families, who were neighbors in town, decided to unite efforts and business locations. "My Dad and Lloyd Heydlauff were great friends," George Winans recalls. The two businessmen divided Winans' store and its rent in half, displaying appliances and refrigerators on one side and jewelry on the other. They maintained this relationship until World War II ended. Meanwhile, as the Winans' space shrank, their lines of merchandise expanded, as the family struggled to discover something that would sell. "During the Depression, who bought jewelry?" Winans points out. "My father sold anything he could to make a buck."

Rolly Spaulding was 10 in 1930, and he remembers that "The old faithfuls in town—the milling company, lumber company, coal yard and Federal Screw—kept their payrolls going. It seemed to me that everyone could find something to do. No one made much, but they could make something."

Throughout the 1920s, the two banks in town had experienced impressive growth. According to Paul Schaible, in 1927, the Farmers and Merchants Bank had total assets of one million dollars and the Kempf Bank's assets amounted to $810,000.

Then came the Depression.

George Staffan remembers that a banker once told his father that his bank had one depositor with $25,000 in savings; if that man had decided to withdraw his money during the early days of the Depression, the bank would have folded—along with the investments of many townspeople.

When tragedy hit the Holmes family in the early days of the Depression, 19-year-old Dudley (left) and Howard (right), pictured here later in life, took over the family business. Courtesy of the Holmes family

The first "Jiffy" baking mix was developed by Mabel White Holmes, mother of Dudley and Howard, in 1930. Courtesy of the Holmes family

In 1930, when the two banks were located on each corner of the west side of the central Main Street block, Claude Sears Rogers was hired by Kempf Bank to cover the two employees' vacation times. Shortly afterward, Rogers recalls, the bank mysteriously began to suffer from a daily shortfall of as much as $20.

"At that time, the two banks cleared their checks daily by exchanging the other bank's checks and giving a check for the differences," Rogers says. "An adding machine tape was made of the checks and sent along with them, showing the total. We would then compare the amount of each check with the amount shown on the tape, as our verification system."

When Kempf Bank's Vice President John Fletcher returned from his vacation and learned of the daily shortfalls, he investigated the matter. "He finally ran a new tape on the checks listed on the other bank's tapes and found the totals were always overstated by the amount of our daily shortages. The young teller at the F&M Bank was somehow entering an amount into his adding machine without having it show on the tape."

Mr. Fletcher confronted Mr. Schaible with the evidence and the losses were repaid and the other teller promptly fired. "I was rehired for the same job the next summer," Rogers remembers, appreciatively. "The $50-per-month I earned on this job about paid my tuition for the fall semester at the University of Michigan."

While neither bank failed during the Depression, their officers decided to unite and operate under one roof. In 1934, they merged to form the Chelsea State Bank, with a total capital of $110,000 and assets worth about one million dollars. P.G. Schaible Sr. was named president of the new bank. Two years after the Federal Deposit Insurance program was established in 1933, the Chelsea State Bank became a member, with deposits insured to $5,000.

Other local business ventures didn't fare as well. Warren Geddes sold his share of the Princess Theater for a penny.

In the days of turbulent union agitation and the emergence of the American Communist Party, many plant owners were concerned about sabotage. The Federal Screw Works beefed up its security. Donald Bacon, who owned Central Fibre, on the other hand, invited the union into his company.

"It was not necessary for the United Auto Workers to have an election to serve as bargaining agent for his employees. Donald Bacon was an outstanding citizen who had the best interests of his people in view," John Keusch says. "He was also responsible for inducing families to locate in Chelsea as employees—people like Harold Jones, Edward Eaton, Robert Wagner, and many others. He also assisted many young people in this community to attend college, Olivet (which he attended), as well as others." Over time, Bacon acquired all of the buildings once owned by his father's stiffest opponent, Frank Glazier, including the Clock Tower.

Throughout the 1930s, John Keusch remembers, William P. Schenk, by now in his 80s, struggled to maintain his department store business. In its golden years, the store boasted 15 full-time employees, three floors of merchandise, a raised office in the rear of the first floor, and a cable system to carry cash from the tellers to the office. By the Depression, Schenk was down to one part-time saleswoman.

"Many times in summer months, I saw him late in the evening going from his home at the end of Orchard Street to the store to raise the awnings," Keusch says. "In the winter months, I saw him go to the store to shovel coal and tend to the fires. His sales were small. His merchandise had been on his counters and shelves for a long period of time. He was unable to replenish his stocks. Yet, I do not recall any complaints. He was cheery and optimistic. He was courageous. He stood the test of the Depression well."

John Keusch graduated from the University of Michigan law school during the year of the Bank Holiday in 1933. In 1935, he went to work for the National Park Service on a Works Progress Administration (WPA) project at Waterloo. "The purpose of the project was to better serve the people living in rural areas with schools and roads. The government wanted to move them to better farmlands," he explains. The government bought 25,000 acres in Washtenaw and Jackson counties, including Crooked Lake, Mill Lake, and Sugar Loaf Lake and formed them into the massive Waterloo Recreation Area. Keusch estimates that his grandmother got "$25, tops" per acre for her 500-plus acre farm.

The Depression did bring other lasting benefits to the community. The Public Works Administration was responsible for building the first sewerage treatment plant in Chelsea, at a cost of $40,000. John Keusch was village attorney. The plant came at the right time, he remembers. The village was being sued by a farmer whose horses had died after drinking in the creek.

"Mr. McKune was mayor during the Depression and he had a Make Work Program," Keusch says. "He had more than 200 people dig West Middle Street five to six feet down with hand shovels. Then they hauled the dirt away in wagons and filled the road with gravel. In Waterloo, we had 2,000 people working. They trucked people in from Jackson and paid them $2 a day."

The Civilian Conservation Corps descended on Chelsea's roads, leveling and paving them. In rural areas, they planted trees and helped create the Waterloo Recreation Area. The "new" post office was built during the Depression and decorated with a mural that illustrates the "workingman's theme" so prevalent in Depression art. The artist, George Fisher, "used the…antigravitational trope for a contemporary family group perched atop a heap of timbers and wheat sheafs in the Chelsea, Michigan, post office," explains *That Abstract Art Stuff*, an authority on Depression-era art.

Fisher had "timeless, emblematic glory in mind" when he painted that mural early in the 1930s and he discussed his Chelsea masterpiece with art historians, explaining, "The title, *Way of Life*, indicates the fundamentals of a system of living and through which are correlated with, and which carry, the possibilities of a great civilization and a strong and happy people. These fundamentals are symbolized by the harvest, the logs, the grindstone, the spinning wheel and the people themselves." On another level, he added, "The mural is simply a picture of a family at rest, with work well done, enjoying the freedom, peace and love which are justly theirs."

Life on the Farm

Four Generations on a German Farm

ALTON AND ARLENE GRAU

Bleating and baa-baaing, several dozen sheep gather for an early dinner in the aromatic basement of the century-old red barn on a crystal-clear winter day. Farmer Alton Grau knows his way in the dimly lit barn as well as he knows his own work-roughened hands. A cat peers down from a loft above the sheep and suddenly the farmer laughs and tells how, as a boy 60 or more years ago, he once dropped a cat from that spot onto the back of an aged, dozing horse and how the horse mustered the vigor of a colt as he flung off his surprise (and surprised) attacker and bolted to safety in a far field.

At right angles to this barn sits another, older red barn with the date "1880" painted on its doors. A handful of outbuildings, tractor sheds, and chicken coops, as well as a pump house, cluster around the two barns. The sturdy, square 85-year-old farmhouse is the second, or perhaps the third, Grau home to survey Fletcher Road, just south of Zion Evangelical Lutheran Church. A long-ago farm wife with an appreciation for nature must have supervised her husband as he situated the buildings, because the house has uninterrupted views in every direction of level, tranquil pastures, fertile fields and faraway wood groves.

"Is this a Centennial Farm?"

Grau repeats the question, then nods and says, "More than that. But we've been too busy to file the papers. You don't need a whistle to tell you you're looking at a train."

The Grau family settled in Freedom Township in the 1840s, when the interior of Michigan was sparsely populated with intrepid pioneers. Grau suspects that his great-great-grandparents left their Prussian home and undertook the long and perilous ocean crossing and then Erie Canal passage in order to escape military conscription and the wars raging throughout Europe at that time. In the basement of his home sits an old pine immigrant trunk with the family name

The wedding of Lydia M. Heller and Albert Schenk was a moment of joy for the young couple. Little would they know that at the age of 26, Albert would die of appendicitis just after the birth of his only son.

Courtesy of the Grau family

hand-painted on its front in an elegant script. That trunk carried his ancestors' precious, and few, belongings on the journey.

After his chores are done, seated in the warm kitchen of the home he and his wife Arlene built a block away from the homestead in 1948, he says, with a nod to his wife, "Up until now, our six children were scattered all over the country. But we're real proud that our son Christopher, at the age of 33, has decided to move into the old farmhouse and take over the farm."

Alton Grau then spreads his family's heirlooms across the kitchen table. He carefully turns the pages of a huge and rare portfolio atlas of Washtenaw County, dated 1874. The book falls open to the page mapping Rogers' Corners and vicinity and he compares the owners' names on the township plots of 1874 with the corresponding map in another county atlas, this one dated 1915. As his finger traces the property lines, he discusses the setting for his family history, referring to a photograph album of his ancestors to illustrate the German settlers in his story.

"All the road names in this area are English, but by the 1880s nearly all the properties were owned by Germans," he points out, adding, "The English were the earliest settlers, but they didn't stay. Either they weren't hardy enough—or foolhardy enough—to stick it out here. Look at the names on the properties."

Meyer, Grau, Eschelbach, Blackwadle, Wiedemeyer, Steinaway, Schenk, Wacker, Koebbe, Liebeck, Heim, Heller, Kaercher are among the names that march across the property lines—and the Grau family tree. "They came for the land. It's heavy clay. Wet. It raises good crops, but you have to be patient with it. This isn't like sandy soil; it retains moisture and you have to wait for it to dry out. But it's good in drought times—and we've had our share of those," the farmer says.

Gotfried Grau, Alton's great-grandfather, was born in Prussia in 1826 and died on the Grau farm in Michigan in 1911. He married Anna Marie Wiedemeyer, whose family owned a farm near the Grau homestead. "My mother told me that the Graus were never wealthy, but we always had the money to buy what we needed. That holds true today," Grau says.

The couple had two sons, John and Christian, who divided the farm when their father died. John, who married Emma Meyer, had a son he named Alton, and when Alton married Irma Louise Schenk, John and his wife moved into Chelsea, a frequent custom for farm families. Alton and Irma Louise had two sons: this Alton, who was born on the farm in 1930, and his brother James, who was born 10 years later. "My mother's people came from the south of Germany, near the Austrian border. Her people were all dark," he says, pointing to photographs in his album. "My father's people were all blonde and blue-eyed. I was the first dark-haired, dark-eyed Grau male ever born."

In the 1930s, on their 87 acres, the Graus raised corn, wheat, oats, hay, vegetables, cattle, hogs, sheep, chickens, and carrots—"*lots* of carrots, to feed the horses," Grau says with a shake of his head. "When I was a boy, it seemed as though I had to weed those carrots from dawn until dusk." Today, the hogs have disappeared ("I got too old for hogs"), the herd of sheep has diminished to 80, the chickens to 30, and the Graus have added soybeans to their crops. Grau also farms a neighbor's land and cuts firewood on the family's 44 acres of woodlands to fuel his home in winter.

Like their neighbors, the Graus spoke German at home, even a century after leaving Prussia—although by the 1930s, Michigan's German was a hybrid of English, German, and Midwestern. In the early years of the twentieth century, when Alton's parents were children, they attended a formal German school, to learn high German. That school had ceased to exist before young Alton headed to Rogers' Corners School at the age of five, but he didn't know much English.

The Rogers' Corners School educated four generations of Graus, including three of Arlene and Alton's six children. At several times in the history of the one-room school, 80 students packed the benches, supervised by one teacher. There were 36 or so when young Alton attended. "Times were so different," he recalls, leaning back in his kitchen chair and staring out the window in the direction of the old school. "We were all like one big family. You couldn't help but learn. The older kids helped teach the younger ones and the older girls kept us all in line. I remember that a little guy named Norman couldn't button well, so after using The Necessary, he would march to the front of the room, exposed to all the world, and the teacher would button his flaps for him. No one snickered—that's the kind of thing a family would do for you. And if we all got wet during recess, which frequently happened, we'd take our clothes off, drape them around the fire to dry, and do our lessons in our long underwear. You sure don't see that happening these days!"

School opened in October, after harvest, and closed in May. Seldom were children kept home to help on the farm. "My father had

Alton C. Grau, Sr. and his cousin, Arthur W. Grau, posed for a local photographer in 1900.

Courtesy of the Grau family

to miss some school, but farming was more labor-intensive in those days," he explains.

His childhood was "a wonderful time, always busy," Grau maintains, despite the fact that his early years spanned the Depression and World War II. "We didn't have a high stress level in those days," he explains. "No one around here felt inferior or superior. We felt we could always hold our own. And when we went to bed at night, we knew who was in charge—that was true at church and at school, too. There's a comfort in knowing that, when you're a boy."

By the time he was seven, Alton was driving the tractor and putting in man-sized work days. "You did what you could to help on the farm and I was the only child there to work," he says pragmatically. "I tipped the tractor over when I was seven. I wasn't hurt. And neither was the tractor." Because he was "low man on the totem pole" on the farm, he reaped the nasty jobs—mucking stables, cleaning corn cobs, filling the wood box, splitting wood, and tending to the three-seater outhouse. "We still use our Necessary today," he says proudly. "It's ecologically sound, you know. There are a couple of active ones yet in the neighborhood."

Young Alton posed with Tom, the horse in July 1933. Courtesy of the Grau family

Except for staples, farm equipment, shoes, and cloth for clothing, which they bought in Chelsea and Manchester shops, the Graus were self-sufficient. "Our diet was horrendous by today's standards—after November, everything was fermented, smoked, salted, or pickled—but my grandmother lived to one month short of her hundredth birthday!" Grau says with a chuckle.

The center of the far-flung German community's social life was the school and the weekly or biweekly services at the Zion Evangelical Lutheran Church. On Lenten Wednesdays, Maundy Thursday, Holy Friday, Ascension Day, Ash Wednesday, Christmas, New Year's Eve, and New Year's Day, the Germans packed the church aisles—"the last thing we did in one year and the first thing we did in the next was go to worship." Women's groups made quilts for Lutheran relief agencies, bandages during wartime. Children presented holiday pageants. For more than 30 years, Alton's mother played the church organ and if her young son wiggled in his front row seat, he knew that he would earn a rap on the head from his father.

In the summers, there were swim parties, ice cream socials, and

Sunday School picnics at the lake. In the winter, everyone climbed aboard bobsleds for wild and raucous rides, skied, hunted rabbits, went ice fishing or donned skates and headed out on the frozen ponds. On quiet afternoons, boys would gather around a workbench to tinker with projects, making everything from waterwheels to miniature wagons and entries for soapbox derbies.

At night, the family read or gathered around the radio and listened to Jack Benny, Red Skelton, the Lone Ranger, "I Love A Mystery," Tom Mix, "The Inner Sanctum," "Gangbusters," and Henry Aldrich. Every summer, an acting troupe set up a tent in town and performed "The Ginnevan Show." Twice a month in warm weather, the little town of Bridgewater had free movies shown on the side of a building, and everyone for miles around would climb into automobiles. Thirty or forty cars would park on a hill to visit and watch the movie.

"Our social life was very meager by today's standards and it was probably lonely—but we didn't know it," Grau says. "If we lacked any skills, it was social skills. We were polite, but we were wary of strangers. And yet there was no prejudice. I remember a neighbor had a prison inmate working for him on the farm, a man as black as they come. My father often hired him to help us. 'He's no different from you or me. He works just as hard,' my father told me. That was what was important."

Charlie Zahn, Herb Hinderer and Harold Eschelbach worked together to get the winter's supply of pork in at Herb Schenk's home.

Courtesy of the Grau family

The Beach Front
GENERAL DWIGHT E. BEACH

Immaculate red barns and outbuildings line up at right angles along the road, in military precision, as neat and spic-and-span as the orderlies that once reported to the resident of the home, General Dwight E. Beach. The Beach farm is seven miles from Dexter, four miles from Chelsea, on Jackson Road. A sign above the large barn facing the road proudly announces its date of origin: 1853.

The general's ancestors were early New England settlers who moved to upper New York State, just outside Schenectady, after the American Revolution, when Captain Joseph Beach was awarded 60 acres of land for his military service. His son, William Green Beach, fathered 13 children, then lost the family farm during the economic panic of the 1830s. Penniless, he decided to move his second wife and

Before and after pictures of the old Beach farmhouse on Jackson Road—the first picture was taken before the future four-star general, Dwight Beach, was born; the second was taken after the General retired.

Courtesy of the Beach family

their children west and start over again. They traveled by oxcart to Lake Erie, which they crossed by boat, spent the winter of 1837-38 in Detroit, then moved west, to Dixboro. By 1853, they had managed to save enough money to purchase 160 acres in Lima Township.

"I remember my grandmother telling me that my great-grandparents had to leave four daughters behind in New York State and they never saw them again," the General says.

In 1853, William and Polly Beach built a quick and temporary house. "My grandmother said that the snow drifted in from the roof in those days," the General recalls. The current home, an L-shaped Midwestern farmhouse painted white with black shutters, cost $1,700 to build in 1886.

Abner Beach, who was 21 when his father bought the property, cut and burned all the white oak and walnut trees on the property, some of them three feet in diameter, in order to clear the land for wheat, which was the only cash crop before the Civil War. The rafters of the big barn on the property are made of tamarack trees cut on the property.

Until the General remodeled the house recently, there were no fireplaces; it had been heated with wood-burning and coal-burning stoves. Registers in the first-floor ceilings allowed any spare warm air to rise to the seven second-story bedrooms. "The upstairs was as cold as cold could be in the winter. Everything we did was done around the kitchen stove," General Beach remembers. "We kept that stove going year-round."

Abner Beach married Cynthia Dixon of Dexter in 1861. They spent their entire lives on the farm and bequeathed it to their only child, David Beach, father of the General.

When David was a small boy, a German family named Luick bought 200 acres of land across the street. "The Luicks spoke no English when they moved to Lima Township and my father spoke no German, but everything worked out," the General says with a smile. David Beach married Bertha Luick in 1896. "Very, very often around here young folks didn't go far to find a wife or husband," he points out. When Bertha died nine years later of "inflammation of the bowel" (probably appendicitis), Beach married her sister Amanda. Together, they had three sons, Dwight (born in 1908), David (1910), and Kenneth (1912).

The farm grew oats, hay, wheat, cattle, fruits and vegetables. David Beach sold cattle to the stockyards in Chelsea, where they were shipped to butchers throughout the Midwest. Jackson Road was unpaved when Dwight and his brothers David and Kenneth were growing up. Once, after a violent ice storm, the three boys skated all the way down the road to Ann Arbor, then paid a dime to catch the trolley home. The Detroit United Railway ran right in front of the Beach home.

A stone's throw away from the farmhouse, Lima Center was the collecting point for social activities. A small church, township hall and store huddled around the corner of Lima Center Road and Jackson Road. The store offered a few staples and a chance to swap news with neighbors. For awhile, a butcher shop operated across from the store and an unusual brick building with a tower, which is now a private home, served as the power plant for the Interurban.

"There were a couple of characters around Lima Center, I remember," the General reminisces. One man, John Brown, helped on the Beach farm. On market day, when David Beach would take the horse and buggy into town, Brown would give him two dollars and ask him to bring back a loaf of bread and a bottle of whiskey.

By the time the three Beach boys were growing up, the farm had a crank telephone connected to the Chelsea exchange. Water was pumped into the kitchen from the windmill outside; the pump house held a tank that was insulated with sawdust. David Beach installed the home's first bathroom. Delco Electric Company provided enough electricity to light the house with two or three glowing bulbs at night.

When the boys were old enough to attend high school, Amanda and David moved their family to Chelsea and rented the farm on shares for 46 years to the Steinaway family. At first, David Beach served as secretary/treasurer for the Washtenaw County Mutual Farm Insurance Company (with offices in what is now the courthouse), but the insurance company closed after a year and a rash of fires and then David Beach found work with Kempf Commercial & Savings Bank.

In the late 1920s, Dwight Beach reported to West Point. He graduated in 1932, began a long and distinguished military career, and established a large and distinguished military family. He retired from the military in 1969.

The future four-star general, Dwight Beach.
Courtesy of the Beach family

When General Beach, his wife Florence and daughter Florence returned to the ancestral farm in 1970, they resumed life much as it had been lived for generations, with a few changes. Interstate 94 now slashes across the farm. Power lines dissect the fields and an oil pipeline threatened another incursion. But, the 47 acres of land on the south side of I-94 and the 107 acres north of the interstate are still cultivated, thanks to a Luick cousin. Until he was well into his eighties, the General kept and rode two horses, cross-country skied, and ran the old cider press. Until his death in July 2000, General Beach maintained a large vegetable garden.

"For years and years, as we moved from army base to army base, the one constant in my father's life was this farm," says the General's daughter Florence, who lives in the old family homestead. "It was important to him that the farm was intact and still in the family after four generations, still being farmed. It gave us roots—and that's important when you're a military family."

Tenant Farming at North Lake
THE NOAH FAMILY

"I hate to see the demise of the family farm, but that's just what we're seeing around here now," says Donna Lane, as she leaves her office at the Lane Animal Hospital on North Main Street and walks next door to her home. "Actually, this land right here originally belonged to the John Hummel Dairy Farm. The demise started long ago."

She was born in 1933 on an ancestral farm on North Territorial that is still maintained by her brother and his wife, Duane and Maryann Noah. Mrs. Lane's memories of farm life turn first to the animals, which is appropriate, considering the fact that her maiden name is Noah and she is the widow of Dr. Wilfred Lane, Chelsea's veterinarian for more than a half century.

"Washtenaw County was the largest sheep-producing county east of the Mississippi," she says with pride. The lambs were shipped to Detroit and Chicago for the Jewish holidays, and the wool was shipped to woolen mills back East. "In those days, lambs were born during the spring months. Now, however, the birth of lambs is orchestrated to satisfy market demands."

Dairy farming has also bowed to modern-day demands. "It used to be very important for dairy farms to have calves born in August, September, and October. That's when we needed lactating cows because the base price for dairy products was formed August 1," Mrs.

Lane explains, adding, "Lactating lasts for 11 months, and anything a farm produced over the base price was considered surplus and earned the farmers less money, so it was important to estimate your herd's yield accurately." Several local farmers, among them the Heydlauffs, raised only Jersey cows because of the cream they produced—until the 1950s, when American housewives started going lighter on cream. At that time, Holsteins took the place of Jerseys on many Washtenaw farms.

"These were very frugal farmers," Mrs. Lane points out. Most farms had mixed, or general, crops. Like the Noahs, their neighbors raised sheep, chickens, dairy cattle, corn, grain crops, and just enough beef cattle for the family's consumption. It wasn't until after World War II, when the demand for red meat began soaring, that herds of beef cattle began appearing on southeast Michigan farms. At that time, the Lesser family became renowned throughout the Midwest for the black Angus they raised.

Mrs. Lane's ancestors were among the first pioneers in the North Lake/North Territorial section of Washtenaw County. Charles ("a very strong, large man, a lay preacher") and his brother John Glenn donated the land and labor for the area's first school and church. Charles gave his son Benjamin 14 acres of land in 1847 when he married Lydia Ann Beakes. Benjamin purchased 160 additional acres, many of them under water, and later added 80 more acres. Benjamin was an entrepreneur who was well known throughout southeast Michigan for his threshing abilities and the nursery business he launched with his cousins Robert and William. They extracted apple seeds from the pulp generated at the cider mill, planted them in crates in the basement of the mill, then grafted stock to the seedlings. Most nineteenth century orchards throughout Michigan were rooted in the Glenns' stock.

The Glenn sons and daughters married the daughters and sons of their neighbors: the Daniels, Wallaces, Bignalls, Schaibles, Burkhardts, Woods, Noahs, Webbs, and Widmayers, most of whom had settled north of Chelsea by following the stagecoach route, which was North Territorial Road, from Detroit. The old Glenn Farm (also known as the Eisenbeiser Farm) and the Riker Farm, both on North Territorial, were stagecoach stops, but when the railroad came into Chelsea, stagecoaches ceased to frequent these roads. The farmers had to haul their produce to the railroad in Chelsea or even as far away as Toledo, Ohio, which was a major collecting point for grain.

Perry Noah, Donna Lane's grandfather, ran the first convenience store north of Chelsea, at the intersection of North Territorial and Noah's Landing. After the turn of the century, when city folk would come to the lake for the summer, they would often drop by his home to borrow a cup of sugar or bottle of milk, so Perry Noah decided to open a back room in his house as a little store. As business began to flourish, he built a store, Noah's Grocery. Eventually, he installed a gasoline pump.

The first convenience store in the farmlands north of Chelsea was operated by Perry Noah, son of Civil War veteran Orange Noah.

Courtesy of Donna Lane

His granddaughter remembers him most, however, for a brave and controversial stand he took in the 1930s. A black family had bought land on Wild Goose Lake and several neighbors started circulating a petition denying African Americans the right to settle in the area. Perry Noah refused to sign, telling them, "My father fought to free the blacks and I intend to help keep them free."

Perry's son Laurence and his wife Esther were tenant farmers on a Burkhardt farm owned by an elderly relative and her blind daughter, who stayed with the Noahs during the summer months and lived in Chelsea during the winter.

On 400 acres of land, the Noahs raised corn, wheat, between 200 and 300 sheep, chickens, dairy cows, a few beef cattle and three children, Duane (born in 1926), Donna (1933), and Lynwood (1936). The Noahs lived about equal distance from Chelsea and Dexter and it was Dr. William Wiley of Dexter who delivered Donna. The bill was $35—it would have been $25 if Donna had been born during daylight hours. "In those days, women stayed in bed 14 days after childbirth," Mrs. Lane explains. "There was an old wives' tale that said that all of the woman's parts went back together after the 13th day. At that time, a lot of women died mysteriously after childbirth, perhaps from blood clots. The two-week stay in bed often meant that phlebitis would set in."

The boys worked in the fields and barnyard. Donna helped her mother can fruits and vegetables, sew, embroider, do the laundry (with a wringer washer and copper pot on the cookstove), quilt, cook, garden, and participate in every farm chore except those dealing with the birth of animals. "My father said birthing animals wasn't fitting for a girl!" Ironically, his girl would grow up to be a nurse, a mother, and her husband's veterinary assistant.

In the 1930s, not all farms had refrigeration. The Noah family kept milk and dairy products in a screened milksafe in the basement, to keep the flies away. There was no indoor plumbing on the farm yet, either. The Noahs used pitchers and bowls in the bedrooms for washing and slop jars in the bedrooms on cold nights to prevent a hike out to the outhouse. Whether they needed it or not, every family member and all hired hands took one bath a week, in the kitchen on Saturday nights in preparation for church on Sunday. "I remember a girl from Ann Arbor came to visit us and said she never wanted to be a hired man because he was the last one to climb into the bathtub on Saturday nights and that water could be dirty!"

An important and cherished feature of families' lives in the 1930s and 1940s was storytelling, she says. "Our evenings and winter days centered around the kitchen and parlor and in the days before television, we had to entertain each other, so we told stories." She and her brothers especially thrilled to hear the Civil War exploits of their ancestor Orange Noah. Occasionally, there would be a school program, square dancing or monthly euchre club meetings ("ten tables with four players each"), with potluck dinners on the second Saturday of each month. Other than these events, farmers' social lives revolved around the churches.

The Noahs' cash crop was wheat, which was sold to the Chelsea Milling Company. At harvest time, John Otto would arrive with his threshing machine and for three days he and the Noahs' neighbors would harvest the grain and the women would prepare elaborate noon meals, complete with roasts, mashed potatoes, gravy, a variety of vegetables and pickles, coleslaw, and pies. Every woman tried to outdo her neighbors, which made for some memorable meals—and they are remembered with relish 60 years later. After the wheat was harvested, the corn was picked and husked. This was a time-consuming, and sometimes dangerous, affair. Donna Lane remembers when Everett VanRiper lost his arm in the cornhusker.

The sheep shearing took place in the winter. Two shearers would arrive at the farm and work from dawn to dusk to gather the wool from 300 sheep. "I remember they had a unique way of tying up the wool, readying it for the wool buyers," Mrs. Lane says.

To make ends meet, Laurence Noah did more than farm. He collected neighbors' milk cans and took them to the creamery, which was located behind the present-day Wolverine Tavern. He collected garbage. And he also cut ice on North Lake, packed it in sawdust, stored it in icehouses, and delivered it weekly to customers, whom he charged $3.25 a season. That ice usually lasted until the end of August.

By the 1940s, Chelsea's lakes were attracting city folks as summer residents and Laurence Noah would occasionally do odd jobs for them. As a schoolgirl, Donna Noah had the honor of shaking the hand of the "Ace of Aces," World War I combat pilot Eddie Rickenbacker, when he visited North Lake. "He shot down twenty-two German planes and four balloons," she remembers.

The Noahs' three children attended Pumpkin (or "Punkin") College, a one-room school on the corner of Island Lake Road and North Territorial that never had more than 16 students in attendance during the years when Donna was a girl. "There were lots of tales about the origin of the name of the school," she says. "One said that it was surrounded by a pumpkin patch in the 1800s when it was built. Another said that at one time boys filled the hall with pumpkins that fell on the teacher when she opened the door and from that point on, everyone called it Punkin College."

The one-room school format has strong advocates in former students. "We learned from each other by osmosis—and there's nothing wrong with that," Donna Noah Lane says. "We all received a fine education."

Laurence Noah was killed delivering a calf at the age of 89. When friends gathered for his funeral, they estimated that he had served as pallbearer at 50 local burials. "He was a good man and he had a lot of friends," his daughter says with pride. His wife lived to be 87 years old. The day she died, Esther Noah had mowed her yard, baked eleven loaves of bread, visited Chelsea to shop for a new car, and renewed her driver's license for another four years. She went to bed that night and never woke up. Her son took over the farm.

A Self-Sufficient Way of Life

THE GUTHRIE FARM

"In the 1920s and 1930s, you could be almost entirely self-sufficient on a small farm, if you were frugal and worked hard. We certainly were self-sufficient," says June Robinson.

She grew up on her family's 40-acre farm, which was located at West Guthrie Crossing on Pierce Road in Sylvan Township. Mrs. Robinson has the original deed signed by her grandfather, Samuel Guthrie, who purchased the farmhouse and 40 acres of land at precisely 1:30 P.M., December 16, 1880. The Centennial Farm remains in the family; June Robinson's daughter and son-in-law, Judy and Kevin Gallagher, live there now with the fourth generation of the family to make their home on the farm: their three sons, Kirk, Todd, and Spencer.

The Guthries were an Irish family whose fore-bears made their way to Washtenaw County before the Civil War, settling along Pierce Road. "My great-great-grandfather was born in Ireland and built the little white house on the corner of Garvey and Pierce, which is where my grandfather was born," Mrs. Robinson explains. Samuel Guthrie moved 90 rods west when he bought his farm. His brother Albert moved into Chelsea and started a dairy that was, in Mrs. Robinson's childhood, run by her second cousin, Ellsworth Hoppe, on Park Street. The dairy made butter and delivered milk, eggs, cottage cheese, and cream to housewives throughout the village and surrounding area.

Samuel Guthrie purchased this farmhouse and forty acres of land at West Guthrie Crossing on Pierce Road in Sylvan Township.
Courtesy of the Robinson and Gallagher families

Samuel and Eva Newton Guthrie had two daughters, Lida and Allie. Lida, who worked at Fenn's Drug Store in Chelsea, became the last woman in Michigan to receive a pharmacist's license without a degree. Allie married Olvien Floyd, a conductor on the Michigan Central Railroad. After losing two babies at birth, Allie moved back to the family farm to be with her mother during her third pregnancy. A healthy little girl was born in 1921 and the family continued to live on the farm.

When June was just a year old, her father returned home from work complaining of terrific pains in his head. He went to bed, became comatose and died two weeks later, on Valentine's Day, diagnosed with "sleeping sickness." Allie and her daughter stayed on the farm, living with Allie's parents and her sister Lida. Lida Guthrie, who said she "never found a man good enough" would in time become known as "Auntie" not only to June, but also to generations of Chelsea children. She worked at Fenn's for 52 years.

Samuel Guthrie farmed his acreage with the help of two horses; he never did own a tractor, although he lived to be 98 years old. He raised hay, wheat, oats, a henhouse full of chickens, generations of pigs, an occasional cow, 25 cats ("to keep down the mouse and rat populations"), as well as vegetables for the family's use. As a girl, June would take a dozen eggs into E.F. Smith's Store in Chelsea on Saturday nights and swap them for three plugs of chewing tobacco for her grandfather.

The Guthries' cash crop was wheat, which would be taken to the Chelsea Milling Company for grinding, and one of the most exciting times in every farm family's life was when the neighbors gathered to thresh each other's wheat. "While the men and boys worked in the fields, every housewife tried to outdo the others with the meals. They were like Christmas feasts," Mrs. Robinson remembers appreciatively.

Threshers weren't the only workers who visited the farm. Maiden ladies traveled from farm to farm, taking up residence for a few days or a week while they sewed the clothes the family would need for the upcoming months. June remembers Ella Freer, a distant cousin, coming to stay with the Guthries while she made the family's summer clothes. "She was the prototypical old maid, very coy."

June attended the Sylvan Center one-room school, which still stands a half-mile away from the Guthries' farm, by the cemetery on Old U.S. 12. Every day children would take turns carrying water from the well across the street and pouring it into the school's crock, where a communal dipper would be used for drinking

When she was "knee-high to a grasshopper," the little girl learned to throw a blanket onto the back of a horse, ride bareback across the countryside and drive horses. Her grandfather placed only two restrictions on her driving: he didn't allow her to operate either the mower or the plow, fearing that a rock from the soil might fly up and injure her.

When she was 12, she started driving her father's Model T and acquired her license when she was 14. From that point on, she drove "Auntie" in and out of town every day while she attended high school and then waited on customers at Fenn's Drug Store until closing time.

The Interurban passed right across the Guthrie farm and offered rides to Chelsea for a nickel, to Ann Arbor for a dime. Often neighbors would stable horses and buggies in the family's barn while they went to town, or wait in the Guthries' home for the trolley on cold days.

During the Depression, the farm lost its original barns in a blaze one terrible night. Samuel Guthrie never knew for sure, but he suspected that vagrant hobos, who often found a bed for the night in his haymows, accidentally started the fire. Hobos were always coming to the back door of the farm, hat in hand, to ask for something to eat—"and we always gave them something, even if it was just bread and butter," June remembers.

Other than the fire, June didn't feel any impact from the Depression. "I was young and it seemed that everyone lived the way we did," she explains. "My mother baked doughnuts, cakes, and bread. Our cows provided all the dairy products we needed. We had a big orchard that produced apples for cider and eating. We grew all our

June Robinson learned at a young age to drive horses as well as ride them.

Courtesy of the Robinson and Gallagher families

own vegetables and we butchered our own pigs, chickens, and cattle. Auntie worked in a pharmacy, so if we ever needed medicines, she could get them there. We truly were self-sufficient. We got by pretty good."

Rural electrification came to Pierce Road in 1928; until that time, the family used kerosene lamps for lighting. Samuel Guthrie installed the farm's first indoor bathroom in the early 1930s. When she was 16, in 1938, June Floyd went off to college for a year, then returned home and found a job at the Chelsea Milling Company at $14 a week—$2 more than the starting salary for women because of her college experience.

Throughout her life, she has lived in the country. After her marriage, she moved to her husband's centennial farm in Grass Lake.

"I love life on the farm," she says. "I love watching the seasons come and go across the fields and orchards. I love animals. When I was a girl, I watched animals being born and I watched animals die. It was the best way for a child to learn about life."

Onion Farming South of Town
THE CHAPMAN FAMILY

In 1863, Arthur Chapman mustered out of the Union Army, anxious to start a new chapter in his life. He found land south of Chelsea, near the Vermont Colony Cemetery on Jerusalem Road, and bought it from the Spaulding family, whose property deed had been signed by President Andrew Jackson.

The land was marshy, with lowlands just right for raising onions. Arthur built a small house and dug a well 13 feet deep for water. He was in business. This place would be farmed by four generations of Chapmans.

"Ours was a general farm, tiny by today's standards—only 50 acres—but it did well," says the founder's great-grandson, Larry Chapman, who was born in 1937 in the Victorian-style farmhouse built in the 1890s, during a period of national and family prosperity. "The farmers of that era lived a hard life, but a good life. They were very independent. They didn't have to rely on anybody for anything. And they were frugal. If they couldn't afford to buy something, they figured they didn't need it."

Most of the Chapmans' neighbors cultivated 100 or 150 acres but they grew the same things the Chapmans grew: hogs for pork, wheat for flour, sheep for wool and eating, cattle for beef and dairy products, and chickens for eggs and meat. "I hated chickens. I really hated chickens,"

After mustering out of the Union Army in 1863, Arthur Chapman was anxious to get on with his life.

Courtesy of the Chapman family

Three generations of Chapmans lived together in this home on original Vermont Colony land.

Courtesy of the Chapman family

Arthur Chapman took this picture of a threshing crew as they began their work on his farm.

Courtesy of the Chapman family

Chapman remembers, 60 years after his boyhood, explaining with a grin, "On our farm, the chickens ran loose and so did I and I was always stepping in chicken manure or putting my hand in it."

When Chapman was a boy, three generations of his family lived together. Larry Chapman's father, Leon Chapman, was a clerk in Merkel's Hardware Store for more than 30 years and farmed during the early morning hours, nights, and weekends. His mother, Dorothy Satterthwaite Chapman, stayed at home when her children were young, and then went to work in Chelsea's nickel-and-dime store. "Both were very hardworking people. When I think of how hard they worked, what they made from scratch and did by hand, I feel guilty with all my modern conveniences," Chapman says.

Larry Chapman's grandfather, George Chapman, supervised the farm and tinkered with interesting projects. He made, among other things, his own camera and film, and he left his descendents exquisitely detailed black-and-white photographs of what life was like between the Civil War and World War I.

In 1998, Larry and Shirley Chapman were browsing at an antique show in Saline when they discovered one of his grandfather's photographs, taken in 1904, showing threshing time on the farm. "That was a wonderful surprise—and a reminder of a special time on the farm," Chapman says, showing the photograph's duplicate. "One person owned threshing equipment and he would go from farm to farm along with the neighbors, for harvest. There was a term that still circulates through this area when a woman is cooking up a storm. People

say, 'She must be cooking for threshers.' Those days were always among the year's highlights."

George Chapman was a member of the area's census team in 1890, and he would tell a story that still makes his family members chuckle more than a century later. "The Prinzing family was a big, wonderful German family. Mr. Prinzing worked in the onion fields here," Chapman explains. "When my grandfather was making his rounds to take the census, he asked Mrs. Prinzing how many children she had. She told him, 'Every two years, vun.'"

As children, Larry and his sister Donna attended the Jewett Stone School, one mile east of the farm, fished and hunted, prowled the fields, swam and sledded. Throughout the winter months, Bertha and Warren Spaulding offered fun and excitement for neighbors' youngsters. Warren would hitch horses to a bobsled, collect all the children he could find, and take them sledding. Then Bertha would make them hot chocolate when they tumbled into her kitchen on South Waltrous Road, tired, cold and happy. "They were wonderful people—just the kind of people you would imagine would establish the Spaulding for Children Foundation."

Social life on the farms during the 1940s was far more active than it is today, Chapman suggests. Three or four nights a week, families would visit. On Saturday evenings, grown-ups would gather for euchre parties, sandwiches, pies, cakes, and coffee, while the children played. "All that stopped with television. That's when the art of conversation was lost," he says with regret. "We were the last family in the neighborhood to get a television set. I remember going to visit neighbors who had bought a television. They kept their eyes on the set the entire time we were there. Afterwards, my Dad said, 'That's the last damn time I go there—that thing is an idiot tube.'"

When Larry and Shirley Chapman married, they moved to town. "I remember when I first lived here, I couldn't sleep at night, between the noise of the trains and the street lights," Chapman says. "I grew up in a dark world and I liked it that way."

Leon Chapman retired from Merkel's in 1964 and died in 1966. For two years, Larry and his uncle continued to plant and harvest wheat, oats, and hay on the family homestead, but when someone broke into the vacant farmhouse and torched the draperies, the Chapmans decided to sell.

Farming during the 19th century required back-breaking labor. At planting time and during emergencies the women joined the men and boys in the fields. Even now, more than thirty years after the Chapman farm was sold to another family, Larry Chapman believes, "There is noting better than the sense of being alone on your own land at night. Nothing."

Courtesy of the Chapman family

Arthur Chapman, a skilled photographer,
captured his family's way of life.

Courtesy of Larry Chapman

Even now, more than 30 years after the farm passed out of his hands, Larry Chapman yearns to climb on a tractor and ride through the night. "I loved doing that on warm summer nights when there was nothing better to do," he says. "My world was only what the headlights would show and there was nothing to distract my thoughts. There is nothing better than the sense of being alone on your own land at night. Nothing.

"I could kick myself that we didn't keep the farm."

Franklin Delano Roosevelt, 1933-45 • Harry S. Truman, 1945-53

1940: Roosevelt elected to third term • Chamberlain resigns; Churchill becomes British Prime Minister • Germany invades Holland, Belgium, Luxembourg • Churchill's 'Blood, Sweat and Tears' speech • Dutch army surrenders • Belgium capitulates • RAF begins night bombing of Germany • Italy declares war on France and Britain • British evacuate 340,000 forces at Dunkirk • France falls

1941: U.S. signs lend-lease bill with Britain • German U-boat attacks intensify • Rommel in Africa • Japanese bomb Pearl Harbor Dec. 7 • U.S. and Britain declare war on Japan Dec. 8 • U.S. Savings Bonds and stamps go on sale • Rubber rationing • Steel prices fixed

1942: The 26 allies pledge not to make separate peace treaties with the enemies • Japan invades Dutch East Indies, Burma • Japanese capture Singapore, Java, and Rangoon • Bataan death march • Tokyo bombed by Maj. Gen. Jimmy Doolittle • Americans win battles of Coral Sea, Midway • Montgomery named Commander of 8th Army • Germans reach Stalingrad • 400,000 American troops land in French North Africa, Rommel in full retreat • Murder of millions of Jews in Nazi camps begins • MacArthur appointed Commander-In-Chief, Far East

1943: Japanese driven from Guadalcanal • Russians destroy German army south of Stalingrad, capture Rosov and Kharkov • Hitler orders 'Scorched Earth Policy' • RAF raid on Berlin • U.S. planes sink 22-ship Japanese convoy in Battle of Bismarck Sea • British and U.S. armies in Africa join forces • Massacre in Warsaw ghetto • U.S. forces land in New Guinea, recapture Aleutians • Allies invade Italy • Italy declares war on Germany • U.S. forces regain islands in Pacific

1944: American Fifth Army launches attack east of Cassino • Americans take Solomon and Marshall Islands • 800 flying fortresses drop 2,000 tons of bombs on Berlin • 700 ships, 4,000 landing craft and allies participate in D-Day, June 6 • Americans capture Guam • De Gaulle enters Paris • Brussels liberated • Americans cross German frontier, and also land in Philippines • Battle of Leyte Gulf • Battle of the Bulge begins

1945: Americans enter Manila • British troops reach the Rhine • U.S. bombs Tokyo, Cologne, Danzig • Okinawa captured • Roosevelt dies, Truman sworn in • United Nations charter signed • Germany capitulates May 7 and "V-E Day" ends war in Europe May 8 • U.S. bombs Hiroshima Aug. 6, Nagasaki Aug. 9 • Japan surrenders • World War II ends Aug. 14

WAR DEAD ESTIMATE:
35 million plus 10 million in concentration camps

U.S. POPULATION
140 million

World War II: 1940-1945

On the Battlefield

Four-star General Dwight E. Beach, West Point graduate (Class of 1932), rises from an antique Windsor chair when the doorbell rings. Ramrod-straight, he advances to guests, offers a steel-like hand grip, then invites visitors to sit by the fireplace in his ancestral home with a voice that has barked orders for more than 70 years. His hair is thick and white, his eyebrows black, his gaze as strong as his grip, and his mind as sharp as ever it was. He might be 91 years old, but few people would guess it—and he doesn't intend to retreat an inch from his struggle with age and time. He remembers the past as though it were last week.

Four months prior to the Japanese attack on Pearl Harbor, December 7, 1941, 34-year-old Dwight Beach had received a promotion to captain of field artillery, U.S. Army, at Fort Clayton in the Panama Canal Zone. Ironically, another Chelsea native and West Point graduate, Brigadier General Herbert Vogel (son of L.P. Vogel) had preceded Captain Beach to Panama, where he was commander of all armed forces there. Beach had spent his years between West Point and Pearl Harbor honing his skills with various horse-drawn field artillery units and starting a family with his wife, Florence Clem Beach, granddaughter of the legendary Civil War "Drummer Boy of Shiloh and Chickamauga," who in time became Major General John Lincoln Clem.

A family memoir notes, "On December 7, 1941, everything changed for all time, for the world—and for the young Beach family. After that date, Captain Beach was always out on maneuvers. Dirigibles hovered over all parts of the Canal Zone. Practice air raids were conducted in which all family members had to get into the bathroom, which was the only interior room in the house. And many times at night the Canal Zone operated under blackout conditions. Florence and her three children were finally evacuated across the Gulf of Mexico (which we were convinced was filled with German U-boats) into New Orleans…Dwight was transferred to Australia."

General Dwight Beach received his fourth star on July 1, 1965 when his family was en route to Korea. As soon as they crossed the International Date Line, Florence beach pinned the star on her husbands uniform.

Courtesy of the Beach family

Kenneth Beach, brother of General Dwight Beach, died as a prisoner of war.

Courtesy Chelsea Area Historical Society

That was January of 1943.

In Australia, Lieutenant Colonel Beach (who had been promoted twice within six months) reported to Brigadier General Cowane, commander of the 41st Division Artillery, which had originally been part of the Washington State National Guard. "I don't like regular army officers. I can't stand West Pointers. And I don't know what I'm going to do with you," Cowane barked at Beach. But Beach set to work organizing the 167th Field Artillery Battalion, at first using wild horses purchased in Australia. ("We gentled 600 horses without much trouble," the General says matter-of-factly.) By the war's end, the unit had progressed to tractor-drawn artillery and its commander had been decorated with the Silver Star for gallantry in action, among other awards.

Beach participated in many of the fiercest campaigns in the Pacific, from Australia through New Guinea, then to the Philippines. Ultimately, he landed in Japan. "I'm alive today because Douglas MacArthur was in command," he believes. "We hit the Japs where we needed to, and let the jungle take care of the rest."

Beach and his artillery command participated in four amphibious assaults, at Aitape, Maffin Bay, Wakde, and Palawan, as well as in the follow-up phase of amphibious operations in Biak and Zamboanga and overland operations at Davao. Those names are familiar only to history books and a few veterans now, but in the tumultuous days of World War II, they were locations known to every newscaster and anxious radio listener.

Meanwhile, General Beach's youngest brother, Kenneth Otto Beach, graduated from the University of Miami Law School and entered the service as an ROTC second lieutenant. He too was sent to the South Pacific. General Beach winces when he tells his brother's story. "He was captured on Bataan when we surrendered there and he was interred on the island in the Philippines called Mindanao, in a prison camp. I finally got in there three months after the Japs abandoned it. I was the first point man to get there, but I couldn't find any trace of my brother."

The Japanese had tried to move all the prisoners of war to Japan. General Beach's brother was with a group of 1,200 Americans in fair shape that left Manila in December 1944. "But only 200 got back to the U.S. after the war," the General says. "They were jammed into unmarked ships and U.S. bombers sank a lot of those ships. The Japs made no effort whatsoever to mark those ships as either hospital ships or ships carrying prisoners of war."

"Kenny survived the Bataan Death March and Mindanao, then survived the bombing of the ship and swam to an island," explains family friend Claude S. Rogers. "The account given to me by Kenny's brother David and by Dwight's son, Col. Dwight E. Beach Jr., says that the Japanese recaptured Kenny and loaded him onto another ship, which was also bombed. He subsequently died from an infected and broken leg."

Dudley Holmes was also in the South Pacific at that time, fighting his way across the islands. Eventually, he landed on Ie Shima ("Shima means island"), where he served as famed correspondent Ernie Pyle's escort the day before Pyle was killed.

"Ie Shima was a beautiful little island, not more than six or seven miles long, next to Okinawa. It was quite a famous place in those days, with a little mountain in the center," Holmes says. "The Japanese entertained us with bombs every morning—their base was seven miles away," he remembers. "We had pretty good underground structures for protection and we had enough brains to use them." He vividly remembers the shock of hearing that Pyle had been shot. "I can remember being so d—d mad that I could have taken on his assailants barehanded. It was a terrible loss. He was a fine writer and a gentleman."

Back in Chelsea…

In the summer of 1943, Richard Kinsey was 18 years old, just out of high school and working for Vogel & Wurster's when he received notice that he had been drafted. The notice was delivered to the store as well as to his home—Uncle Sam wanted him and the town was small enough to know where to find him.

"I remember talking with my friends about going to war right after Pearl Harbor. Everyone was so excited, almost wild to get involved. We knew that the war would offer us a chance to show our patriotism. We also hoped it would mean better times, a chance for people to make money again," Kinsey says. "But we had no idea what life on the battlefield would be like. We were just country kids."

At about the same time, Rolly Spaulding was working in his father's car dealership when the draft board called him into service. After he reached Fort Moxie in Texas, he sent for his sweetheart, Gretchen Burg, and they were married before he shipped out to Europe with an evacuation hospital unit. He saw the Battle of the Bulge firsthand. Through Belgium, Holland, Luxembourg, France, and Germany, Spaulding supervised the hauling of wounded soldiers and supplies as part of General George S. Patton's Third Army.

Richard Kinsey was 18 years old and tending Vogel & Wurster's Store when he received his draft notice. Courtesy Richard Kinsey

Drafted in 1942 at the age of 20, Congdon descendent Merle Barr remembers D-Day "like it was yesterday." Courtesy of Merle Barr

George Winans was flying a B-24 in the skies over the same Normandy beach on D-Day.
Courtesy of George Winans

Spaulding's best friend, Wilfred Lane, was part of the largest amphibious assault in the history of the world. He left Chelsea in March of 1942, assigned to the 164th Signal Intelligence Corps. After training camp, in November of that year, Lane sailed to England aboard the luxury liner *Queen Elizabeth*, which had been drafted into wartime service. He became part of the Allies' priceless ultra decrypting operation, which deciphered key German secret signals. Three days after D-Day, he landed on Omaha Beach and remained in Europe with the Signal Corps until the close of the war.

Merle Barr, then Captain Merle Barr, remembers D-Day like it was yesterday. Drafted in 1942 at the age of 20, he had trained at Fort Belvoir, Virginia and attended Officers Candidate School before joining the former Cleveland National Guard in Ireland in October 1943. "They had been the first American troops to land in Ireland and they were seasoned," he says. Together, they trained in southern England, in preparation for the invasion of Europe. At 40 minutes after H-Hour, Barr was standing by the railing on a naval landing craft off the coast of Omaha Beach. As he was exchanging words with the sailor standing next to him, the sailor was shot and killed. Barr was the second man off the right side of the craft and immediately after he exited, the ship was hit by 88-millimeter shells and exploded.

"I was under water at that point and fortunate enough to make it to shore," he says. Until 5:00 that night, he was pinned on the beach, then slowly began fighting his way inland with the combat engineers, who were responsible for locating mines. "I still can picture every detail of that beach on that day. I'd like to go back and see it again," he says, staring off into distant memories.

While Barr was pinned down on Omaha Beach, George Winans was flying a B-24 in the skies over the same Normandy beach. "It was an undercast day and we could only catch glimpses of the ground, so we had no idea where our bombs hit," he recalls. "But it was an amazing, awesome sight to see the tremendous numbers of planes and ships off the coast of France on D-Day."

Winans had enlisted in the Army Air Forces in 1943, when he was 21 years old. "I chose the Air Force because I thought it sounded glamorous and I didn't want to be a ground pounder," he says with a grin.

After training in Enid, Oklahoma; Garden City, Kansas ("It was no garden!"), Pampa, Texas, and Boise, Idaho, he headed for England and combat. Winans flew 13 missions with the Army 8th

Air Force. His plane was hit two different times while aiming at the same German industrial spot, a synthetic oil refinery ("which was absolutely critical for Germany by this time in the war") in Politz, on the Baltic Sea. The first time his plane was shot, his engineer, an inventive—and, no doubt, desperate man,—transferred gas back and forth from the various engines until the 10-man crew could see the White Cliffs of Dover. There they bailed out and watched their plane crash. The second time Winans' plane was hit, the damage was more severe and the crew knew they couldn't make England. They headed in the direction of Sweden, 100 miles away.

"We saw a plane up ahead and I shouted to my crew, asking if they saw a swastika. Someone said it had a yellow and blue flag painted on the side. Then we knew we'd be all right," Winans remembers. "The plane dipped its wings, indicating that we should follow, but we had to bail out long before the pilot noticed we were gone." Winans and his crew spent five months in Sweden, grateful to be alive, before the Army Air Force managed to secret them out of the country, in mid-November 1944.

"We got word a few days in advance that they were going to fly a converted B-24 to the air base in Stockholm and pick us up," George Winans says. "Sweden was neutral, and my guess is that the Swedish government alternated letting German and Allied planes retrieve soldiers."

On D-Day + 3, Richard Kinsey was a member of Company A, 116th Infantry, 29th Division, and he too was pinned down on Omaha Beach under murderous German fire. The unit was heavily hit that night by German artillery. "They would light up the area with flares and then lob 20-millimeter shells at us," he says. "By the end of a day there, only five or six of my unit were left on their feet." The 19-year-old was badly wounded and evacuated to a hospital in England.

"I clearly remember my first thoughts after I was wounded," he says, a half-century later. "I wanted to go home. I wanted my family so badly. Yet, as terrible as war was, I knew that I would miss the excitement, the camaraderie and the feeling that I was doing something important." Three months later, after recuperating, he was sent with occupation troops to Paris.

A lawyer in private practice, John Keusch volunteered for service in the Navy in 1943, when he was 32 years old. He served as a legal officer and worked in the Naval Air Stations at Quonset Point, Rhode Island; Norman, Oklahoma; Memphis, Tennessee; and Glenview,

Brigadier General Herbert Vogel (shown here as a toddler) helped convince Dwight Beach to leave the University of Michigan and enroll at West Point. Both of them earned stars during World War II. Courtesy of the Vogel family

Illinois. During his military years, he began his acquaintance with Gerald Ford. His service was stateside.

Dr. A.A. Palmer had a distinguished military career, serving in both World Wars as a medical officer. During World War II, he was part of a command in India that flew supplies to Chinese forces resisting the Japanese. He was a charter member of Chelsea's American Legion post.

After D-Day, Florence Vogel, R.N., sister of Brigadier General Herbert Vogel and a graduate of the University of Michigan, disembarked on the Normandy beaches, to care for Allied wounded. She served with the Army Nursing Corps throughout the war.

Ellis Boyce was one of very few officers who not only survived a highly dangerous position with the joint assault signal company, but managed to serve both in Europe and the South Pacific.

≈

On a cold winter day, as the winds howl around the shores of North Lake, Ellis Boyce and his two sons, Alan and Floyd, sit in front of a cozy wood-burning stove and discuss the story that Ellis Boyce couldn't bring himself to relate for more than four decades. "My memories of those days during World War II were horrible. For a year or more after the war, I had nightmares every night," he says.

It wasn't until historian Stephen Ambrose began advertising for D-Day stories that Ellis Boyce decided it was time to tell his tale.

On June 6, 1944, Second Lieutenant Ellis Boyce was standing aboard a naval carrier on heaving seas, watching Omaha Beach loom in the distance. He and the other members of the 294th Joint Assault Signal Company (JASCO) had been assigned to make up part of the second wave of Americans to hit the beach, as part of the 2nd Battalion, 16th Infantry, First Division.

Boyce's job was to lead six enlisted men to rendezvous with a naval liaison officer who had already landed. Equipped with field glasses and radio, Ellis would serve as a forward observer and radio instructions to artillery units based on ships off the coast about where to fire on the Germans.

The seas were rough and men suffering agonizing bouts of sea-sickness were forced to embark on small landing craft farther out to sea than expected. Clinging to cargo netting, Ellis was lowered into his landing craft, just as two of his men were swung against the side of the ship and their legs were broken. Not an auspicious start, but there was worse to come.

As his unit's landing craft and two others neared shore, a German obstacle under the water forced his unit's craft to halt. Burdened with 60-pound packs, the men were unloaded in water up to—or over—their necks. Many of them drowned. Others were gunned down by murderous German fire, and, Boyce believes, so were the men in the other two landing craft. He managed to grab hold of debris and float to shore with only his nose and eyes above water.

Alan Boyce pulls a history of World War II out of a bookshelf and the volume falls open to a page of photographs by *Life* magazine photographer Frank Capa. "We are convinced that this is my father," he says, pointing to an officer with a distinctive arch on his helmet swimming to Omaha Beach while clinging to debris. "This insignia on the helmet denotes his rank, that he was part of amphibious forces, and the fact that he was a field observer. The other two fields observers from the other ships were landed knee-deep in water and they never made it."

When Ellis Boyce reached the beach, he discovered that his communications equipment had been lost in the landing. Meanwhile, the Germans' artillery was even more murderous on shore. He ran to join an officer lying on the beach and as the man turned to speak with him, a bullet shot through the officer's helmet and out his ear. He was dead.

Boyce flattened himself on the ground and waited for an opportunity to advance and meet his naval liaison officer. Finally, he saw the only one of the unit's 32 tanks to reach the shore intact. He ran to the tank, followed by his men, and used it as a shield until they could reach higher ground. The men followed a line of markers that indicated land mines had been cleared from a path, but one of Boyce's enlisted men running right behind him stepped on a mine and his legs were blown off. The five remaining men quickly dug a hole in the sand for the soldier, administered morphine, and continued running up the hill.

No naval liaison officer could be found. Boyce managed to locate the officer from an adjacent team which had lost their forward

Life *magazine photographer Frank Capa took this picture of American GIs clinging to debris from sunken ships as they swam to Omaha Beach on D-Day. The Boyce family is convinced that the photograph shows Ellis Boyce.* Courtesy of the Boyce family

Some of the war's most harrowing battles—both in France and in the South Pacific—were witnessed first-hand by Ellis Boyce. Courtesy of the Boyce family

observer, so Boyce took his place. He glanced back at the beach and saw a radio, then dashed back down the beach, bullets flying, to retrieve the equipment. He gave it a quick inspection; it was intact. He ran past the spot where his wounded man had been left and saw a gaping crater—the soldier had been blown to pieces. By the time Boyce reached a point of safety farther up the beach, the radio on his back had been smashed by bullets.

"Those bullets were meant for him," Floyd Boyce says. His father nods.

After several days in Normandy, his job was complete. He was ordered back to England and then to the South Pacific. He mailed home a notebook written in an eastern European language, and what he believes to be a French dueling pistol. In 1999, he donated those items to the new D-Day Museum in New Orleans.

"I had thought that nothing could be worse than D-Day, but my experiences fighting the Japanese were worse," he tells his sons.

On October 28, 1944, Boyce arrived in Hollandia, New Guinea and shortly afterward was attached to the Second Battalion, 20th Infantry, Sixth Division. When his unit advanced to the northwest side of New Guinea, there was little initial opposition by the Japanese at the landing site. They had retreated into the jungle. Boyce's unit stayed there until early January 1945, when they joined a huge convoy headed for Luzon. Japanese planes bombed and strafed the American convoy and kamikaze pilots smashed their planes loaded with explosives into the ships.

Boyce's Shore Fire Control team was aboard a landing ship tank ("LST#667," he recalls, as though it were yesterday) that stopped 4,000 yards from shore, transferring the soldiers onto open-topped tracked vehicles that could move on both sea and land. In the meantime, the 20th Infantry had run into stiff opposition and the 51st Field Artillery Battalion had lost all of their forward observers. On January 14, Ellis was assigned to replace them.

"During that time, there were five days that stand out in my mind," he tells his sons. "On one of them, we were getting some small arms fire. Lieutenant Colonel Floyd Simmons ordered a flamethrower team to flush them out."

The team leader, Lieutenant Frankel, led the way and stayed well out in front of the rest of his team. Suddenly, out of the brush came four Japanese with swords, running toward Lieutenant Frankel. He waited calmly until they were several yards away, then zapped them with his flamethrower. "It was a horrible thing to witness. Horrible. I had nightmares about that for years."

In the first contested assault in which Boyce participated, the American infantry lined up in waves, the leading wave firing their rifles straight ahead. "This was done to keep the Japanese from firing," the veteran explains. "However, they were able to bring us to a halt."

Huddled down, Boyce took out his field glasses and saw a building ahead, with Japanese soldiers constantly going in and out. He radioed back, suggesting that it might be a command center or an observation center for their artillery. He was given the order to destroy it.

"I blew the building into a pile of rubble," he remembers. "We could see bodies and parts flying out of it. That was the only time in the war that I could be sure that I was responsible for killing anyone."

Several days later, his unit walked into a trap in the Cabaruan Hills. "There were Japanese to our left and our front," Boyce says. "When they started firing, men started dropping all over the area."

The wounded were calling for medics, but any movement in the grass brought a hail of bullets. "It's a soul-searching experience to be lying there in the grass and see stems shot off by bullets flying past your head," he says. "We stayed there until dark and made our way back to battalion headquarters. The Battalion Medical Officer said the wounded were the worst he had seen. I found out later that he suffered a nervous breakdown."

The following day, Boyce's radio officer, Pete Waleski, was sent out with a jeep to retrieve the dead from the fighting that took place the day before. Ellis Boyce carried his radio and together the men ran into heavy fire from the Japanese. As he tried to get a better vantage point to relay information to headquarters, he was separated from his unit, isolated on a dry rice paddy. If he moved an inch, the Japanese fired at the spot.

Just as he realized that he probably would die, a tank pulled up next to him. He crawled around to the back of the tank, which was drawing heavy fire, and "ran until I couldn't run any more. But it was far enough."

"Comparing this experience with D-Day is like comparing a battleship to a child's toy boat," he says. "I never really thought I was going to die while I was in France. But the action in Luzon seemed more brutal."

Several months later, he was issued plans for the U.S. invasion of Japan, but feels immensely grateful that he didn't have to use them.

Ellis Boyce returned home late in 1945. The following year, he enrolled in college and to outsiders it looked as though he had put the war behind him. But he suffered from recurring nightmares, visions of Japanese soldiers armed with swords coming at him, and in the dreams, he had no weapon. By June of 1946, he had lost 50 pounds and was suffering from insomnia.

"I was certain that I was going to die. Here. Back at home. Far from battlefields. But, somehow, I did not."

≈

War, like life, can be full of coincidences and quick (and often unexpected) reunions with friends from home.

While Edward Visel was serving on the hospital ship the *U.S.S. Hope*, which transported wounded soldiers from the battlegrounds in the South Pacific to military hospitals, one of the passengers was David Winans from Chelsea.

Rolly Spaulding and Wilfred Lane, best friends from boyhood days in Chelsea, ran into each other in Germany after D-Day.

Captain Merle Barr was eating donuts and sipping coffee at a Red Cross station in Germany when a nurse heard his voice, turned around and said, "You're Merle Barr!" "You're Irma Fleming, from Chelsea!" he answered, astonished.

Jim Daniels was sitting in a café in Paris after its liberation when he saw Bob Foster walk by.

≈

Fifty years after D-Day, Wilfred Lane was asked to address the community about the momentous events of that day, that war, and all wars.

"I am proud to say that I was one of the thousands upon thousands of Allied Forces who were poised on the British Isles, ready to be launched across the English Channel to take part in the largest amphibious assault in the history of our universe," he told his audience at Oak Grove Cemetery.

"Many of my newfound comrades never returned to their loved ones," he noted. "Some of my high school classmates are lying here in this very cemetery, while others are resting where they fell on foreign soil or in the oceans where they fought and died...In the nine wars that the United States of America has been engaged in, the common citizen soldier, the lifeblood of the American military, in wartime has always been given a reason to bear arms, a goal to attain, an ideal to uphold. And they have always done their duty."

He ended his speech with a challenge to future generations. "Remind your children and your grandchildren when they are enjoying their freedoms—the right to vote, the privilege of attending a meeting, to read a book or newspaper with differing points of view—that these are some of the blessings of living in our democratic society. Remind them, too, of the sacrifices that made these blessings possible. These are the freedoms we must cherish!"

On the Home Front

Together, Howard Holmes and George Staffan drove to the Army Recruiting Center in Ann Arbor to register for the draft. "We were the only two to get a deferment that day," Staffan recalls. "Howard got his deferment on account of the business he was in—food was essential to the war effort—and I was working with the health department both in Chelsea and Ann Arbor. The other embalmer had gone to war, so I got a deferment."

Over the next few years, Staffan helped lay more soldiers to rest than he could count. In his offices, as well as in homes and businesses in Chelsea and throughout the nation, there was a constant concern that a friend or family member would be the next to arrive at the local funeral parlor.

Staffan remembers a carpenter by the name of Koch who was told that his son was missing in action. A day or two later, the father said, "I know he's dead now." The Army confirmed his intuition the following day.

White hearse—George P. Staffan's first motorized "Michigan" hearse built in the 1920s.

Courtesy of Ann Arbor Federal Savings Village Book

Often, the home front and the war front were indistinguishable. Virginia Barr and Edward Visel had dated for six years before he enlisted. They planned to marry when the naval officer was home on leave from duty in the South Pacific for two weeks. But his leave was shortened, so Visel was married the day after he arrived home and he left two days later for the *U.S.S. Hope.*

Even during a routine day at home, the war cast its shadow over everyday life.

Children from German-speaking families like the Graus of Freedom Township were warned not to speak German outside the home.

Families would crowd around the radio at night to learn about the Allies' latest maneuvers.

They scanned newspapers for lists of casualties and consulted atlases to discover just where a brother, father, husband, cousin, or friend was fighting.

Stars hung in windows, indicating the number of family members in the service; a gold star meant that the family had lost a member to the war.

"I had a brother in the Army, in the African campaign," Marjorie Hepburn says. "I remember a current of worry that ran throughout all of our lives. We would wonder what our brothers or sweethearts or friends were doing in the war and worry about their safety."

"People were very patriotic," George Palmer says. "I remember seeing people buy Savings Bonds and then light a match to them, they just wanted to help in every way they could. Every woman who could do it got a job at a factory, to do her part. You can't imagine the single-minded purpose of every single person here: to beat Hitler."

As a boy, Palmer stood by the railroad tracks and watched long lines of Sherman tanks pass through town on freight trains bound for the tank arsenal in Detroit. "But my clearest memory is looking out the window and seeing a B-24 built at Willow Run fly past. They rolled out one complete bomber every hour and they were always testing them, seven days a week, three shifts a day, every day."

For those four years, the pace of life in Chelsea picked up dramatically. Chelsea's families, industries, and businesses left the Depression doldrums far behind.

"The Midwest—that includes Chelsea—became the breadbasket for the Allies," Dudley Holmes points out. "Farmers planted more crops, herded more animals, produced more wheat and did their part."

Factory workers, some of them moving up from the South, began pouring into town. War-based industries ran shifts around the clock. The war ended the tradition of the Catholic angelus, the bells that traditionally chimed every six hours throughout the day. "The factory workers were sleeping at all hours of the day and night and the angelus was stopped so the bells wouldn't awaken them," John Keusch says. "It was never resumed after the war."

As many as 100 trains a day roared into, through, and out of Chelsea, carrying heavy materiel and farm produce to shipping points, and then, eventually, to the war fronts in Europe, Africa, and the Pacific. Restaurants stayed open around the clock, cooking meals any time of the day or night for shift workers just getting off from work.

Many housewives in town earned spending money by renting a room or two out to boarders employed in the now-booming industries in town. Larger homes, including the Franks' and Myles' brick Victorian homes on East Middle Street, were chopped up into apartments to accommodate Chelsea's growing population. The mobile home park was planted on the site where Chelsea homeowners used to dump their ashes from chimney stoves and fireplaces.

Despite the undercurrent of worry, life went on pretty much as usual for children at home. They still played in the peat bog in summer, sledded and skated in the winter, worked at their chores at home and ran errands or took part-time jobs for busy shopkeepers in town.

In 1944, Marjorie Whipple (now Hepburn) became a member of the Congregational Church and graduated as salutatorian from Chelsea High School in a class consisting of 44 students, two-thirds of them girls. Most of the boys had already left for battlefields.

During the war years, Marjorie had worked evenings until 10 P.M., bagging groceries at Kroger's, then hurrying home to do her homework. Still, once in awhile she managed to attend a high school dance or meet friends at "John the Greek's" for an ice cream sundae.

Throughout the country, the mercantile and grocery businesses were regulated by government pricing and rationing. "Each item was allotted a certain number of points, which were stamped on the can," Marjorie Whipple Hepburn says.

Every family was given a ration book with the number of points depending on the number of people in the family. Cashiers would have to add up the points as well as the prices, then collect the coupons from the ration books. People would swap or share their stamps, she recalls. "I had a shoe stamp, but no money to buy all the shoes I could have, so I gave that stamp to a friend's family."

Customers would line up outside the stores long in advance of opening time, hoping to get scarce items, such as bananas. "The Kroger's manager got to the point where he would only put out half the day's stock in the morning, to keep some for the people who couldn't shop until later in the day," she says.

Shortages led to a brisk black-market trade. Alton Grau remembers that his father once traded a ham for a pair of shoes from a Chelsea shopowner. Cigarettes and liquor were particularly scarce and often acquired in nonregulation ways.

Until he was drafted, Rolly Spaulding worked in his father's car dealership in town and he and George Palmer share memories of those years. "There were no cars to sell, so we turned to repairs. There was a lot of scraping going on to keep in business," Spaulding says. "If we had something a customer needed and the customer had no money, we just passed out the parts and kept track of what they owed until times were better. We'd fix tires that today would have been long since junked."

"The government allowed us to buy a few parts so we could keep people going back and forth to work, but that was all," Palmer adds. "Those were four very dry years."

Wartime Industries

When war was declared, the entire Barr family went to work at the Federal Screw Works. Merle Barr Sr. became a shipping clerk. His son worked in the purchasing office until he enlisted in 1943. His wife, daughter, and mother-in-law worked as inspectors. And, as the Screw Works' workforce swelled, the government munitions plant took over more and more buildings in town. They burst out at the seams of the building on Main Street and moved into the Clock Tower, the Welfare Building, the old Hoover Ball plant on Hayes Street and even into an old building on the peat marsh. At its peak, Federal Screw ran around the clock seven days a week with 1,600 employees working full time.

"We made firearms ammunition and the cones for artillery shells," Virginia Barr Visel says. "This was the first time that I saw more than a handful of women working. Federal Screw Works had a great many women working there, especially as inspectors."

"You can't imagine the dedication on the part of every person," George Palmer says. "People weren't making a lot of money by today's standards, but they were working long hours, seven days a week, helping to win the war."

Central Fibre Products had moved into former Glazier industrial buildings lining the railroad tracks in 1936. In 1940, the company expanded once again. During the war, Central Fibre manufactured parts for the 90-millimeter antiaircraft gun and for various tank models. The Dexter Machine Company, located at Old U.S. 12 on the borders of the village, manufactured high-precision shaved gears used in fire control and the turret drive mechanisms for the B-29 Super Fortress, which George Winans would fly. The Rockwell Spring Company ran four round-the-clock shifts.

The war also had far-reaching effects on long-established hometown businesses. As many as 100 trains ran through town every day. Many of them stopped to load farm produce, flour, and animals, as well as the war materiel being manufactured at record rates in Chelsea industries. Grocery stores, restaurants, boarding houses and hotels were packed with customers. Shortages, rationing, and federal price regulations strongly affected the fate of small businesses, however.

"During the Depression, we had jewelry but no one could afford to buy it. During the war, people were making money again, but we couldn't get jewelry to sell to them," George Winans of Winans Jewelry says. "Metal was vital to the war effort, so we saw a lot of wooden jewelry."

The government rationed the number of watches the jeweler could sell and the Office of Price Administration required permits before jewelers could set prices on watches. "We sold magazines and greeting cards and other things, just to keep the business going," Winans says.

Farmers broke new ground—literally—in raising crops for the war effort. Anyone who wanted to work could find any number of jobs.

"It is impossible for folks today to comprehend what those times were like—the intense feeling of patriotism, the push everyone felt to do everything they could for the war effort, the fear for family members and friends on the battlefields," John Keusch says.

During World War II, Central Fibre Products manufactured parts for the 90-millimeter antiaircraft gun and for various tank models.

Photograph from the 1959 Chelsea High School Yearbook

Harry S. Truman, 1945-53 • Dwight D. Eisenhower, 1953-61

U.N. General Assembly holds its first session in London, 1946 •
Nuremberg Trials, 1946 • Churchill delivers the 'Iron Curtain Speech' •
The Marshall Plan, 1947 • Tennessee Williams wins Pulitzer for *Streetcar
Named Desire* • Michigan defeats Southern California 49-0 to win Rose
Bowl, 1948 • America sings *Some Enchanted Evening, Diamonds Are A
Girl's Best Friend*, and *Rudolph The Red-Nosed Reindeer*, 1949 • U.S. liter-
acy rate is 96.8, 1950 • J.D. Salinger writes *Catcher In The Rye*, Catherine
Marshall writes *A Man Called Peter*, 1951 • Stalin dies, 1953 • Queen
Elizabeth II crowned • Vietnamese rebels attack Laos • Eero Saarinen wins
award for General Motors design • U.S.S.R. explodes hydrogen bomb,
1954 • U.S. Supreme Court rules against segregation by color in public
schools, 1954 • Senator McCarthy on witchhunt in Senate • Bikini bomb
tests • U.S.S.R launches Sputnik, 1957 • Alaska becomes 49th state, 1948 •
Fidel Castro becomes Cuban premier, 1959 • America sings *Everything's
Comin' Up Roses*, 1959

U.S. POPULATION
150,697,999

The Post World War II Years: The 1950s

America Reinvents Itself

Ask anyone born before 1940 where they were when V-E (Victory in Europe) and V-J (Victory over Japan) were declared and they will remember. They'll tell you that they were dancing, kissing, pumping hands, hugging, laughing, crying, lighting bonfires, banging on kettles with spoons, shouting, singing patriotic songs, praying, visiting a soldier's grave site, marching or driving down Main Street, blowing horns, and maybe even firing a hunting rifle into the air, jubilant that the war was over.

The honor roll for the American Legion lists names of 136 Chelsea men who gave their lives during World War II and are buried at home, at sea, or in graves on foreign soil.

On December 2, 1945, a greyhound bus dropped Wilfred Lane off on "Burg's Corner" of Main Street. "I vividly remember everything about that night," he told the Rotary Club exactly 50 years to the day later. "It was a cold, clear night and a light snow was falling as I stood on the corner admiring the little village I had missed so much while I was away…"

On the northeast corner of Main Street, Lane noticed, Charlie Bycraft was displaying the Christmas trees he offered for sale near his taxi stand. The stores were closed and the streets were deserted. At about the time the soldier was ready to pick up his barracks bag and start the trek home, a black sedan came around the corner, a window rolled down, and a voice inquired, "Going somewhere, soldier?"

"Heading for home, sir," Lane answered, as he stepped toward Chelsea's police cruiser.

The officer was the first to greet the four-year veteran. "Jump in and I'll take you home." That was music to Wilfred Lane's ears. "That Christmas was the happiest holiday I had spent in many years," he told his audience.

On another night, this one in 1946, Sgt. Richard Kinsey found himself on the corner of Michigan Avenue, discharge papers in his pocket and a duffel bag in his hand. A car pulled up and the voice of a high school friend Kinsey hadn't seen in three years asked, "Who's home from the service?"

"That's how I was reintroduced to civilian life," he says.

Within a year, he and Ilene Loeffler, like countless other couples, had driven to Angola, Indiana to get married. "It was quick and we didn't want to wait. We were anxious to get on with our lives," Kinsey explains.

Richard Kinsey had worried about readjusting to civilian life as he left Europe for the United States. "As terrible as war is, it is also very exciting," he says. "I thought it might be hard to give all that up and return to a normal, everyday kind of life." Eventually, after hanging up his uniform, he became a beer salesman for O&W Inc.

One of the first changes Kinsey noticed in town was what every young man would notice: the price of automobiles. "In 1943, a car cost $900. In 1946, a car cost $1,700—when you could find one." He still appreciates the fact that Warren Daniels would allot one new Buick or Oldsmobile a month to a local veteran at the time when automobile manufacturers were slowly converting from wartime material production to peacetime automobile production and every-one wanted a new car. "That generosity on Mr. Daniel's part was something that I will never forget," Kinsey says.

When Merle Barr's tour of duty in Europe ended, the 24-year-old U.S. Army captain spent his time on the troopship sailing home from Europe wondering what to do with the rest of his life. "It was actually more difficult to readjust to civilian life than it had been to adjust to the life of a soldier," he remembers a half-century later. "As a soldier, you were housed, clothed, fed, and you knew exactly what you were supposed to do. As I rode that troopship home, my future seemed questionable. I had no job, no money, no idea of what the future would hold."

Despite his concerns, Barr was welcomed back at the Federal Screw Works in Chelsea, where he had worked prior to the war, and he stayed there, with only a one-year separation, until his retirement in 1987.

Rolly Spaulding returned home from war to discover that "a lot of wonderful people" had moved into town from the South, particu-larly Kentucky and Tennessee, to work in wartime factory jobs. Many of them decided to stay and make Chelsea home.

Although many of the local industries cut back on the number of employees and shifts after the war, the companies continued to thrive. America was feeling good about itself. Soldiers were returning home in waves, taking off their uniforms, rolling up their sleeves and heading back to work. They needed jobs. They needed homes and cars and food and appliances for their new families—and they were in a hurry to get them. Many women—willingly or unwillingly—turned their factory and defense jobs over to men and retired from the workplace.

"Once the country settled into peacetime existence, the postwar years were good years," Spaulding says. "Things changed a little—some longtime clothing stores went out of business or changed owners—but Chelsea was still Chelsea."

The Korean Conflict

When Captain Merle Barr returned to Chelsea in 1945 after three years of duty in Europe, he never envisioned that he would be called back into uniform for another war. He had picked up where his career had left off at the Federal Screw Works, married, and started his family. Then the Korean Conflict was ignited and his life was once again interrupted. In 1952, he was recalled into active service and sent to Alaska to install sophisticated monitoring equipment.

"There was no question that World War II was a necessity. It was a foregone conclusion that we had to go to war. I didn't feel that way about Korea," he says, nearly 50 years later. After his year of service, he returned to his position in the purchasing office of the Federal Screw Works and retired his uniform permanently.

Florence Vogel, a Registered Nurse with the Army Nursing Corps, boarded a ship bound for Korea. At the end of the war, she retired with the rank of lieutenant colonel.

By the early 1950s, Dwight E. Beach was a brigadier general in the U.S. Army. In 1953, he was placed in command of the 11th Airborne Division and, later, the artillery of the 45th Infantry Division in Korea. He moved up in rank, serving as Artillery Officer and Deputy Chief of Staff for Plans and Combat Operations, Eighth Army, in Korea. Then, in November 1954, he was appointed Chief of Staff of the Eighth Army. At the time when General Beach decided to retire in 1968, he was serving as Commander-in-Chief of the U.S. Army, Pacific.

Brigadier General Herbert Vogel left Panama when he was promoted to head the Army Corps of Engineers.

Bob Daniels spent 37 months on a destroyer off Korea. Afterward, he worked as an engineer elsewhere, but decided that his heart still belonged to his hometown. He settled down in Chelsea in 1955, joining his father and brother at the Chelsea Lumber Company.

George Palmer graduated from the University of Miami, returned home for a year, and then received his draft notice in 1952. "I spent all my military time in the States, so I can't say the war changed me," he says with a chuckle, then adds on a more serious note, "People were highly critical of that war, though it wasn't like Vietnam. The military managed some colossal boo-boos, including the situation with General Douglas MacArthur, and that raised criticism. There were a lot of doubts about fighting someone else's war, though I have no trouble with the justification. We made a statement. We went there to be counted. And we were."

The count of Chelsea natives who gave their lives to their country during the Korean War totals 13. For the first time, a woman's name is on the honor roll. Martha Stevens Holbrook.

The Life of Reilly

In 1950, the United States boasted 1.5 million television sets. One year later, the number had jumped to 15 million. By 1960, there would be 85 million televisions in American homes. A generation of children sported Davy Crockett coonskin caps and Mickey Mouse ears, played cowboys and Indians, scanned cereal boxes for decoder rings, and sang "It's Howdy Doody Time!" The Salk vaccine was created to fight polio and schools began administering the polio vaccine on lumps of sugar to all children. Elvis Presley sang to swooning teenagers while Perry Como crooned to their mothers. The daddy of the "Lone Ranger's" horse Silver was laid to rest out by Grass Lake, amid local fanfare. The Baby Boom had begun and life was looking good.

"The biggest changes after the war?" Rolly Spaulding asks rhetorically. "People got older. Cars got bigger, newer, shinier. Kids grew up. And so did the town. It began to bother me when I heard people call Chelsea a "*quaint* little town."

Chelsea bowed to the Baby Boomers and built a new elementary and high school to educate the postwar generation of children. Charles Cameron was superintendent of schools in those days. When Paul Schaible Jr. thinks of outstanding events taking place in the 1950s, the new schools top his list. During this decade, school buses also made their first appearances. One-room country schools, which had flourished throughout Washtenaw County since its pioneer days, began closing and increasingly more students boarded buses to attend Chelsea schools.

One of the most important and far-reaching changes during this decade occurred south of Chelsea, along M-52. One farm after another was purchased, their homes and barns either moved or demolished. But the reason for the land consolidation, all the bulldozers and secrecy, remained unknown for months. Amidst wild rumors, the Chelsea Proving Grounds broke ground on its 4,000-acre laboratory on the Vermont Colony lands south of town.

In the early 1950s, the Fisk farm was one of more than 20 farms purchased south of Chelsea to make room for the Chrysler Proving Grounds.
Courtesy Chelsea Area Historical Society

"The land was bought through an independent broker, John Hannah, who was very close-mouthed," Larry Chapman remembers. "There was tremendous talk about what was going on there and a lot of the speculation centered on the idea that it was going to be a nudist colony." Chapman grins and adds, "Everyone said that John Brookes would put a telescope on the cupola of his house (just south of I-94) and charge people for a look at the goings-on."

One farmer who declined the purchase offers and decided to stay put was Lloyd Grau's father, Arthur Grau, who had purchased the 120-acre Chase farm on M-52 in 1929. He and several other neighbors banded together, refusing to sell their lands to the mysterious entity. "Every day every person had a different idea about what was going on," Lloyd Grau remembers. "That affair stirred up a lot of people." Grau's farm is adjacent to the Proving Grounds now and recently he purchased John Brooke's farm and its 90 acres on the other side of Chrysler's property on M-52.

The Proving Grounds changed the complexion of the land south of town and it opened up hundreds of jobs to Chelsea residents, among them Larry Chapman and Michael Kushmaul. According to the literature Chrysler published for town residents as an explanation of its movements,

The Heim family posed for an unknown photographer on their farm—one which was purchased by Chrysler. Courtesy of the Grau family

The qualifications for the site stacked up clearly. It would be big enough to permit construction for many different kinds of tests, level enough for long, turnpike-type straight-aways, hilly and rugged

The Chrysler Proving Grounds eventually swallowed up 4,000 acres of farm land and opened up hundreds of jobs to Chelsea area residents. Courtesy Chelsea Area Historical Society

enough to let us test cars on just about every kind of terrain they'd be likely to encounter in service. It would have to be no further than 60 miles from Detroit…And finally, it would have to be close to a town—a firmly established, forward-looking community."

Chelsea's 125th Anniversary

At about the time all this was happening, Chelsea celebrated its 125th anniversary with the biggest party the community has ever seen.

"Rolly Spaulding ran the whole shebang and he was fantastic. Russ McLaughlin was another who did a great job. In fact, everybody in town played a part in the success of the 125th in 1954," Bob Daniels says. He remembers the excitement of the big day and the early morning hours when he sat in the back of a pickup truck with pages of the town history hot off the presses, collating and stapling the books, then handing them out as fast as he could. "People couldn't get enough of them that day, so we authorized the printing of thousands more—and we had massive piles of the histories sitting around for years. The passion was spent on the big day, I guess," he says, with a grin.

For months in advance, men began growing mustaches and beards as "Brothers of the Brush." Ladies sewed and sashayed in old-fashioned dresses and bonnets. "A firm from Ohio came to produce the extravaganza and stirred the town up to a fever pitch months in advance of the official celebration," Daniels says. "They made a big presentation and announced how much the townspeople would need to contribute. Ahead of time, they had convinced certain people in the audience to speak up and say, 'I'm ready to go! Here's my money!' And the celebration was underway."

Chelsea Lumber Company donated all the materials to build a house the size of an average settler's cabin, 30 by 20 feet, and Spaulding marshaled forces to construct the home in record time in Heydlauff's parking lot. "It was built in one day and painted in four short minutes," Daniels remembers. "Rolly had everyone in position with a paintbrush and an allocated two feet of space, some on scaffolding, others on the ground. Someone fired a gun and the painting began."

"There was more paint on the participants than on the house," Larry Chapman says.

Then the parties began. The whole downtown hosted concerts, dances, concessions, and parades throughout the year. "There were parades in town almost every week," Daniels says. "I remember one being led by a fellow named LaBonne, who served as a majorette, carrying a toilet plunger to lead the band."

One Chelsea resident who asked not to be identified, also noted, "There were more divorces from that celebration than ever before in the history of Chelsea. Men and women starting working together on big projects that year and got to know each other. Then the divorce rate started to rise."

The decade of the 1950s was also notable for the establishment of a permanent home for the Chelsea Library. In 1958, Mrs. E.J. McKune willed the McKune House, which was the former Elisha Congdon home, to the town. Her niece, Katie Staffan Wagner, helped orchestrate the renovation of the home and the organization of the library, which had been itinerant since 1932, when the Woman's Club of Chelsea opened a lending library in a downtown storefront with 20 donated books and 100 volumes provided by the State Library. In those Depression days, patrons had been served by two volunteers during the three hours a week (usually Saturday nights) when the library was open. When the McKune House was transformed into the McKune Library, its doors were open six days a week.

Business Moves into a New Age

"Through the first century of Chelsea's history, the town survived because of the support of prosperous farmers," George Heydlauff says. "Chelsea businesses served good, hardworking families who lived for miles around the village and came to town for supplies once a week and to attend church on Sundays. As the economy grew during and after the war, the entire complexion of the town began to change. We saw more people moving to town and commuting to Ann Arbor or Jackson for work. Full-time farmers kept the jobs in industry they had held during the war and farmed early in the morning, at night, and on weekends. Our customer base not only began changing, but growing. And that was true for the other businesses in town."

In 1946, Walter Leonard, an Iowa native who had apprenticed on a Linotype machine as a boy, bought the *Chelsea Standard* from M.W. McClure, who had been responsible for reporting local news since 1921. For $50,000, Leonard acquired the masthead, a 1920 Linotype machine, one job press that was hand-fed, a newspaper press, a folder, and one employee, an alcoholic who periodically went on week-long binges.

Leonard and his wife Helen added the *Dexter Leader* to their masthead in 1955 (purchased for $15,000) and were responsible for introducing the small, old-fashioned local newspaper to the age of computers, automated presses, cell phones, fax transmissions and e-mail. By the time they left the office for the last time, the *Standard* had ten employees and four printers.

One of the most memorable of the Leonards' early staff members was Emma Oesterle, a housewife who lived on Taylor Street and worked out of her home. "She was an excellent writer, a natural, and she took care of writing all the society news, gossip stuff, and activities," Walter Leonard recalls. "After she retired, we never had anyone local again. We could only afford to hire entry level writers who could live on what we could pay."

For years, the newspaper was housed at 108 East Middle Street, but as it expanded its coverage, the paper began bursting the building's seams. In 1960, Donald Bacon sold the Leonards Frank Glazier's Welfare Building, which had housed the Federal Screw Works during the war.

"The move was a wild gamble for us. We worked around the clock—literally—to make it happen and meet all of our deadlines," Leonard says. "We shut down the paper Wednesday night. The movers arrived right away, and we were operating at full strength by Monday morning."

At first, the paper took more time to print than to write, the publisher remembers. The press would print four front pages, then the pressman would flip them over so the back pages would be printed. Later, new machinery allowed the pressmen to hand-feed pages through the folder. About the time they moved, the Leonards bought an eight-page printer that would print and fold at one pass, producing 4,500 pages per hour.

"We put our necks on the line for the $40,000 to buy that machine—but it paid off," Walter Leonard says. "We had the last letter press of any small-town paper in Michigan and we couldn't wait for offset to be perfected."

When Walter Leonard arrived in Chelsea, it was a country town with a handful of industrial operations, he recalls. "Chelsea Milling

Company, Federal Screw, Rockwell Spring Company, and Central Fibre Products were running great guns and bringing workers into town. There were five grocery stores here, several good clothing stores (Dave Strieters' men's store and Helen Vogel's women's store), Vince Burg's drugstore on the corner of Main and Middle, a pub where Cleary's is now, the Muleskinner, the Chelsea Bank, and a couple of restaurants."

~

With World War II at an end, the small family-owned businesses in town also began expanding, as local servicemen returned to a peace-time existence.

George Winans remembers that he had no plans when he returned home from Europe. "I had no idea of joining the family business, but my father and grandfather taught me what they could and watch repair came easy to me," he says. After his marriage, he and his wife Jeanette moved to Peoria, Illinois for two years, so he could attend watchmaker's and engraver's school. "I wasted a year learning to engrave—it's a lost art now. Machines do it all," he says.

In George Winans' day, as well as in the days of his father and grandfather, the jewelers in town were often the first to know about who was planning an engagement—"and I learned the hard way not to ask a wife if she liked the ring her husband had bought," George Winans remembers. "I quickly discovered that not all the jewelry was intended for wives!" Once, after George mounted a diamond for a Chicago customer who paid the bill with a check for $1,000, his grandfather told him, "That's the kind of money I used to make in a whole year."

Local industries quickly converted to peacetime manufacturers. Central Fibre manufactured its last antiaircraft guns and tank parts in 1945 and then returned to its original line of work, producing paper fleece twine, as well as new products such as paper and tissue seam cord, tacking strips, bare wire and paper-covered wire.

With the end of the war in sight, in 1945, the Central Fibre Company had sold its Power Take-Off Division to local businessmen, among them Howard Holmes, R.W. Wagner, E.W. Eaton, P.G. Schaible, and E.A. King. Renamed Chelsea Products, Inc., the new enterprise manufactured take-offs for every make of truck and, later, airplanes. The company suffered a huge fire in 1947 that destroyed

90% of its buildings, but the plants were rebuilt and business resumed. The firm was sold to the Dana Corporation in 1958.

The Rockwell Spring Company, which had started in business as the Chelsea Spring Company, continued manufacturing mechanical springs, wire forms, moulding clips, wiring clips, and small stampings under new ownership after the war.

Chelsea Heat Treating was launched in 1953 by Wayne Gow and Elden Heller. Dozens of other small businesses made appearances. Some flourished, some moved away, some failed.

The Chelsea Lumber, Grain & Coal Company extracted itself from the coal business, then the grain business. "We were in direct competition with the Chelsea Milling Company and it made no sense," Bob Daniels explains. "The milling company was growing very fast at that time. So, sometime in the 1950s, we decided to concentrate on what we did best."

Glazier's monument to Chelsea's industry, the Clock Tower, represented the booming postwar times just as it had represented the booming turn-of-the-century industries. In the 1950s, local businessmen contributed enough money to bring the clocks up to modern-day standards, so that they would once again keep perfect time. America was in a hurry and time was money.

Main Street looking north in the 1950s.

Courtesy Chelsea Area Historical Society

Dwight D. Eisenhower, 1953-61 • John F. Kennedy, 1961-63
Lyndon B. Johnson, 1963-68 • Richard Nixon, 1968-74
Gerald Ford, 1974-77 • Jimmy Carter, 1977-81

Americans sing *Itsy Bitsy Teenie Weenie Yellow Polka Dot Bikini* • Arnold Palmer wins U.S. Open • Cuban missile crisis • Berlin Wall constructed • Irving Stone writes *The Agony and the Ecstasy*, Harold Robbins writes *The Carpetbaggers*, Joseph Heller writes *Catch-22* • 200,000 freedom marchers descend on Washington • U.S. spacemen Glenn, Schirra, and Carpenter orbit the Earth • Kennedy assassinated • Lee Harvey Oswald killed as Americans watch on TV • N.Y. World's Fair • Artificial heart beats • Vietnam escalates • America watches a *Hard Day's Night*, *Goldfinger*, *Mary Poppins* • North Vietnamese shoot down U.S. jets • Student protests • Riots in Detroit, Cleveland, Newark • Robert Kennedy assassinated • 75,000 American troops sent home from Vietnam by end of 1969 • Neil Armstrong walks on the moon • U.S. bombs Cambodia • Pentagon papers • By 1972, fewer than 24,000 troops left in Vietnam • Watergate • Energy Crisis • Muhammad Ali reclaims heavyweight title • Unemployment rate highest since 1941 • U.S. Bicentennial • Cost of mailing U.S. letter: 13 cents • U.S. spacecraft land on Mars

U.S. POPULATION
1960: 179,323,000
1970: 205,000,000

The Vietnam Years: The 1960s and 1970s

In the Service, in the Rice Paddies, and in the Jungles

"I owe everything to the Marine Corps. The Marines made me who I am today," says Bill Abernethy without hesitation. "I went into the Corps as a wise guy, a 17-year-old who thought he knew everything, and I was forced to grow up—and grow up fast—in a very unforgiving environment. I had two choices: to shape up or not. I shaped up. I would never have gone to college, let alone graduate school, I would never have taken my career path, if it hadn't been for the Marine Corps and Vietnam."

After being expelled from high school in 1965, 17-year-old Bill Abernethy decided to ignore his family's advice to enroll in an Eastern prep school. Instead, he convinced his mother to sign the necessary papers so he could join the Marine Corps. His father, a World War II veteran and a psychologist, opposed the war and opposed his decision.

"Why the Marine Corps?" Abernethy repeats the question, grins, and answers, "Youthful romanticism."

The young recruit trained in San Diego, then shipped out for Vietnam in March 1967, assigned to an antitank battalion. He agreed to a six-month extension of his 13-month tour of duty in order to trade assignments and join a Combined Action Platoon, CAP for short. "This was a famous program at the time and people still speak highly of it," Abernethy says. "The Marines sent squads of 12 to 15 men to live in villages and train and operate with Vietnamese Popular Forces, which were similar to a National Guard. The idea was to counter guerrilla warfare by encountering guerrillas at our discretion, not in the way that line infantry troops traditionally would." He divided his service between two CAP units that operated between Dong Ha and Quang Tri City.

Typically, CAP units were responsible for three or four villages within their tactical area of responsibility, Abernethy explains. His first unit worked within three villages and the Marines were headquartered in a miniature compound, surrounded by barbed wire and trenches. The second CAP unit, christened Romeo 4, was a roving CAP. "We lived out of our backpacks."

Although living, training, and fighting with South Vietnamese troopers, the language barrier kept the Marines from making close friendships, he says, "We did have favorites among the South Vietnamese troopers, but real friendship was impossible without a shared language."

Abernethy vividly remembers the "very, very intriguing and beautiful country," the stomach-knotting patrol duties with his squad, eating C-rations endlessly ("canned meals that were horrible—their only merits were that they were prepared to last for decades"), struggling through tremendous rains and floods, and living on a daily basis with a constant, gnawing sense of great danger.

At the age of 17, at the height of the Vietnam war, Bill Abernethy shipped off for the rice paddies and jungles as a Marine.

Courtesy of Bill Abernethy

"CAP units made frequent contact with the Vietcong—there were always small groups involved in fights. And because we were small units, we could be overwhelmed. There was no rest from the sense that anything could happen at any time," he says. "In fact, our unit was taken out shortly after I left."

When he sailed for home after 18 months in the jungle, the teenager was a corporal, up for sergeant. "I had no thoughts of staying, however," he adds. "I remember being in the bush when a gunny came out and gave me the reenlistment papers, but I didn't think of changing my mind for a second. I was ready to get out into the real world as an adult. I didn't want to be a high school dropout for the rest of my life."

During his three years with the Marine Corps, Abernethy somehow managed to complete his GED. ("My transcript reads 'no accredited high school.'") When he left the service, he enrolled in a teacher's college for a year, then transferred to the University of Oregon, where he earned his undergraduate degree in English and German, a master's degree in linguistics, and a doctorate in English literature. After his appointment to a research position at the University of Michigan, he moved to Freedom Township. He now heads the English department at Washtenaw Community College and teaches classes on Shakespeare.

Abernethy lives with his four-year-old son, teenage daughter, and his wife, writer Laura Kasischke, in an old farmhouse at Rogers'

Corners that once served as a blacksmith shop. Every once in awhile he will pull out a picture of his platoon standing around a mortar unit and study the young faces. Recently, he discovered a web site that links former CAP veterans and he has tracked down several of his friends.

"I have no ghosts to lay to rest," he says firmly. "Much of the time I was scared to death, but I have a great deal of loyalty to the Corps. I had a very interesting war and I wasn't injured—which makes a profound difference, probably, in a person's perspective."

"The politics of Vietnam have always been murky to me, but I would have hated to miss the war—after all, war is one of the great archetypal experiences a man has," he adds. "As more than one man has said, Vietnam was dirty little war, but it was all we had."

~

"The Vietnam War was just heating up when I became eligible for the draft. I took the honorable way out. I didn't want to serve in Vietnam, but I refused to run away to Canada, either. So, I enlisted in the Air Force," says Michael Kushmaul, the son of a World War II veteran (Nelson Kushmaul), who had served with an engineer outfit on Omaha Beach during the Normandy invasion and in Europe afterward. "My father didn't say a whole lot about the war, but I knew he was proud that he had served his country," the son says. "I am, too. But I have put those years far, far behind me."

Kushmaul enlisted almost immediately after graduating from Chelsea High School in 1966, during the escalation of antiwar rallies around the nation. "Chelsea was a pretty conservative town and I didn't have anyone trying to convince me not to enlist," he says. In fact, he never saw signs of antiwar sentiment here, he adds. After receiving his training at Lackland Air Force Base in Texas and Chanute Air Force Base in Illinois, he was stationed in Germany as a buck sergeant supervising parachute preparations.

In Frankfurt, he saw his first antiwar demonstrations. "I didn't like the war, but I thought I was doing my duty," he says. When his tour of duty ended, he considered reenlisting, but felt sure that would mean Vietnam and by that time he and his wife Rose were expecting their first child. He left the service.

When Michael Kushmaul arrived home, he got rid of his uniform as fast as he could and settled down quickly to civilian life. "I felt sorry for the Vietnam vets who were fighting wars on two fronts—in the jungles and at home. That wasn't fair," he says. Although the recession of 1970 meant that jobs were scarce and hard to find, he eventually became a mechanic at the Chrysler Proving Grounds. For a time, he belonged to the local VFW (Veterans of Foreign Wars) post, but eventually dropped his affiliation.

"At the time when I was in the service, I was probably as patriotic as the next person," he says, three decades later. "I thought that I had done my part by enlisting and serving. Then I left that behind me, to get on with my life."

≈

Michael Kushmaul's cousin, Bobby Kushmaul, wasn't so lucky. He was killed in Vietnam while serving on a patrol boat that was ambushed on an interior river in Vietnam. "He had joined the Navy in 1969 and he was killed just as his tour of duty was about to end," Michael Kushmaul says. "The story I heard was that the person who was supposed to be on that boat got sick and Bobby either volunteered or was ordered to take his place. He never left the ship alive." Bobby Kushmaul's body was shipped back home. He was buried in Oak Grove Cemetery.

≈

Chelsea Village Manager Jack Myers joined the Marine Corps 13 days after graduating from high school in June 1962, just before the Cuban Bay of Pigs crisis. He retired 20 years and 17 days later. His occupational specialty was finance—"but when you are a Marine, you are always prepared for fighting," he says. That was certainly the case when he served in Vietnam.

He was there at the peak of American involvement, which included the Tet Offensive in 1968. During those dark days, the North Vietnamese raised their flag a quarter-mile from where Myers was stationed, at Namo Bridge, close to the Ho Chi Minh Trail.

"I wouldn't say that we lived in a constant state of fear, but the atmosphere was always hot. You just hoped that there wasn't a rocket or a bullet with your name on it," he recalls.

Five days after Myers' arrival at Red Beach, not far from the South China Sea, the Vietcong launched a mortar attack on his command post, with major casualties. One night, the battleship *U.S.S. New Jersey* shot rockets from 22 miles off the coast, over the heads of American personnel to an invisible enemy just beyond their compound. One morning, on his way to work, Myers got halfway to the office, but decided to turn around and make certain a friend was awake. As he retraced his steps, his office was blown up. "If I'd kept on going, I wouldn't be here today," he says, with a trace of awe in his voice still, after all those years. The list of near-saves and near-misses goes on and on as he remembers his tour of duty.

Nearly four decades after he arrived in Vietnam, retired Captain Myers vividly remembers the details of life in Southeast Asia. The shots that thinned Americans' blood so they could cope with the intense heat. ("They felt like syrup injected into your hip.") The weather. ("Some days were 130 degrees in the shade, and then we would freeze when the temperatures dropped to 60 at night.") The monsoons that dumped rain for two and three weeks at a time. The Marine Corps food—and, in particular, the night that the commanding general learned that huge quantities of delicacies had been shipped to the base. ("That was a highlight—everyone in the compound had their fill of lobster and steaks," he says with a laugh.) Myers also remembers the crowds of Vietnamese who waited by the gates of the compound every day, hoping for work. He employed them to fill sandbags for bunkers. ("We hired them. We did our best by them. But we never totally trusted them," he says.)

To this day, Jack Myers isn't convinced that Americans should have been sent to fight in Vietnam. His fellow countrymen's opposition to the war and to those who were fighting in the war still bothers him. "But I was a Marine and I went where the Corps sent me," he says. He served in Vietnam for 13 months and to this day he appreciates the intense loyalty shared among his comrades there. "The Marine Corps is famous for that sense of loyalty, but there was an entirely different environment in Vietnam, like nothing you would ever find in a garrison stateside," he says. "We would do anything for each other."

"I don't talk about Vietnam much, but I think of the people," he admits. Outside the gates of his compound, Americans had built an orphanage that Myers and others would visit on Sundays, carrying boxes of cookies, candy, or other treats. "Tears still come to my eyes when I think of those babies without arms or legs," he says quietly. "One little boy always came up to me. To this day I wish I'd brought him back with me."

Myers entered the Marine Corps as a private and left as a captain. Now a member of the United States Marine Corps Association and the Retired Officers Association, he says, "The Marine Corps changed my life. It made me grow up. You either loved it or you hated it. I loved it. Sometimes I still miss it."

~

By the time the U.S. and South Vietnamese government signed the cease-fire agreement on January 23, 1973, American losses from combat deaths totaled 45,948, with an additional 303,640 wounded, while noncombat causes resulted in 10,298 deaths. More than a dozen Vietnam veterans are buried in Chelsea cemeteries.

Back at Home with the Baby Boomers

During the first half of the twentieth century, 87% of Washtenaw County—and even more of Chelsea—was composed of native-born white residents. But, by 1960 that figure was dropping, due in part to Appalachian natives who immigrated to the area to work in the war industries. In 1960, the percentage of blacks in the county rose to 11% and Eastern Europeans and Asians were also gaining in numbers.

But life in Chelsea went on much as it always had. Boys like Scott Otto who grew up in the 1960s and '70s spent their after-school afternoons and long summer days doing the same things John Keusch, Rolly Spaulding, and George Winans had done as boys. They played hockey in the peat marsh on the present-day hospital grounds. Played baseball in a nearby farmer's field, dodging manure as often as they dodged well-thrown balls. Rode their bikes through town, exploring all the cracks and crevices. Worked an occasional odd job. Chatted with the shoe repair man whose business was above Merkel's. Cheered at the Memorial Day and Fourth of July parades, then ate their fill at chicken barbecues afterward.

They turned to George Gooden, a sympathetic neighbor who lived on Wilkinson Street, to repair their bikes. Checked on the peat fires that seemed to burn for years. ("Old Julius Rule—we called him Czar—told the town that they would have to dig trenches all around it and fill them with water if they wanted the fires out," Otto remembers. "The town never did it.") Boys still occasionally helped with the asparagus or onion harvests on farms bordering the village. And they avoided the bigger boys.

Girls joined the Girl Scouts, helped their mothers with chores, played dolls, took dancing lessons, babysat little brothers and sisters or the neighbors' children, climbed an occasional tree, wrote in their diaries, stood in line to see Disney movies, listened to transistor radios, experimented with makeup, and fell in love with movie stars and rock 'n roll.

Those were the days when allowances were hot topics among parents and the lucky kids got a quarter a week. Kool-Aid was the normal alternative to milk. There were only two types of sneakers for girls and boys—PF Flyers and Keds—and they were only worn during gym class. It took televisions five minutes to warm up and even then, there were only three channels to choose from. Laundry detergent came with free dishes or dishtowels. Parents dressed for dinner. Boys wore suits and ties to church. Mothers wore dresses, heels, hose and pearls to wash kitchen floors in television shows and hats and gloves to go shopping. Any parent could discipline anyone's child, feed them, or ask them to carry groceries and the children did it. Candy bars and popsicles cost a nickel. Ice cream cones and comic books cost ten cents. Math students did calculations with slide rules. Cashiers in department stores used adding machines. Just about everyone watched "Today on the Farm" before heading off to school.

"Chelsea was like the ideal 'Leave It To Beaver' town in those days," says Jeff Daniels, who was born in 1957. "All the kids in the neighborhood would ride their bikes to school—and everywhere else in town—play army in the backyards and woods, go on exploring expeditions. This place was very safe and it seemed very far away from the big city of Ann Arbor. Everyone's parents were wired into the entire community and everyone knew everyone in town."

During his middle school years, in the 1960s, Jeff Daniels discovered he might have a flair for acting.

DiAnn L'Roy, the middle school's chorus director and manager of the Chelsea Players was "a one-person force who lived to put on musicals and I was the main beneficiary," Daniels remembers. "Somehow, when I was in sixth grade, she saw something in me."

One day, Miss L'Roy decided to do improvisations with her class of restless sixth graders and she chose Jeff Daniels to play a politician giving a speech while his pants are falling down. Long beyond his allotted three minutes, he kept the class—and stray visitors who heard all the commotion—laughing uproariously at his skit. Later, his teacher went to his parents and suggested, 'Don't let this go unnoticed.'

"Had I not met this Chelsea teacher, quite possibly I wouldn't be where I am today," the actor says.

Forensics teacher Bill Coelius next took the boy in hand and introduced him to film making, on a homemade level. "When a couple of teachers take an interest in you and tell you they see talent, it can do great things for a kid," Daniels says.

~

Life in Chelsea during the 1960s and 1970s was quiet, secure, leisurely, and business saw a continuation of the boom days of the 1950s—for most people.

"The 1960s were great times for men to find work, but hard times for women," Marjorie Whipple Hepburn remembers. Despite the fact that she had been salutatorian of her high school graduating class, scholarships had been scarce for women in 1945. When Marjorie Whipple graduated from high school, she went to the University of Michigan, but as a glass washer in a laboratory rather than a student. She married Max Hepburn and together they had six children. When her husband was disabled and her little boy was diagnosed with leukemia, she returned to the university and eventually headed a laboratory, a position she earned by hard work rather than by an academic degree.

Working women were relatively rare in the 1960s. Another exception was Lida Guthrie, a single lady who had earned her pharmacist's license in 1940, 30 years after first going to work at Fenn's Drug Store. She retired about the time that Marge Hepburn returned to the workforce.

A landmark in the business community for 64 years renowned for its order and organization, Fenn's Drug Store had long glass-fronted shelves lining the north wall of the store that displayed all the drug stocks in "apple-pie order." Cosmetics and other home necessities lined the south wall. The Chelsea institution closed its doors at 116 South Main Street for the last time in 1962 and the week the drug store closed, Miss Guthrie told a *Chelsea Standard* reporter that when she had first started working there, customers arrived by horse and buggy and tied their rigs to the hitching posts that lined

Fenn's Drug Store was a landmark in the business community for 64 years. "Auntie" Lida Guthrie poses on far right.

Courtesy of the Robinson and Gallagher families

Main Street-which was still gravel. "Merchants started their business days by sloshing water in the stone gutters to clear away the previous day's refuse," she recalled.

Times had changed dramatically.

≈

Several years after Lida Guthrie retired, so did Brigadier General Herbert Vogel. After leaving the military, he served as chairman of the board of the Tennessee Valley Authority and as an advisor to the World Bank on flood control and water quality. He died one day after his 84th birthday, on August 29, 1984, and was buried in Arlington National Cemetery.

The Grove family owned and operated the last dime store in Chelsea until the 1980s—by that time the 5-and-10-cent-store had gone up to $1.00. Courtesy Chelsea Area Historical Society

Four-star General Dwight E. Beach left the U.S. Army and his command in the Pacific in 1968, then took a year to consider his options. He moved his family back to the ancestral farm in Lima Township. "This place has been in my family for nearly 150 years. It was the land that called me back," he says.

"No matter where in the world Dad lived, he managed to find a little bit of land for a garden—his roots to this farm ran very deep," adds his daughter Florence, whom he calls Twinkie. "He would have my mother mail him seeds even when he was in the jungle. And he had wine-making apparatus in most of the cellars where we lived." ("It wasn't drinkable, except by Navy people," the General adds with a grin.)

But when the veteran of countless South Pacific campaigns landed in Chelsea, he discovered that times—and Interstate 94—had made major inroads in the appearance of his farm as well as in the lives of many other farmers. The Beach farm, along with many others, was cut in two by the highway.

The next threat to the farm came when the power company informed the General that it was going to install high-tension power lines across his farm. "My father used his best Army vocabulary to dispute them," Twinkie Beach says, laughing. The General took them to court and the electrical company was only awarded a right-of-way, not ownership—and it was forced to pay seven times what had originally been offered as compensation.

Later, in 1990, another knock on the door informed the General that a crude oil pipeline was about to be installed on his property—and that his hedges and a good number of the 3,000 trees that he had planted would be demolished. Once again, he went to battle and won his case—though not, as of yet, all the trees that were casualties in that battle.

"I remember that all through our years of moving from base to base, my father would say with pride that not one acre of our farm had ever been sold. These incursions were terrible for him," his daughter says, adding, "On top of these personal things that happened to our farm, one of the biggest changes I've seen since moving here is the price of real estate. I read the Sunday ads and I'm astounded at what an acre of land will sell for."

≈

The same year in which General Beach retired, the current district court system was created. In 1968, Chelsea became eligible for a court. When the Chelsea State Bank moved to its new building on the corner of Orchard and Main Street, the bank's board of directors offered the old Glazier bank building to Washtenaw County as the 14th district court.

≈

Chelsea's quality of life took a significant step forward when the Chelsea Community Hospital welcomed its first patient on Tuesday morning, September 21, 1970. The hospital was a new tenant in the east half of a 40,000-square-foot building erected on the former peat marsh that had been a favorite haunt for generations of children.

Throughout the twentieth century, Chelsea village leaders had intermittently discussed the need for a local hospital. The nearest was at least a half hour away and during times of crisis—such as when the Interurban collided or flew off their tracks—local farmers or automobile owners would be pressed into service to rush accident victims to emergency rooms. Some died on the way there. By the time the discussion of a local hospital resurfaced in the 1960s, Washtenaw's population had mushroomed by 35% during the previous decade and Chelsea was home to three times as many people over the age of 65 as the county itself averaged. Partners and fellow physicians Michael Papo, Bruce Stubbs, and Jim Shadoan pressed for better facilities and more acute-care beds.

On June 10, 1970, village officers Paul Mann, Ferdinand Merkel, and Harold Jones met to charter the Chelsea Community Hospital, which was incorporated 16 days later. During the first year, one-fifth of all admissions were made by doctors Joseph Fisher and Charles Krausse.

The squat, H-shaped facility had been built for a franchised 110-bed skilled nursing, or extended care, unit, but within months of its founding, the community began demanding more. On January 1, 1973, the hospital's governing board purchased the hospital's building, equipment and 10.5 acres of land, making the Chelsea Community Hospital a private, nonprofit corporation, and plans developed through the years for expansions of facilities, health professionals, and staff.

In 1975, Willard Johnson became the first full-time administrator. When he took the job, he announced, "We want people to feel this is more than just a place to come when someone needs medical attention. We want it to be a pleasant place, a spot to hold a meeting, to eat a meal, to jog or walk our nature trail. We want to get away from the concept of being one of those dreary, fearful places."

Jimmy Carter, 1977-81 • Ronald Reagan, 1981-89
George Bush, 1989-1993

Carter declares embargo against U.S.S.R • U.S. refuses to attend Moscow Olympics • 52 Americans held hostage in Iran for 444 days • Divestiture of AT&T • ERA defeated • Sally Ride becomes first woman in space • U.S. peacekeepers killed in Lebanon • Grenada invaded by U.S. • "Live Aid" concert • Space shuttle *Challenger* explodes • AIDs • Iran-Contra hearings • Stock market on phenomenal rise • *Exxon Valdez* spills oil, covering 45 miles of Alaska's waters • Gen. Colin Powell becomes first black Chairman of the Joint Chiefs of Staff

U.S. POPULATION
216 million

Change Comes to Chelsea: The 1980s

Changes Come at a Dizzying Rate

John and Gloria Mitchell moved their family to Chelsea in 1981, the year they bought the Staffan Funeral Home on Park Street, much against the wishes of Gloria. "I had grown up in a tiny farming community in the thumb of Michigan and I always said I'd never subject my children to a tiny town," she says. "I quickly learned that this was a much more progressive area. We experienced firsthand the positive aspects of living in a farming community that also had access to Ann Arbor."

She remembers sitting in the office of the funeral parlor across from George and Catharine Staffan on George's seventieth birthday, February 12, 1981, while the Staffans advised the newcomers to go out into the community. "People are more willing to find you and welcome you," they urged.

"That was good advice. I've found Chelsea very accepting," Gloria says. When the Mitchells moved to town, they had one child in high school, one in middle school, and one in elementary school. All three couldn't wait to get away from the small town after graduation, their mother remembers. "Yet now our two boys are back and our daughter says that when she starts a family, she wants to move back here, too," she says with a smile.

"I came to Chelsea crying, but now I can't imagine living anywhere else. The downtown is wonderful. So are the people. You have the access to Ann Arbor for shopping and the lakes for recreation. There is so much available to us."

≈

Shortly after they arrived, the Mitchells co-chaired the Sesquicentennial committee and joined the belles and beaus who participated in the year-long celebration in 1984. Townsmen grew beards, women donned old-fashioned gowns for the series of parades, festivals, lectures, and community projects that marked the anniversary year.

One of the most significant projects to emerge from that celebration was the restoration of the Chelsea Depot. By the 1980s, it was only used for storage. An earlier restoration project had ended before the building was half done and some village people were calling for it to be torn down, Gloria Mitchell remembers.

She credits Will Connelly, a public relations expert and local newspaper columnist, with promoting the Depot's restoration. "Will Connelly had the vision. And he had the expertise to convince people to actually do something about it," she says. But first, the town had to determine just who owned the Depot, which had been built on former Congdon land. U.S. Representative Carl Pursell discovered that it was the property of the Michigan Central Railroad, and in 1985, the railroad sold the building to the town for $15,000.

The newly formed Chelsea Depot Association members decided to open a museum at one end of the building and a community room on the other. To do this, they raised $160,000 and formed a group of hardworking volunteers to renovate and restore the building. They sold bricks to raise funds and contacted railroading groups to help scrape peeling paint, fix trim, clean up the exterior and interior, and brush on a fresh coat of color. "It's an ongoing project," Gloria Mitchell says, 12 years after joining its board. In 1998, the association installed a kitchen in the building and raised $20,000 for a new roof.

～

"The last good time that everyone in Chelsea shared was the Sesquicentennial in 1984," says Steve Otto emphatically. "My friends and I were in our young twenties then and we had a blast. We dressed up as Keystone Cops and joined a caravan that went through Manchester and out to Waterloo. There were contests and picnics at the lake. It was a great time."

The biggest changes in those years?

"Too many new people. Too much building. I don't know everyone any more, like I used to when I was a kid," Otto says.

"People are getting older. Cars are getting newer and shinier. Kids are growing up. Building is going on. New people are moving to town. But I think we've had nice, steady growth," believes former village council president Rolly Spaulding.

"I served on the Economic Development Committee when I was

on the Village Council for two four-year terms in the 1950s and 1960s and I fixed the idea in my mind that we had to bring in more industry and get the town to grow," says Larry Chapman. "Now, I think we were wrong to do it. Why do we have to grow any more? I'd like to go back to the way it was."

In the 1980s, Chelsea saw more losses in the business community than the village had witnessed since the Depression years. At the end of that decade, Walter Leonard chronicled the changes in the business community in the pages of the *Chelsea Standard*:

Chelsea Pharmacy moved. So did the hardware and department store. Rockwell Spring Plant moved. Central Fibre went to Indiana. Except for the Chelsea Milling Company and Chelsea Products (which was sold to Dana, which built a 54,000-square-foot plant on Sibley Road under the name Ann Arbor Machine Company), Chelsea became a sort of ghost town.

When John and Gloria Mitchell moved to town with their children, seven empty buildings stood on Chelsea's Main Street.

H.S. Holmes built this exquisite Queen Anne Victorian home in the 1890s.

Courtesy Chelsea Area Historical Society

Architecture

To Preserve and Protect

Throughout the 1990s, the sounds of hammers, sandblasters, wallpaper scrapers, carpenters, painters, woodworkers, and metalworkers resounded through the East Middle Street neighborhood as John and Jackie Frank and Kim and Jim Myles began the lengthy and costly restorations of their nearly identical brick Queen Anne Victorian homes. Both couples are committed to preservation, but they took very different approaches to the renovations of their homes.

"During those years, we purposely didn't cover our first-floor windows so that people could see what we were doing," Jackie Frank says with a smile. "Our renovations quickly became community projects."

The Frank home, at 138 East Middle Street, and the Myles' home at 118 East Middle Street, were built by the same builder—whose name has disappeared into history—several years apart during the exuberant post-Civil War era when Chelsea began to boom. Originally, they were placed on adjacent lots; over time, the lots were subdivided and newer homes intervened.

The Myles' house is the older one, built around 1878 for Michigan State Senator J.S. Gorman, a politician, lawyer, and cigar manufacturer who made a substantial fortune with his tobacco business, which was located in the commercial building right next to his home. The house passed through a number of hands and during World War II, when housing was in short supply, it was divided into apartments.

The Franks' home was constructed sometime between 1885 and 1891 for Dr. George W. Palmer and his family. A village trustee, Dr. Palmer was a prominent physician and for many years the town's health officer. In 1900, the family moved to 145 Park Street and Daniel and Emma McLaren bought the house. McLaren was a businessman who headed McLaren & Son (dealers in hay, straw, and potatoes) and the McLaren-Holmes Bean Company, a joint venture with Harmon S. Holmes, McLaren's new next-door neighbor.

In 1936, Nettie Irene Notten moved the first hospital in Chelsea from the site of the present-day post office to 138 East Middle Street. Within the upstairs rooms babies were born, elderly people died, and residents were treated for every kind of medical complaint. The Franks have kept the surgical sink in place upstairs, as well as some medical supplies dating to that era.

After World War II broke out, this house was sold and divided into a rooming house for women who worked in Chelsea's defense industries. Later, it became a chiropractic clinic and apartment house, which is how the Franks found it when they moved to town in 1991.

According to architectural historian Lloyd Baldwin, who was hired to submit the home's application to the National Register for Historic Places,

The house reflects the popular Queen Anne style, expressed in a less common medium, brick. The house is less exuberant than one would commonly associate with the style, but still carries key features such as the broad overhanging roof with multiple gables, bracketry, large window openings, colored glass, and ornamental brick work. The interior retains a tremendous amount of historical integrity, and is outfitted with moldings, doors, and mantles that were purchased from one of the popular catalog suppliers of the day, as it appears the house plans themselves were obtained.

When the Franks bought their house in the early 1990s and the Myles bought its twin, the homes were begging for owners who would appreciate their history and correct the changes brought by time and circumstances.

The Franks had moved from an antebellum home in Kentucky and while there had become committed to historic preservation. Jim Myles was a builder with an appreciation for fine architecture and he had all the relevant skills to restore a home; Kim was a mortgage broker who knew the other side of the restoration process: the financing. Together, as the two couples planted their roots in the community, they founded Preservation Chelsea, an organization dedicated to protecting and preserving the historical character of the village. In their "leisure" time, they concentrated on restoring their houses.

"We wanted an 1880s Victorian, as authentic as possible to the period, with just enough adaptations to make the house livable for us," Jackie Frank explains.

The Myles, on the other hand, bought their home with the intention of opening a bed and breakfast. "We wanted to restore the house to its original structural appearance, but make the interior comfortable for modern-day living and entertaining," Kim Myles says.

Because many changes had been made over the course of a century, the couples researched the history of their homes and their neighbors' homes and consulted experts in historic preservation and decorative arts. "This kind of project is like fitting pieces of a puzzle together—it takes a while to get the whole picture intact," Jackie Frank says.

Arriving in Chelsea three years after the Franks had begun their work, the Myles were able to use the Franks' house and research as a starting point. In return, Jim Myles shared his building expertise with the Franks.

After the research, the real work began. The Franks carted 500 pounds of lead from the walls lining the former x-ray room, which had been installed in their home's original library. Both couples tore down fake paneling, ripped out tiny kitchens and bathrooms that had been wedged into nooks and crannies for latter-day apartments, removed old linoleum to find beautiful parquet floors, took down false ceilings, refinished original woodwork, rehung original pocket doors between parlors, updated existing plumbing and electrical systems, replaced roofing, rotting porches and ornamental work. The Myles also designed and began constructing a two-story carriage house that reflects the Victorian architectural style of the town.

The Franks did the initial deconstruction work themselves, then turned to subcontractors. Kim Myles estimates that her husband did 70% of their home's restoration himself, with the help of her father, repairing the original plaster walls, restoring woodwork, molding, and wrought-iron work that had disappeared over the years. They installed a brand new kitchen (though keeping the flavor of a turn-of-the-century kitchen) and enough bathrooms to accommodate bed-and-breakfast guests. Then they turned their dusty, musty third-floor attic into a spectacular master bedroom suite. Their innovations are not authentic to the original house, but harmonious with both the Victorian era and a twenty-first century lifestyle.

Then the decorating began.

The Franks wanted to replicate the decor typical of a late nineteenth century Victorian. They collected decorating hints from the scraps of wallpaper and colors they found when removing dozens of layers of papers and paint and they catalogued samples of every piece of wallpaper, paint, and fixture they removed—including a 1960s plastic chandelier—for future preservationists. Then, when the preparation work was done, they combined and installed 35 different wallpapers and borders in the four downstairs rooms, giving them an authentic Victorian appearance. Their decorating scheme is ornate, stunning, and historically accurate.

The Myles chose to bypass the traditional elaborate Victorian interior decor in favor of a simple paint scheme that calls attention to the home's elaborate woodwork, hand-grained doors, faux-marble mantles, stained glass windows, parquet floors, ornate staircase, and built-in cabinets. They also chose to retain several minor changes made to the exterior of their house over the years, among them an enlarged front porch and an enclosed back porch.

The Myles replaced the missing cast-iron roof crests and fence and then chose a typical Victorian color scheme for the exterior of the house. "A woman who had been a life-long member of the Congregational Church across the street came up to us after we had painted the beadwork, scrollwork, and woodwork and asked why we had added all those details. When we told her they had always been here, just obscured by dirt and white paint, she was astonished," Kim Myles says with a smile. "We have found treasures beneath a century of dirt, grime, and alterations."

The one original feature on both homes that bowed to modern costs and technology is the roof. Originally slate, the old roofs are tremendously expensive to replace. Jim Myles tracked down an asphalt shingle manufacturer who could replicate the look of a Victorian roof without the cost of a Victorian roof. The Franks followed suit. "You always have to make compromises when you're dealing with an entirely different time period. You just need to do it thoughtfully," Jim Myles says.

"This has become our life's work, our fun, and our passion," Jackie Frank says with a smile. "Before we bought this house, our children had grown up and moved into homes of their own and we decided that finally we could live the way we had always dreamed of living."

Like many homes in Chelsea, the Myles house has undergone several transformations in its long life. Courtesy of Jim and Kim Myles

"There are special challenges in restoring and renovating old homes—and often many surprises along the way—but the effort pays off in intangible ways," Jim Myles adds. "You form a link with the past when you do this kind of work. And you preserve a little corner of the past for future generations to see, appreciate, and perhaps, to understand."

~

When Elisha and James Congdon were growing up in Connecticut, just about every New England town shared a similar layout and pattern of development. A white church or two with tall steeples pointing to heaven stood at the head of a town green. Nearby would be a town hall and probably a schoolhouse. Homes and shops were clustered around the town green or on winding back streets running off from the green like crooked spokes radiating out from the center of a wheel. New England streets could never be relied upon to go in any particular direction; their rambling gaits usually followed cow paths or Indian trails.

New Englanders had immigrated to the New World because they were seeking freedom of religion and free speech. The visual prominence of the church, the town hall and the school in New England villages reflect the central position those institutions held in colonial lives.

A century or two later, when the Congdons moved to Michigan, America's focus had changed. Newcomers came looking for economic opportunity and land, for a place to settle down, raise families and make a living. The Congdons consciously designed their town to reflect those priorities.

There is no central town green in Chelsea. The village's shops and banks have always lined Main Street, the narrow road that runs straight between Stockbridge, to the north, and Manchester, to the south. The railroad runs east-west as it intersects the town. The depot, not a church, sits close to the village center. Originally, churches, schools, and the town hall were situated a block or two away from Main Street. Looking at Chelsea, there is no doubt that business was its business and that its founders were practical businessmen first of all.

The Congdon lands were surveyed in December 1849 and the village was platted in 1850. The original town consisted of six blocks, three west and three east of Main Street. Elisha Congdon took the eastern half, his brother the western.

The earliest homes were hastily built structures, designed to provide shelter just until time and money could be spared for something more ambitious. Elisha Congdon lived in three different houses at the 221 South Main Street site and their progression illustrates the changes taking place in the community. The father of 15 children built a log cabin as their first home. That burned to the ground in 1850, and he erected a typical modest Midwestern Victorian frame house. In 1860, with his village progressing well and money in his pocket from the sale of wheat and real estate, Elisha moved that house and built his dream house: a substantial square colonial home made of red brick. This house is an exact replica of one on West Huron Street that he passed many times on his way into Ann Arbor for supplies, but homes of these dimensions, made of brick, would have been familiar to him in his Connecticut home town.

The Congdons set the standard to which many would aspire, but few would equal—until, that is, Frank P. Glazier built his mansion on South Street.

The earliest homes in town contain some elements of the Greek Revival architectural style that was in vogue back East when the early settlers headed to Michigan. These homes are symmetrical two-story clapboard buildings, with a steeply pitched roof, a gable end that faces front, long and narrow small-paned windows, wide cornice boards, and often columns supporting a square front porch or side porch. The two earliest Greek Revival homes sit on Jackson Street, at 122 and 128. The Farmers' Supply building is a Greek Revival relic from the 1850s, originally used as a hotel on Main Street, although you have to know what you're looking for to see the original design beneath the changes. Next door, at 128 Jackson, is a "frame vernacular Greek Revival temple-front and wing" that stands one and one-half stories tall, according to Lloyd Baldwin. One of the finest residential Greek Revivals that is still a home sits at 160 East Middle Street.

The majority of the buildings in the original downtown, homes as well as businesses, rose between 1870 and the 1890s, following major fires. In the 1870s, the Italianate style arrived in town. Brick is used in both residential and commercial Italianate buildings, both as a deterrent to fire as well as a sign of prosperity. Outlines are tall and narrow. Windows are also long and narrow, often with arches at the top or ornamental brickwork. Roofs are flat and supported by ornate roof brackets or decorative details.

The next architectural trend to settle in town was almost strictly residential: the flamboyant Queen Anne style, where everything but symmetry and predictability could be incorporated into a house. This style was an architect's playground, with its varied combinations of steeply pitched roofs, interesting porches and balconies, ornate gingerbread trim, unusual windows (often stained-glass), heavy gables, and fancy chimneys.

Chelsea has fine examples of the Queen Anne style. While Elisha Congdon built a Georgian style home whose architectural roots are back East, his brother James built a Queen Anne Victorian. Other Queen Annes include the Frank and Myles' homes on East Middle Street, which may have been modeled after the architectural pattern books being published and circulated during America's Gilded Age. The Holmes House, at 146 East Middle Street, is an example of the same style. This residence, which gave Harmon S. Holmes' rival (Frank Glazier) a run for his money, has many of the trademarks of the Queen Anne style, inside and out: an elegant reception room, heavy ornate woodwork, pocket double doors, elaborately turned banisters rising to the second story in a hand-crafted staircase, stained-glass windows, bow windows, eyebrow windows, sleeping porch, nooks and crannies, high ceilings, elaborate built-ins, examples of early plumbing and a water cistern the size of a swimming pool to accommodate early plumbing facilities. The exterior is a blend of shingles and clapboards, with complex roof lines, a miniature balcony, ornate trim and gables facing in different directions.

The house also has a one-of-a-kind feature for Chelsea. "Every house in town had its own well, but my grandfather wanted to make sure that his family got the best water the town had to offer—after all, the privies were uncomfortably close to wells in those days," Dudley Holmes explains. The separate gray shingled structure immediately behind the house is actually a well house that once had a windmill to pump water directly into the house.

At the peak of the Queen Anne style in Chelsea, however, was the Glazier home on South Street, which was probably designed by Jackson architect Claire Allen. This was a joyously ornate Victorian with unusual and varied windows, tower rooms, nooks and crannies, gables, brackets, balconies, and a wide front porch. Originally, the house shared its large town lot with an elegant carriage house and formal gardens.

Unfortunately, some of the exquisite windows have been broken or obscured, the unusual front porch has been enclosed, and time, neglect and twentieth-century additions and changes have caused the home to lose its distinction. Now hidden at the back of the property behind a home and garage, the exquisite Glazier carriage house sags and crumbles, just barely able to hint at the high style in which the original owners' horses and carriages were maintained.

Architecturally and commercially, Frank Porter Glazier ushered Chelsea into a new century. His first building project, his home, reflected national tastes. His later projects, most of them commercial or public, reflected Frank Porter Glazier's taste. Just as Congdon had molded and shaped the village of Chelsea in its early years, Frank Glazier became the village's molder and shaper at the turn of the twentieth century.

By the time Glazier took over management of his father's drugstore on Main Street in 1880, the original wooden shops on both sides of Main Street had been destroyed by fires and replaced with fairly typical Midwestern Italianate brick storefronts.

In 1891, Glazier entered into partnership in the Glazier-Strong Oil Stove Company, with production facilities on the north side of the railroad tracks. The following year, Glazier bought out his partner and launched Glazier Stove Works, manufacturers of "brightest and best" oil and kerosene stoves. Fires in 1894 and 1895 destroyed the early plant buildings and Frank P. Glazier used this as an excuse to rebuild Chelsea in his own image.

He hired notable Jackson architect Claire Allen to spearhead this ambitious building project. A self-taught professional, Allen is responsible for designing a half-dozen courthouses in southeastern Michigan. Ironically, his first project for Glazier was a bank that would later became the courthouse here in Chelsea.

Glazier very deliberately made his mark on every direction of the compass in his home town: on the north, south, east, and west entries to the village as it existed in his day.

For the east-west road that cut the Congdons' village layout into two equal parts, Glazier commissioned the Eisele brothers, Alsatian-born and trained stonemasons, to build ornate stone gates. The gates on East Middle Street lead to Oak Grove Cemetery. The gates on West Middle Street lead to the Chelsea United Methodist Retirement Home, for which Glazier had provided the land and $5,000 to construct the home as a memorial to his mother.

The southern boundary of the village at the turn of the century-and the most eye-catching spot for visitors arriving from that direction—was the intersection of Main and South streets. Glazier commandeered the northwest corner for the Chelsea Savings Bank, a memorial to his father.

At the northern entrance of the village, he erected a massive, attention-grabbing industrial complex for the Glazier Stove Works. Glazier obviously wanted his hometown to put its best foot forward to visitors and customers coming from all directions.

Glazier also had his hand in just about every other major building project that occurred during the turn of the century.

A member of the Methodist Church, he had been urging church members to pull down the original church, built in 1858, and build a new one. Some of the congregation voiced their reluctance and the matter seemed to be in limbo until circumstances forced their hand. The church caught fire on January 8, 1899, and burned to the ground. Rumors circulated about Glazier's possible role in the fire, but nothing was ever proved. Glazier joined forces with George and Ida Palmer to help fund the construction of the new church and Glazier offered the services of his favorite architect, who designed a castellated bell tower and round rose window for the Romanesque-style building. The stones for the church were supplied by local farmers.

After the enthusiastic response to the new stone church, Glazier asked Claire Allen to plan the bank building. Allen's design speaks of strength, stability, age, power, and money—everything an investor wants his bank to have. The Beaux Arts Classical building, two-and-a-half stories high, was built of rock-faced granite laid in a random pattern by stonemason George Hindelang.

Twenty-five years earlier, Glazier's rival in the local banking industry, the Kempf Commercial & Savings Bank, had been erected on the southwest corner of West Middle and Main streets. This building, composed of yellow bricks, shows the simpler lines of the Classical Revival style then in fashion for commercial buildings.

Glazier also had Allen design a home for his daughter across South Street from his own palatial residence. The industrialist then planned his masterpiece: the redesign of his entire industrial complex. He wanted to let the world know his philosophy of life, labor, and rewards. Claire Allen designed monumental brick and stone buildings with traces of Flemish Revival features.

The first of the new generation of industrial buildings was

Glazier's office, at 113 Main Street. This was a building for the ages, a monumental stone building with a rounded end, again made of randomly dispersed rough-rock granite. Unfortunately, years later, even the granite stones couldn't prevent it from burning to the ground when the Heydlauff and Frigid Products stores suffered a fire in 1970.

The Clock Tower warehouse opened in 1906. Allen designed the building using the new and revolutionary Kahn System, which called for concrete reinforced with steel rods. The warehouse stands three stories high with inset bays, limestone detailing, and large windows (good lighting was a revolutionary concept for factory owners to consider offering their employees).

In 1907, the Clock Tower itself was finished. It rises 120 feet from its base to the top of its octagonal convex roof and has four Seth Thomas clock faces that are seven feet in diameter. They are capable of ostentatiously showing the entire Chelsea area—not to mention the employees who were paid by the hour—the correct time. Glazier was not just a philanthropist, but a pragmatist: after suffering heavy losses from two fires, he incorporated an enormous tank in the tower to hold 35,000 gallons of water.

Under construction at the same time was the adjacent Welfare Building. This facility was dedicated to the welfare of Glazier's employees, many of whom shared rooms in inexpensive boarding houses in town during the week and commuted to their homes and families in Detroit on weekends. Glazier decided to create a recreation center where his men could have wholesome, respectable entertainment. The Welfare Building was equipped with a swimming pool, theater, reading room, basketball court, billiards room, and meeting rooms.

Architectural historian Lloyd Baldwin credits J.H. Patterson, owner of National Cash Register of Dayton, Ohio, with the origin of the idea. Baldwin explains, "It was an example of corporate paternalism designed to counteract growing interest in unionism." It was also probably a mark of Glazier's sincere concern for his workers' well-being. Unfortunately, his employees had barely moved into the building before Glazier's financial scandal closed the doors of his stove works and Welfare Building.

Glazier's name can still be seen, engraved in stone on many of the buildings and his clock tower still towers over nearly every point in town. Glazier's monumental building phase peaked the year of his political downfall, and in part, caused the downfall, as he reached into state funds to underwrite his massive expansions.

~

Many other names through the years have also been associated with the buildings that make Chelsea special. The Maroneys, Irish immigrants, built many of the early frame homes in town. Frank Staffan was a skilled carpenter who slipped into the mortuary business through the back door, by constructing coffins for customers, as early as 1852. John P. Foster was another local builder whose imprint rests on many Chelsea landmarks.

According to John Keusch, "John P. Foster was a member of an Alsatian German family who is credited with building the Congregational Church, St. Mary's Parsonage, and numerous large buildings in Chelsea. Edward Beissel, John Foster's grandson, still lives in Chelsea."

Among others whose names are cast in stone are Joseph and Martin Eisele, gifted Old World stone cutters and masons who were trained in their native homeland, Alsace-Lorraine. The Eiseles arrived in Chelsea in time to help make Frank Glazier's monumental projects a reality. Their legacy can be seen throughout Washtenaw County as well as within Chelsea: in the entrance gates to the cemetery and Methodist Retirement Home, in the walls of the Glazier bank building, and the Chelsea United Methodist Church. Their nephew, Paul Hoffman, wrote in 1978, "In the years of 1918 and 1921, respectively, Martin and Joseph, two kindly old men, their bodies bent and maimed with the hazards of their occupation, were summoned to their last journey, taking with them their skills."

~

"The downtown is what attracted me to Chelsea," says modern-day architect Scott McElrath, a University of Michigan School of Architecture graduate who moved to town in 1994 and opened his own shop, Dangerous Architects, on Main Street. He takes a swig of coffee and an early-morning break from his telephone, fax machine, computer, and design board, leans back in his chair and discusses Chelsea's architectural heritage and future.

"Chelsea's architectural fabric is eclectic, with a little bit of every-

Time transformed the Maroney's small but elegant Greek Revival gem into a contemporary-looking home. Often in Chelsea, detective work is necessary to date a building and trace it to its architectural roots.

Courtesy Chelsea Area Historical Society

thing," he says. "The courthouse is Romanesque, heavy and very masculine, for example. Many of the downtown buildings are Italianate. The Sylvan Town Hall is not quite like anything else I've ever seen before, certainly not a building that you can put a label on."

But, McElrath quickly adds, "What is just as impressive as the village's architecture is the town planning and the street layouts. Everything is plotted on a grid. What is incredible about Chelsea are the nice, well-kept perpendicular streets that form symmetrical blocks. The street widths and scale are inviting and they give a personal atmosphere that you don't see in surrounding towns, which are designed with broad avenues that can feel threatening or remote. This is a place that invites people to stroll down streets, visit with neighbors, greet strangers.

"In fact," he continues, "I can't praise the forefathers enough for their design. They did a great job. And the local builders gave a harmonious look to the town by being fairly consistent in the buildings' height and setback. There is a very nice sense of proportion here."

Unlike the early builders, McElrath is working hard to avoid being painted into a niche. "I think that's the kiss of death for creativity," he says. "I'm always researching new ways to do things." The projects on his drawing board include the formulation of a master plan for a teen facility on the University of Michigan campus; the renovation of Chelsea's village office building housing the police department; the design for Jim and Kim Myles' carriage house; the creation of the shrine dedicated to St. Mary for the town's Catholic Church; the blueprints for several residences on the outskirts of town; and the renovation of the old Sylvan Town Hall. ("We have tried to be sensitive to its history as well as its architecture, but the bleachers on the second floor, for instance, had to go. Ultimately, the owners need to make money to stay in business.")

"I love designing unusual, one-of-a-kind buildings, but since taking up residence in Chelsea, I have developed an affinity to historic commercial buildings and old houses," the architect adds. "I think the name of my firm, Dangerous Architects, says it all—that architecture can be emotive, not just mundane. Good architecture, no matter what the style, is charged with emotion, passion. You see that here in Chelsea when you walk down the streets of town."

Fire!

Fires were a devastating reality of life in a small town, as well as on the outlying farms. Most houses and all early shops and businesses were wooden buildings heated by wood or coal and lighted by kerosene lamps—all of them frequent causes of fire. Untold numbers of times, soot-plugged chimneys would catch fire and homeowners would scramble onto their roofs to put blazes out. Other times, sparks from fast-flying trains ignited roofs or piles of building materials sitting too close to the tracks. It wasn't uncommon to see homes with ladders permanently leaning against the home for emergencies.

Chelsea's first major recorded fire took place in 1870 and destroyed the entire west-side business district of Main Street, including the town hall, which contained all of Chelsea's early public records. Another devastating fire took place six years later, destroying the northeast business district and the Congregational Church and parsonage. But it was not until May 4, 1888, that the first fire station was built, on the back of the town hall on West Middle Street.

According to Jim Gaken, a longtime volunteer fireman and fire chief, the building was made of corrugated sheet iron at a cost of $344.65, which included $4.00 for painting. In July the village purchased a hook and ladder wagon for $268.00. Firefighters would unwind a rope according to the number of men available, then each grabbed part of the rope and pulled the wagon to the fire. The wagon carried ladders, buckets, pike poles, and kerosene lanterns.

In 1988, Jim Gaken wrote a history of the first century of Chelsea's Fire Department, the best record of the ups and downs, good times and hot times the volunteer company endured in its first 100 years. Gaken was a third-generation firefighter. His grandfather, Ed Gentner, joined the department March 2, 1907, and served 35 years. His Uncle Floyd Gentner was a member for 30 years. Gaken himself served with the fire department from 1947 until 1981; during 18 of those years, he was chief. His son, Larry, joined the department in 1978.

Gaken wrote that in 1889, the town purchased two chemical wagons for $1,108.45. Although he never saw a photograph of these wagons, he believed that they were hand-drawn and equipped with soda-acid fire extinguishers. The bicarbonate of soda and sulfuric acid reacted and produced carbon dioxide gas with sufficient pressure to expel the extinguisher's water.

The bell in the town hall belfry sounded the alarm and summoned help in the early days of the village. When Frank Porter Glazier

Office Hours from 9 A. M. to 12 M., and from 1 to 5 P. M. Saturday Evening from 7 to 8 o'clock.

Office of Chelsea Municipal Electric Light and Water Works Plant,

Folio *130*

M *Woodman Hall*   Chelsea, Michigan, MAY 20 1907, 190

To Chelsea Municipal Electric Light and Water Works Plant, Dr.

For Electric Lighting
For Water from APR 1 1907, 190, to MAY 1 1907, 190, as below specified:

Received Payment, *J. D. Watson*, Collector.

Electric Light Rates must be paid the last of each month.

Chelsea's first electric lights were brought to town by Frank P. Glazier. So too was the public water system. In 1898, Glazier sold his Electric Light and Water Works Plant to the village.

Courtesy of Scott Otto

sold the electric light and water works to the village in 1898, a steam whistle became the official announcement of a fire. Later, the woman serving at the telephone switchboard became responsible for answering the fire phone and blowing the fire whistle.

One of Chelsea's most civic-minded citizens, Howard F. Brooks, served as fire chief from 1904 until 1944 and participated in the fire department until his death in 1954. He was also a justice of the peace, and all hearings dealing with minor law infractions, for speeding, drunkenness, assaults, and minor thefts, were held in his home or the town hall. He presided over all elections, administered oaths, and in his spare time worked as a masonry contractor and founded the Crescent Sporting Club at Blind Lake. "Fires were far more frequent in those days, with coal- and wood-burning stoves and furnaces," John Keusch remembers. "Howard Brooks was a busy man. He was active and in charge when fires occurred."

In 1917, during Fire Chief Brooks' years on the force, the fire station was moved to a wood frame structure behind Merkel's Furniture Store. By this time, the hand-pulled hook and ladder truck had been converted so that it could be drawn by horses. The person who hitched his team of horses for the fire call was paid 50 cents.

After the water system was installed in Chelsea, fire hoses, with a nozzle at one end and a hydrant wrench at the other, were rolled around large spools secured to the back of the fire wagon, and later, fire truck. When firemen reached the site of the fire, they attached the hoses to the nearest fire hydrant.

Once, Ed Gentner responded to a fire alarm and saw a team of horses hitched to the post that was reserved for the fire department. "He thought he knew the owner, so he hitched the team to the hook and ladder and proceeded to the fire," Gaken wrote years later. "Upon returning to the station, he found, much to his amazement, that the team of horses…didn't belong to a friend, but to a stranger. The gentleman told him it was alright (*sic*) to use his team for the fire and if the occasion arose again, to go ahead and do it again. That, my dear readers, is how close my grandfather came to being hung for a horse thief."

Ed Gentner had a close call in the fire that destroyed "John the Greek's" candy and ice cream parlor. According to Gaken, the fire caused the floor to collapse. The ammonia cylinder required for the manufacture of ice cream and candy exploded, releasing a devastating cloud of ammonia gas. Ed Gentner was trapped in the basement of the building, carrying a kerosene lantern and a two-and-a-half-inch hose line. The ammonia extinguished the lantern, warning Gentner of the lack of oxygen in the air. He put his head over the nozzle tip of the hose and managed to get enough oxygen from the water flow until he could crawl to safety in the pitch dark by following the fire hose out of the building.

At first, firefighters wore their everyday clothes when they responded to a call. Later, the regulars purchased their own rubber boots and rubber coats. In time, a rubber hat similar to a sailor's sou'wester was added to their ensemble. Eventually the town agreed to purchase one dozen fire helmets and a dozen boots, which were stored on the trucks. "But, there were times when someone that normally wore a size 12 ended up with a size 10 boot. Also remember that a dozen of each were purchased, but there were 18 men on the department," Gakan wrote.

From the Merkel's location, the fire station moved to Palmer's Garage and the equipment was updated. In 1918, the first motor truck (a combination chemical and hose cart mounted atop a Model T Ford chassis) was purchased for $2,000. By 1942, Chelsea's newest fire truck was mounted on a Chevrolet chassis. It had a front mount pump and was equipped with a 500-gallon tank so that water could be carted to rural fires. For many years, when large fires burned outside town, milk haulers would respond and fill their milk cans with water, dipping them into a creek or lake, then dumping the water onto the tank at the back of that fire truck.

The Chelsea Fire Department stopped its training exercises to pose for this photograph in 1909. Long-time Fire Chief Howard Brooks, in a white straw hat, stands in the front and center, holding a coat.

Courtesy Chelsea Area Historical Society

Mechanization offered a whole new set of challenges for fire-fighters, Gaken pointed out in his memoirs. Occasionally so much time elapsed between alarms that the gasoline would, unbeknownst to the firefighters, evaporate from the fire truck or the battery would lose its charge. These circumstances could result in costly delays.

In the Gaken/Gentner home, when Jim Gaken was a boy and the fire whistle blew at night, Grandmother Gentner would call "central" to learn the fire's location. Jim's job was to grab the red fire coat and rubber boots and position them at the front door so his grandfather could put them on before dashing to the fire station. The whistle blew a certain signal to indicate the ward in which the fire was located.

Once the telephone switchboard was automated, fire phones were placed in private residences where homeowners would be paid to answer the calls.

"A lot of the firemen's residences had storm windows and were better insulated, so the whistle couldn't be heard as well," Gaken wrote. "Another whistle was installed on South Main Street…Even then, it seemed hard to hear. The wives started a phone system of calling to help alert the men when there was an alarm."

Even with the improved alarm system, tragedies occurred. During World War II, the Stofer farmhouse at 20900 North Territorial caught on fire. Neighbors were unable to extinguish the flames because their water source, North Lake, was frozen solid. Probably because of the frigid weather, the fire burned slowly enough that the men were able to save everything in the house—including the bath-tub—except for the things in the bottom kitchen cupboards. ("Perhaps because they were unaware that cooking utensils were stored so low," one wife later speculated.) When Irene Stofer returned home from school that day, all that was left of her home were smoldering ruins, the stone chimney and the bathtub in the front yard.

In 1945, the village bought the municipal building and remod-eled it for use as a fire station, but as fire trucks became larger, the station's floor joists were unable to support the vehicles' weight. Floors started cracking and walls started buckling. A second drawback was the station's single door, which meant that if the truck in front of the door failed to start, it had to be pushed out of the way in order to make way for the other two trucks.

Finally, on November 2, 1963, the Chelsea Fire Department moved into a new station, with four bays. Eight years later, firemen were equipped with small radios, which could monitor calls. These, in time, were replaced with pagers.

Throughout the history of the fire department, volunteers like the Gakens and Gentners raised much of the funding for new equipment and facilities themselves, through carnivals, car washes, dances, feather parties (playing bingo with turkeys, chickens, ducks, and geese as prizes), homecoming celebrations, and even a wrestling match.

The biggest fire George Staffan ever saw—and he was born in 1911—was the fire that destroyed the old wooden warehouse situated alongside the railroad tracks, where several grain elevators now stand. "It was a large wooden barracks and when it caught fire, it exploded with flames. The wind was from the north. My father—and everyone else in town—kept a sharp eye on the roof of his home. The trains had to stop so that the firemen could run a hose across the railroad tracks."

Staffan, like many other longtime residents, remember the day in 1970 when the Heydlauffs' appliance store on Main Street, just south of the railroad tracks, burned to the ground. The beautiful two-story stone building with a curved north side burned with such intensity that even the stone walls couldn't be salvaged—they were reduced to ashes.

One of the most devastating fires in recent memory occurred at Heydlauff's Appliance in the former Glazier office building during the 1970s. Courtesy of the Heydlauff family

Operation Desert Storm • Dow Jones Industrial tops 3,000 for first time • Clarence Thomas is nominated to the Supreme Court, resulting in charges of Sexual Harassment • World Trade Center bombed • Congress votes to reduce federal budget deficits • "Brady Bill" is passed • Sexual harassment suits are filed against President Clinton • O.J. Simpson is charged with murder • Major League baseball players strike • Americans flock to see *Titanic* • *Seinfeld* shoots its last episode • Monica Lewinski and the Clinton scandal consume newspaper headlines • Millennium fears and fever shake the world

U.S. POPULATION
263,814,032

The Close of Another Century: The 1990s

The Purple Rose Blooms—And So Does Chelsea

By the beginning of the twentieth century's last decade, downtown Chelsea was looking bleak. Residents will tell you that five, seven, or even a dozen storefronts were glaringly empty and other local business people were considering a move from Main Street to a new commercial area just south of town. Malls in Jackson and Ann Arbor began infringing on local businesses. Main Street was deserted by six o'clock every night. Real estate prices were dropping. The town was peppered with "For Sale" signs. Local businessmen and Chamber of Commerce members were increasingly concerned about the future of Chelsea.

Was it destined to become a ghost town, reduced to serving as a bedroom community for the cities to the east and west?

"The early 1990s was a time when we saw more housing was for sale and businesses closing than at any time in our history," Larry Chapman remembers. "With more cars and greater affluence, people were more mobile. New malls and shopping centers were pulling people away from the shops and businesses in our downtown."

The Downtown Development Authority gradually became a visible and influential presence in the community, working hard to convince taxpayers to improve sidewalks, plant trees, and publicize the benefits of a beautiful Midwestern downtown. Newcomers like Jim and Kim Myers and John and Jackie Frank joined with others to form Preserve Chelsea, a community action group committed to the preservation of the historic fabric of the town. Old-timers argued with newcomers over some of the suggestions for improving their beloved town—but all agreed that it was a place worth saving.

"It's amazing how many businesses here have lasted a century or more, into the third and fourth generation," says Mark Heydlauff, citing the Winans, Holmes, Lanes, Merkels, Staffans, and Daniels families as examples.

A member of the third generation to run Heydlauff's Appliance

Store on Main Street, Mark Heydlauff's family has weathered years of door-to-door sales, the Depression, two world wars, the passing of the railroad age, the coming of the age of mega-malls and on-line shopping, and a devastating fire that destroyed their store and all its inventory, causing the family to start all over again in 1970.

For many years, Chelsea Lumber Company was operated from this building across from the clock tower. Courtesy Chelsea Lumber Company

"There is a camaraderie within the Chelsea business community that was forged long before my generation," he says, leaning back in his office chair early one Saturday morning. "There is a commitment here in town to support local businesses—and that dates back to the early days of Chelsea's founding. That commitment is what has kept us—and others like us—in business so long."

He believes that each generation within a family business feels increasingly more responsibility to maintain that community relationship and their family business. "We all know that studies prove there is a very low percentage of success when a business gets to the third generation," he points out. "Chelsea's record is extraordinary, really. But it's not easy."

"As a viable, thriving, independent downtown, Chelsea has succeeded where others have become a disappearing breed," says Lloyd Baldwin, historic preservation consultant responsible for researching and writing Chelsea's Historic District Review. "In part," he adds, "the economic downturn of the village in the 1980s saved the town. It was preserved in its original form until the 1990s, when a nationwide movement renewed commitment to preserving and highlighting the village's architectural and cultural resources."

Then, at the right moment, along came a great idea and the people who could implement that idea.

∼

On the walls of Bob Daniels' office at the Chelsea Lumber Company are mementos of his family's history in Chelsea. A 1924 poster illustrates another Daniels endeavor: "Dodge Brothers Motor Cars, Chelsea, Michigan." A framed advertisement for the lumber company's predecessor, the Chelsea Lumber, Grain & Coal Company, announces its motto: "Where The Home Begins." A newspaper clipping from 1917 announces the marriage of Gertrude Estella Storms to Warren Ruel Daniels, and points out,

"The wedding was a complete surprise to even the nearest and most intimate friends...Both are popular young people and graduates of the Chelsea High School. The groom is a successful young businessman, treasurer of the Chelsea Elevator Company and serving his second term as village clerk. They will live at South and Grant Streets."

"Actually, the name was originally *McDaniels*," Bob Daniels says, as he catches a visitor glancing at the historical materials. "My grandfather was an auctioneer named Edward who liked the name on the sign 'Eddie Daniels, Auctioneer,' and kept it."

Eddie's son Warren in time became secretary/treasurer of the Chelsea, Lumber, Grain & Coal Company, whose headquarters was a three-story brick building at the corner of Main Street and the railroad tracks, where the Chelsea Milling Company grain elevators now sit.

My grandfather, W.R. Daniels, was someone who had great respect in the town," Bob Daniel's son Jeff says. "People called him 'Sporty' and I've heard stories about how he'd go to Jack & Sons Barbershop during the Depression, hear about someone down on his luck, and slip the guy $20. When he was told that he couldn't be sure when he would see the money again, he always said, 'It doesn't matter.' He taught my father and my father taught my brother, sister, and me not to lend money expecting to get it back. 'It's not about getting it back. It's the giving that's important,' W.R. always said."

Warren's son, Bob Daniels, born in 1929, was inducted into the business world at an early age. In the 1940s, when Bob was 15, his father gave him the authority to receive, test and dump wheat into the elevators and to load beans onto rail cars. On the other side of the grain elevators ran the bean track, which had a chute going right into freight cars to load beans.

After the Korean War, when Bob Daniels returned to his roots in Chelsea, his family's business had begun to focus exclusively on the building trades. They sold off their interests in the grain storage business, the bean business, and the coal business and created the Chelsea Lumber Company.

Through four generations, the Daniels family has numbered among Chelsea's prominent families and among the leading agitators for gentle change—occasionally, a change back to the original vision of Chelsea's founders.

"In the 1960s, when times were hard for young families, Bob

Daniels would help a couple get a start in life, by lending the capital to build a home because banks wanted 30% down and that was a stretch for some folks," Larry Chapman says. The lumber company provided the materials and financed the new homeowners until the structure was up. Then the banks could see equity and would agree to a mortgage." The Daniels family, Chapman believes, is responsible for the first postwar building boom within Chelsea's village boundaries.

"In my estimation, there are four men in Chelsea who made a significant difference here—and who could have gone anywhere and done just as well," says John Keusch. He lists Bob Daniels, banker P.G. Schaible, industrialist Larry Dietle, and auto dealer George Palmer. "They are all members of the same generation, interestingly. Together they worked to make a positive difference in their hometown."

⁓

By 1990, Chelsea was a community struggling to maintain its identity. "We had a terrific downtown, a strong history in business, 50 lakes within a 10-mile radius, the Pinckney and Waterloo recreation areas," Bob Daniels points out. "But the downtown was nearly dead and we faced a major decision. We could let it die. Or we could figure out new uses for the downtown and how it could complement, but not try to compete with, the malls."

One day in 1990, after discussing Chelsea's dilemma with friends and speculating about the possibility of luring a sit-down restaurant to town, Bob Daniels began casting feelers to entrepreneurs who might be interested in taking a chance on Chelsea. One well-known Ann Arbor restaurant manager told Daniels, "Chelsea is too small." But a day or so later, he walked past the restaurant table where Daniels and his wife were sitting and placed beside his plate a business card with the name "Craig Common" and his phone number written on the back.

Within days, Daniels and several other Chelsea businessmen had given Common and his wife a tour of Chelsea. Common was hooked and told them he had a financial backer.

The backer, however, told Common that Chelsea was "too small."

"Give me 24 hours," Daniels told Common.

He sat down with a piece of paper and wrote down the names of six people he thought would be able—and might be interested in—putting up $30,000 to launch a restaurant.

They all said yes.

"Craig is a master at running a restaurant," Daniels says, simply. "Chelsea is a jewel and sometimes the people closest to it forget that. Sometimes, it just takes a little reminder to get it moving. My goal is always to urge people to imagine what we can be—and then reach for it."

"Bob Daniels is a master at seeing what needs to be done and then quietly setting out to get it done," John Keusch says.

≈

At the same time, another Daniels family member was beginning to make plans for his hometown. Actor Jeff Daniels and his wife Kathleen had moved back to Chelsea from New York City in 1986. "I spent the next four years, between movies, playing golf. I loved being here, but I missed the creative energy that comes from being with other actors," Jeff Daniels explains on a break from filming *Escanaba in da Moonlight.*

He began working on an idea to create a regional theater that would help develop local and regional talent, not only actors, but also stage managers, scene painters, playwrights. He searched for a location to stage his idea and bought an old, abandoned garage across from the Staffan-Mitchell Funeral Home, on Park Street.

One day shortly before the curtain went up on Jeff Daniels' idea, a man walked up to him in the theater and introduced himself as Craig Common. He said he was thinking about opening a restaurant in town and asked Jeff Daniels if he would still be here in five years.

"I can remember thinking, 'I have put out $300,000 of my own money and I have absolutely no idea if this theater will fly…'

"Of course I will," the actor told the prospective restaurant owner with a bright smile. Common opened his restaurant in W.P. Schenk's former department store on Main Street. Within weeks, restaurant critics and theater critics from throughout the region had visited, sampled and written rave reviews—of the theater and the restaurant. Chelsea was once again on the map.

"I didn't dream up the idea of the theater just to revitalize Chelsea—but I was pretty confident that when people had a reason to come to Chelsea, its businessmen and civic leaders could find a reason for them to stay and look around, maybe spend some money," Jeff Daniels says.

Chelsea native Jeff Daniels opened the Purple Rose Theatre Company during the early 1990s. Courtesy of Photographic Works and the Purple Rose Theatre Company

The newly renovated Purple Rose opened in 2001. Courtesy of Purple Rose Theatre Company

"The theater opening was scary for Jeff and Kathleen in the beginning," his father acknowledges. "They were experimenting with a pretty novel idea—to turn their backs on New York and L.A., and promote Midwestern actors and playwrights. But they had a dream. Jeff wanted to use his career to communicate with—and help—people back home. And he has. Most theaters in Michigan struggle to stay alive. But not this one."

"From the time my father was a little kid, his father told him, 'Make sure you leave a place better than you found it,'" Jeff Daniels says. "My father told his kids the same thing. And we have all tried to follow that advice."

Several years after opening the Purple Rose Theatre Company, when Jeff and Kathleen Daniels knew that their venture would be a success, they decided to make another move to benefit people in the arts. Kathleen Daniels, who had attended St. Mary's Catholic School, as had generations of Chelsea's children, worried about the fate of the old building as it stood vacant. The Daniels bought the school and turned it over to the Chelsea Center for the Development of the Arts.

"I had a great teacher who helped me discover acting and encouraged me when I needed encouraging. We wanted to do the same thing for the boy who wanted to play the piano or the girl who was great at the saxophone," Daniels says.

∾

One cold afternoon in January, longtime friends Julie Sverid and Mary Lou Severin sip tea in Sverid's dining room and reminisce about their years in Chelsea. These women represent a new breed of community-minded activitists: newcomers who have made volunteering a full-time job.

When their children were small, they joined play groups and Bible studies. When their children were toddlers, they pushed them on park swings while discussing community projects. They have worked for the Educational Foundation; participated in school programs, planning meetings, and the PTA; and helped orchestrate the mammoth community project called Timber Town.

"Timber Town, in my eyes, was one of the highlights of life here in Chelsea in the 1990s," Julie says.

John and Mary Lou Severin moved to town in 1985, when their son was a baby. "We had been living and working in Ann Arbor, but I went very part-time and we were ready to settle down when J.P was born," Mary Lou says. "We didn't know exactly what we wanted, but we knew that we'd recognize it when we saw it."

Their realtor drove them to one new subdivision after another and Mary Lou said no—again and again. Then the realtor brought the couple to Chelsea and drove up to the 1920s-era house where they now live. "I saw the old trees, kids playing on the sidewalks, the big front porch, porch swing, and basketball hoop, and I didn't have to see anything else. I knew this was the place for us," Mary Lou remembers.

A native of Detroit, it took her awhile to adjust to small-town life, she recalls. "I was walking the baby when a woman I had never seen came up to me and told me how much she liked the flowers I'd been planting. That was my first introduction to small-town life, where everyone knows what everyone else is doing."

At first, she was taken aback—"but I quickly discovered that it wasn't claustrophobia I was feeling, but a wonderful sense of security, stability, and safety," she says.

Julie Sverid moved to Chelsea several years after the Severins, when her husband, John Rutherford, took a job with the Chelsea Milling Company shortly before their two daughters were born. "We had lived in the Ann Arbor area and knew all the options available, so coming to a small town was a personal choice," she explains. "What I like here is how people all feel that we can make a difference, that our voices aren't lost in a big city. There's a sense of intimacy and immediacy that you don't see in a lot of other places."

The first joint project shared by the two friends was the elaborate children's playground north of town, known as Timber Town. It took a year of organization, tremendous community participation, and one very long week to accomplish. Julie Sverid served as the motivating force and organizer, Gloria Mitchell as her co-chair and coordinator of the project, Jim Myles as construction superintendent, Mary Lou Severin in charge of public relations and communications, hundreds of children wearing hard hats collecting signatures for volunteers, local businessmen contributing materials, prison inmates toting telephone poles, and hundreds of volunteers who did everything from scrutinizing blueprints to preparing the land, carrying lumber, sawing lengths of timber, babysitting volunteers' children, mixing gallons of lemonade, hammering countless nails, trucking materials, and a hundred other jobs.

"The main reason I wanted to get involved was to promote a

chance for natives to get to know newcomers. This was a community project that really did involve the entire community, in a wonderful and positive way," Julie Sverid says. "This was the closest thing I've ever seen to an old-fashioned barnraising."

Everyone involved still cherishes memories of faces from that week. The look on the prisoners' faces when they earned a standing ovation for their hard work. The faces of the hundreds of volunteers when the ribbon was cut and they watched an army of kids dash onto the playground, laughing and shouting. The joy of the children.

~

"The town is getting too big. I hate to see the farms replaced by urban sprawl," Merle Barr says.

"I used to know everyone in town. Now my wife and I can go to the Common Grill for dinner and not see one person we know," observes George Staffan.

"I appreciate the fact that newcomers think the town is beautiful and they want to preserve it the way it used to be, but we've done just fine all these years and I don't want any regulations telling me what I can or can't do with my business," George Winans says. He is referring to the controversial historic district ordinance which has been presented to the village for approval.

As an example of the way strict preservation regulations could affect local businesses, he points to the rebuilding the Heydlauff family had been forced to do after their original store, which once served as Frank P. Glazier's offices, burned to the ground. "If they had been required to rebuild a replica of that two-story stone store, they could never have done it."

~

"There's a bit of push and pull going on between the newcomers and the old-timers these days," Julie Sverid acknowledges, quickly adding, "but I think that's true anyplace you go. We all know that we can learn from each other, share a vision, and work together to make good things happen." She lists countless examples: the level of cooperative effort that went into building Timber Town, the restoration of Chelsea's Main Street, the public meeting in 1995 where community members shared their vision for the future, school and community activities, restoration of the Depot, the goals and activities for the Community Endowment Fund and the Educational Foundation.

Bob Daniels once wrote me a letter that I still cherish," Mary Lou Severin says. "In it, he outlined what every public citizen should know, that *'Striving to make the Chelsea area what it is capable of being is a never-ending process that demands the attention and the efforts of all who are willing to contribute their time.'*

"That says it all, in my estimation."

"There are so many well-meaning people and we all share a deep love of Chelsea," Julie says, with a nod toward her long-time friend. "This isn't a place to pass through. It's a place where you settle and put your roots down."

"The newcomers are just like the first settlers who came to Chelsea. They want a good place to raise their families, to be able make a living, live comfortably and have a voice in what is happening—and will happen—in their community. I would imagine that that is what every person throughout Chelsea's history has been searching for."

≈

One of the Cavanaugh Lake cottages owned by Frank Porter Glazier is now the home of David and Kathleen Salsburg Clark, president of the Chelsea Historical Society and a writer who has chronicled Chelsea's people and places for years in the pages of the *Chelsea Standard*.

Although she lived in Detroit while growing up, she spent summers on the lake with her grandparents in the cottage they bought from the Glazier family in 1917. Kathleen Clark cherishes a deep and abiding interest in Chelsea's history and a passion for preserving it for the future. On Saturday afternoons, either Clark, Marjorie Whipple Hepburn, or Preservation Chelsea President Kim Myles open the town's museum in the old village Depot and welcome visitors.

On the days when the OPEN sign sits in the Depot window, tourists passing through town spend a quiet half hour scanning the old photographs, inspecting the displays, and comparing former pictures of the town with what they see when they walk up and down the sidewalks. Sometimes a member of the team who restored the Depot in the 1990s will drop in. School children come armed with questions for a classroom project. Or an amateur genealogist digging for a root or two will come with questions or old photographs. Thanks in large

Renovated in 2000, Glazier's Clock Tower building remains the focus of Chelsea's downtown.

Courtesy McKinley Commercial Properties

measure to the efforts of Kathleen Clark and Marjorie Hepburn, the historical society has amassed a treasury of old pictures, papers, and memorabilia.

"We're at an important crossroads in Chelsea's history right now," Kathleen Clark says, as she catalogues a collection of antique postcards recently donated to the museum. "Times are changing very fast—and Chelsea is changing very fast, too. When that happens, memories and memorabilia slip through our fingers and are lost to history forever. Our job is to remind people of the treasures associated with our past. And our job is to preserve the stories of days that are now gone by, so that future generations will understand what life was like here, what the people were like here. I think that is vitally important."

The New Millennium: 2000 and Beyond

Childhood in the early days of the New Millennium has probably changed more than at any other time in Chelsea's history. Saige and Jenica Rutherford love to play with dolls (American Girl Dolls these days), engage in imaginative games, pore over homework assignments, swing on swings, rollerskate, fuss with their hair, giggle with friends, and walk their dogs. All of these are activities that generations of little girls have pursued in Chelsea, but now their attention is also claimed by video games, computer games, and schedules. The Rutherfords play soccer, take dance lessons, swim on teams, attend Girl Scout meetings and Sunday School classes. "Some days it just seems that we get up, look at our calendar and run. And we keep checking our calendar until bedtime," their mother, Julie Sverid, observes at the end of a hectic day.

Boys' schedules are just as full, with Scouts, the variety of sports programs, organized clubs, and leagues.

And, meanwhile, increasingly more families have two working parents, or only one parent. Divorce, remarriage, stepchildren, stepparents, stepbrothers and stepsisters complicate the family tree.

~

Grown-ups' lives are also complicated by changes taking place in society. Soon after his reelection as Chelsea Village president, Richard Steele outlines some of the most pressing challenges the village council faces. "There is a lot more pressure now for growth," he observes. "Chelsea and the area around Chelsea are hotbeds for growth. The biggest change of all is the disappearance of the farms that have been here for generations."

Steele also cites the issue of a bypass around Main Street. Under discussion for decades, the bypass idea has renewed interest since traffic jams began to plug Main Street between the hours of two and six o'clock P.M., on weekdays. "We're discussing where the southern terminus of a bypass should be located—and where it should run west of town. We all agree, however, on the northern end. It should be Werkner Road."

Although a bond issue to renovate the old Village Hall for $1.8 million was defeated, the village needs a larger police station and village hall, Steele says. The Historic Preservation Ordinance is still under study. There have been rumblings about moving the Depression-era post office. "When a post office leaves the downtown, something very important goes with it—a chunk from the heart of the community," Jackie Frank says, firmly.

"There's no question that the village council has a full workload ahead," Steele acknowledges. "Lots of changes are in the air."

≈

But still, life in Chelsea goes on at a slower and more stately pace than lives in many larger communities around the nation.

Every weekday morning, 90-year-old attorney John Keusch leaves his home on Washington Street and walks briskly to his office at Flintoft & Keusch and puts in a good half day's work before he returns home for lunch with his wife Madeleine, whom he met when she was Madeleine Boilore, a teacher in Chelsea's elementary grades. More than 70 years ago, on the eve of the Great Depression, Keusch learned that he had passed the bar. He has been practicing law ever since.

"I have enjoyed the practice of law here in Chelsea—I still do," he says thoughtfully, leaning back in his leather office chair. "I am satisfied with the choices I have made and the choices made for me by events such as the Depression. The experiences were satisfying and I value the many acquaintances I have made. If it weren't for the concerns and talents of Peter C. Flintoft, my legal activity for the past 25 years would not have been possible. He is one of my life's blessings. Nowadays, I am, however, disturbed by some recent legal trends, such as "See Lee Free" huckster TV ads and the multitude of class action suits."

Meanwhile, down the street, the Chelsea Milling Company is being run by fifth generation Holmes', and turns out more than a million boxes of Jiffy Mix a day.

A surprising number of other Chelsea businesses have names that have been around since John Keusch and George Staffan were boys riding their bicycles up and down Main Street. The Staffan-

Mitchell Funeral Home is the oldest business in Chelsea and the eighth oldest in the state. In 1852, carpenter and home builder Frank Staffan built a coffin for a friend's funeral. That service launched a business that would serve generations of Chelsea families.

At the time Staffan was swinging a hammer, John Winans was establishing a general store on Chelsea's new Main Street. No record exists of how long that store stayed in business, but through the last years of the nineteenth century, John's grandson, Larry Winans, ran a drug store that in time would carry a few pieces of jewelry. Gradually, as market demands and local economic conditions permitted, the store evolved into a jewelry store. During the Depression, it shared quarters with the Heydlauff family's appliance store to make ends meet. During World War II, it could find little jewelry to sell. But the Winans family persevered. Now the family's fifth generation is running the business.

The Chelsea State Bank traces its heritage back to 1894, when one of its predecessors, the Kempf Bros. Bank, received its charter. Years after John Mann followed his father into the banking business there, he now serves as president of the bank. The third generation of Schaibles is also associated with the bank. P.J. Schaible Sr. helped launch the predecessor bank in 1921 and served as its cashier. His son, Paul, carried on the family commitment to banking, serving as president of the Chelsea State Bank. The third Paul Schaible also works there.

Palmer Family Ford, which began in business as a gas station and repair shop, holds the oldest Ford franchise in Michigan. The company received the franchise on the very day in 1912 when the *Titanic* sank. Unlike the unfortunate ship, the car business has not only floated through icy economic times, but even flourished. Throughout the last decades of the twentieth century, Palmer Ford kept its historic business location, but expanded to other locations outside of town for truck and used car sales. Bill Weber now runs the company along with his wife, Susie Palmer Weber.

Now a fine-quality furniture and flooring store, Merkel Furniture and Carpet One opened its doors in 1924 as an auto supply, gas and hardware store. When Tim Merkel's grandfather took over the business in the 1940s, it offered farm implements, hardware, and a few pieces of furniture. By the 1950s, the company had shifted its focus to furniture.

Heydlauff's Appliance Center has been on Main Street for more than 60 years, but the business actually began when Lloyd Heydlauff began door-to-door sales and repairs. Eventually he moved into basement quarters, then in with his friend and neighbor as they struggled to weather the Depression together. At the end of World War II, Heydlauff moved into the old Glazier Stove Works office building, a magnificent stone building adjacent to the railroad tracks on the west side of Main Street. In 1970, the store burned to the ground in one of Chelsea's worst fires, but the Heydlauffs rebuilt and reopened. These days, Lloyd's son George and George's three sons run the family business. It continues to flourish, serve children and grandchildren of its original customers, and expand its customer base.

New businesses have been attracted because of the customer base here. In the last year of the old millennium, two hotel chains, an enormous new grocery store, small shopping strips with restaurants and a bookstore appeared. The Clock Tower has been restored and has become headquarters for Sleeping Bear Press and other local enterprises. Realtors and property owners have long waiting lists with names of small businesses hoping to find a storefront on Main Street, another list of large businesses looking for rural settings for major headquarters complexes, and a third waiting list of prospective customers who hope to find a charming old Victorian on a residential street in Chelsea or to build an impressive new home on the shores of one of the nearby lakes.

"Chelsea has always been home to entrepreneurs. It has always attracted business people with dreams and ambition who have set down roots and become a valued part of the community," Ann Feeney, director of Chelsea's Downtown Development Authority and former executive director of the Chelsea Area Chamber of Commerce, told the *Ann Arbor News* recently. "I think it's an immensely healthy sign that Chelsea continues to attract new businesses."

≈

In the 1990s, Walter and Helen Leonard sold the *Chelsea Standard/Dexter Leader* newspapers to the Heritage Company, which owned Manchester's newspaper and a string of others.

Walt Leonard, editor of the *Chelsea Standard* and *Dexter Leader* for 48 years, now lives with his wife in Silver Maples, the retirement community built on lands once farmed by Chelsea's earliest settler, Cyrus Beckwith. Although he spends his days in a wheelchair, his mind is sharp and his feelers are still out for news of what's happening in town. "Once you've been a newspaper man, you're always a newspaper man," he says with a grin.

"The biggest change that I've seen in Chelsea is the disappearance of full-time farmers and the growth of the suburban area," he adds, after contemplating the long list of possibilities. "When I came here right after the war, the farmers were very prosperous and the farms were passed from father to son to grandson. I remember seeing Don Whitaker, who was 85 or so, still working 12 to 15 hour days. Every three years he would trade in a harvester and the equipment had risen in value so much that he bought the new equipment for practically nothing."

Another prominent farming family, the Trinkles, also supervised a large and prosperous farm—"raising mostly dairy cows and the crops to feed them," he recalls. The Leonards' close friends, Dorothy and Anton Nielsen, moved to Chelsea three months before the Leonards did. "They made a good living running the Farmers' Supply, supplying farmers. Nowadays, I imagine, the business caters to suburban homeowners with flower beds and vegetable gardens as much as it does to farmers."

Life on the Farm

THE RODGERS FAMILY

Noon. A rooster cock-a-doodle-doos in the still chill of the country air and the belated wake-up call seems to resound for miles. In response, an invisible but tremendous chorus of sparrows bursts into song from the rafters of barns and outbuildings. Chickens cluck-cluck-cluck. The fuzzy, furry blonde dog howls. An enormously fat pot-bellied pig rolls over and snorts.

Exactly halfway between Chelsea and Dexter on the Dexter-Chelsea Road sits the Rodgers' farm, composed of 100 acres of level fields and woodlands, a newly dredged pond, a cluster of barns and outbuildings, an uncommon conglomeration of farm animals, and a cream-colored Victorian farmhouse topped by a large bell that still calls family members from the fields to dinner.

Cats and kittens roam the property, looking for a tasty luncheon morsel. Somewhere out of sight are rabbit hutches, assertive roosters, a 450 Ferguson tractor a bobcat for hauling manure, hay mower, binder and baler, three rototillers, a plow, cultivator, and mulcher.

A U-shaped barnyard is planted behind the farmhouse. Its windmill stands tall, trying unsuccessfully to shield prying eyes from the old red outhouse it supports.

An aging silver-gray New England-style cow barn faces east; it boasts a new overhang to shelter the half-dozen sheep, ten Scotch Highlander cows, and two ponies.

A gambrel-roofed barn with fading red paint and a new shingle roof looks south, at the road. Its double-wide doors stand open, revealing a peacock perching on an aging red-and-white Massy-Ferguson tractor. Two llamas, two donkeys, a humpbacked zebu, and a couple of chickens and ducks cuddle around the tractor like kittens around a mother cat.

A small granary on wooden legs, a miniature chicken coop, and an assembly of small wooden houses completes the fenced-in barnyard. Off to the side, a modern farmstand sits closer to the road, with a sign announcing that vegetables are for sale here, at Rodgers' Corner.

To make ends meet, Doug Rodgers holds two full-time jobs, one on the farm, the other at the University of Michigan Medical Center. Right now, he is at the hospital. Sue Rodgers works on the farm, works in the house, works part-time at the Chelsea Hospital, works as a substitute bus driver, works as a volunteer in her children's classrooms, works with the county 4-H clubs, and runs the Chelsea Farmers' Market in season.

"I was raised on a 300-acre farm on Guenther Road and the one thing I *didn't* want to do was live and work on a farm," she says with a grin as she settles down for what must be a rare moment of relaxation on her living room couch. Her father, Bob Heller, farmed not only his own 300 acres, but his father's farm next door and a neighbor's land as well. When Sue grew up in the 1960s and 70s, the Hellers raised corn, wheat, oats, hay, and dairy products. Now, Bob Heller plants and harvests corn, wheat, and soybeans and he feeds out cattle.

Sue Heller went away to school, to distance herself from the farm and from farmers. In Grand Rapids, she met Doug Rodgers while they were both studying radiography. He was a city boy from Linden, she was delighted to discover. They married and bought a home in the city on an acre of land.

Soon afterwards, Bob Heller had a calf with hoof problems that needed some loving care, so the Rodgers agreed to take it in.

Next, they inherited an orphaned lamb. Then four chickens.

They moved to Howell and a home on five acres. Doug bought Bob Heller's flock of sheep and tried his hand at construction work. He didn't like it.

The Rodgers moved closer to the farm and Doug spent a year or two farming with his father-in-law. Then, a dozen years ago, after their first baby was born, they learned that the decrepit old Taylor farmhouse on Dexter-Chelsea Road in Lima Township was for sale, complete with 100 acres.

Sold.

It took the six months to make the kitchen, bathroom and a community bedroom inhabitable. "This house is still a work in progress," Sue Rodgers says, glancing around the front room. Two staircases on opposite walls lead to what was originally a divided upstairs—"one staircase and one upstairs for the hired men and boys, the other staircase and upstairs for the farmers' daughters," she explains, adding, "I'm amazed at how many people stop by and tell us that they once lived here." The farmhouse was rented to a succession of tenants during World War II.

What started as a hobby quickly grew into a vocation for Doug Rodgers and his reluctant wife. "Living on a farm is hard, hard work," she says. "Every other day I ask my family if we shouldn't sell. But my husband and the kids love it."

The road from avocation to vocation hasn't been easy. Five years ago, the farm's original barn burned to the ground on Christmas Eve, when the pot-bellied pig knocked a bale of hay onto a heat lamp that was nurturing baby chicks. Fortunately, Sue saw the smoke in time to rescue the animals and the Dexter Fire Department's volunteers were all at the firehouse celebrating the holiday, so they responded instantly, along with Chelsea's firefighters. Otherwise, more of the farm might have gone up in flames.

Once the rubble was cleared away, the Rodgers learned about a barn preservation society that places endangered barns with new owners. They were able to move an old bank barn from the corner of Ann Arbor and Saline Road to their land, thanks to the assistance of the preservation society and an Amish crew of carpenters, who took the barn apart board by board and reassembled it on the Rodgers' property. "It probably cost us the same price as a new barn, but we wanted to maintain the character of the old farm," Sue explains.

Twenty acres are dedicated to raising vegetables. Hay is harvested on additional land. Cattle and sheep have their own pastures. The Rodgers' three children (Ben, 13; Austin, 11; Alyssa, 8) are responsible for chores, animals, and a patch of land where they can raise their own crops.

The farm is large enough to be productive, but not large enough to warrant (or afford) the investment in modern-day planters, combines, threshers, huskers, and plows, the Rodgers believe. "So, from practicality as well as from principle, we buy old—some would say antique—farm equipment, fix it up, and use it," Sue says, as the telephone rings.

She gives the caller directions to the farm, books a spring tour for a Saline preschool class, writes the information on the back of an envelope, then hangs up and explains, "The money these days is in entertainment farming, where a farm offers fresh vegetables for sale, hayrides, haunted pumpkin patches, festivals, crafts, jams and jellies, maybe a petting zoo." The Rodgers do a bit of all this, offering vegetables for sale at the roadside stand, barnyard tours for school children ($1.50 apiece), and fall hayrides out to their pumpkin patch. "It works out so that the revenue from these activities pays for the animals' feed. We can't make this farm fly without working at outside jobs," she says.

Sue Rodgers knows of a newly established farm couple in Manchester who have managed to be self-sufficient on their farm, raising and selling produce, growing potted plants in greenhouses, offering a haunted corn maze in October, and participating in local farmers' markets. "They make a living—but no one will say a good living," she explains. "Your gross income can look good—but when you determine what your net income amounts to, it can be very discouraging."

The Rodgers' vegetable gardens yield beans, peas, carrots, beets, squash, melons, tomatoes, pumpkins, sweet corn, cucumbers, peppers, zucchini, yellow squash, and asparagus, all of which are offered for sale at the stand (with an honor system can for payment) and at the Chelsea Farmers' Market.

Occasionally, at a customer's request, the Rodgers will experiment with a new kind of bean or pepper—"white beans were a real disappointment." Doug Rodgers applies fertilizers to the land, but no sprays to the vegetables. "Our customers would rather pick an occasional worm out of their corn than eat products that were grown with chemical sprays," Sue says.

Her grandmother, Clara Heller, is her inspiration, she adds. Clara Heller was a good person who loved her children and made everything—clothes, food, even all her noodles. "I like the idea of being self-sufficient, but I wish it didn't cost so much," Sue says. "The price of animal feed is high. Gasoline is high. Then there are the modern-day costs that our grandparents didn't have." On her fingers, she counts off the costs of raising and transporting modern-day children, the fees for their participation in sports and camps, taxes, seed costs, and "a hundred other things."

She cans tomatoes, makes jams, stores squash in cool places for the winter, and freezes enough fruits and vegetables to get the family through the winter and spring months until the next year's vegetable crops are ready for harvesting. The Rodgers raise a steer for butchering and buy a pig each year for its bacon, pork chops, and hams. Sue makes bread—but with a breadmaker.

"I think I'm wearing myself out," she admits with a sigh. "My husband tells me to cut back on the vegetables, but the sale of the vegetables helps to pay our bills.

"My three sisters are all professionals with 401Ks and stocks. Those are their investments for the future. This land is our investment for the future. I can't see sitting on 100 fallow acres. I would feel as though we weren't allowing the land to do what it was intended to do. We believe that we have a responsibility to maintain this land."

Out With The Old, In With The New?

Many of Chelsea's farmers have not been as fortunate as the village's downtown entrepreneurs in maintaining their business and their way of life. Developers and realtors are pounding at their doors continuously. Public utilities challenge them for rights-of-way upon their property. When Interstate 94 slashed through Washtenaw County, it divided many farms and exposed them to development challenges these farmers had never anticipated facing.

1990s Main Street looking south.

Courtesy McKinley Commercial Properties

Mobile home parks. Industrial centers. Hotels. Mobile home parks. Residential developments. New grocery stores. Mobile home parks. Convenience stores. Zip strips. A gravel pit. A bypass. All these projects are covetously eyeing farmers' fields.

"The demand for growth is unbelievable," observes Lima Township Supervisor Gary Adams. He speaks for the entire Chelsea area when he says he is bombarded with development proposals.

In response to the tremendous demand for the land, the four townships ringing Chelsea united with the village to form an innovative and groundbreaking team to pool resources and plan wisely for the future—together.

The Chelsea Area Planning Team, CAPT for short, is composed of representatives from the municipalities sending children to schools in Chelsea: Lima, Dexter, Lyndon, and Sylvan townships as well as the village. The Chamber of Commerce, Board of Education, library, fire authority, and other area service organizations also send representatives to the monthly meetings.

"Everywhere you look, there are things happening, land being bulldozed, phones ringing off the hook," Adams observes. "The question is: how do we make coherent sense of it all? And, with limited personnel and increasing pressure from the courts, how do we accomplish all that needs to be done? Our answer was to form CAPT."

It was an idea whose time had come—and it came from different sources. Anne Feeney, former head of the Chelsea Chamber of Commerce and director of Chelsea's Downtown Development Authority, suggested pooling resources, ideas, and plans at about the time that Maryann Noah, supervisor of Lyndon Township, attended a statewide convention on land use plans.

"For three days I heard nothing but townships being blasted and blamed for suburban sprawl," Noah says. "The speakers and agencies didn't look at the other side of the coin: that the courts have made every township responsible for providing high-density housing, mobile home parks, residential settings, and commercial development. It made no sense to me to blame the townships when we all know that the courts will step in if we don't accommodate all those requirements."

At first, it was a temporary union with fellow Chelsea area municipalities to dispute an easement for Toledo Pipeline. A 120-foot easement already existed between Stockbridge and Freedom Township, but the new company didn't want to share that easement. They proposed to take 206 acres of forest land, bisect a number of farms—among them General Dwight Beach's farm—and take 60-foot strips from home lots as small as two acres.

Together, the municipal officials jointly protested, filing the protest as an intervening party. The Public Service Commission told them that they were the first townships to come to them with an objection to the pipeline route. They won their case and saw the kind of impact they could have if they were united. CAPT soon became a working reality.

In May of 1999, more than a hundred residents of Chelsea and the surrounding area gathered in the new high school to discuss the direction people thought their community should take.

"It was a fascinating process," says District One County Commissioner Joe Yekulis. "We broke into 10 groups to pinpoint issues, then put together one rough map for the entire area, based on all input, to create a vision of how we wanted to build our community. We tried to put growth in logical areas."

The municipal officials took that rough map to the Washtenaw County Metropolitan Planning Commission and asked for assistance in drawing up a logical master plan for the growth, development, and preservation of the entire area. Their timing was crucial. CAPT was anxious to put their master plan into place before another zoning issue arose or another developer came along.

Dexter township supervisor, Robert Tetens notes, "CAPT is a remarkable example of intergovernmental collaboration, but it is just the beginning."

Will 175 years of farming disappear entirely from the landscape surrounding Chelsea?

"I don't think we can preserve agriculture as we know it," Dresselhouse suggests. "The pressures for development are too great and we have no right to dictate to farmers what they should or should not do with their land. What we can do is plan for the future wisely and preserve open space wherever we can."

～

"Farmers are under tremendous pressure these days—and farming itself is in jeopardy," says Lima Township Supervisor Gary Adams, a retired engineer who raises beefalo on 220 acres of land. "We are all constantly being approached about development. The township gets calls every day. We have farmers who need to split their property up in order to survive—for a time, for the short term. There is also a lot of interest in the preservation of open space. Everywhere you look, new things are happening. The question is: how do you make coherent sense of everything, and what is the best thing to do?"

Despite the booming economy in southeast Michigan, farmers face Depression-level prices, with no relief in sight. Meanwhile, property values are rising so that young people can't afford to go into farming—or stay in farming, Adams points out.

Sylvan Township Supervisor Gerald Dresselhouse owns 85 acres and raises beef and grains. "I farm, but I don't call myself a farmer," he is quick to say, explaining, "I don't depend on farming for my

1990s Main Street looking north.

© 1999 Andrew Sacks

livelihood." After watching what is happening in Sylvan, he has concluded, "We won't be able to preserve farming here, but we can preserve open space, by having developers set aside 10, 20, or 40 acres. I hate to see it—and to say it—but you can't farm on 200, 300, or even 400 acres if everyone on your periphery is residential. The farmer just will not be able to survive. Newcomers won't accept the smell of a manure field, the dust from plowing, the noise from harvesting crops late at night, and the grain dryers running all night long. Eventually they will make life miserable for the farmer."

Beyond those incompatible lifestyle situations comes the fact that if a farmer is the only one left in a township, he has to go far afield for machinery, parts, and fertilizer—not to mention fellowship. "Farming requires an infrastructure, with services available in close proximity," Dresselhouse points out.

"I don't foresee an end to the encroachment of development," he says, shaking his head. "It's gone too far for us. Right now in the Chelsea area, the big focus is on the land."

The land.

The land is what brought the earliest settlers to the area. And it is the land that will determine its future.

About Memories

Chelsea was ushered into the twentieth century in style, by a man who seemed larger than life then, and continues to today. In October 1999, the *Ann Arbor News*, which had been founded by Frank Porter Glazier, carried an article that reviewed his life as though he were still alive today. His name is still a household word in Chelsea.

An extraordinary entrepreneur, consummate politician, empire builder, and member of Michigan's uppermost social circle, Frank Glazier's impact on his hometown spanned the nineteenth and twentieth centuries and continues to influence Chelsea history, even as businesses belonging to a new generation take up headquarters in his Clock Tower building, as people discuss renovating and preserving the streets he once knew, and as residents argue about what is best for the village's rapidly changing future.

Without Elisha Congdon's vision and drive, and without Frank P. Glazier's vision, drive, ambition, and commitment to his hometown, Chelsea may well have faded into the state of semiobscurity that so many of the neighboring villages have experienced in the past three decades. But Chelsea is still upheld by the vision of its two strong-willed, hardheaded founding fathers.

Congdon's vision carved Chelsea out of the wilderness, launched the village structure and organization, established the grid of streets and services, lured and diverted transportation networks into town. Thirty years after he died, Frank Porter Glazier appeared on the scene as Congdon's spiritual heir and Chelsea still has one resident who remembers him personally. She called him "Papa."

Ninety years old and blind, Geraldine Kraft lives on the third floor of the Chelsea Methodist Retirement Home. Her memories linger fondly over what she calls, in a teary voice, her "best years," the years when she was the grandchild being raised by Henrietta and Frank P. Glazier.

She was born several years after the financial scandal that sent her "Papa" to prison. The father/grandfather she knew was a tender,

Like many of their friends, Frank Glazier's granddaughter Geraldine and her first husband eloped to Indiana soon after the war, impatient to get on with their lives.

Courtesy of Geraldine Glazier Kraft

fun-loving friend who wiped away her tears, listened for Santa on rooftops, and loved her very much.

The family never spoke to her of her grandfather's financial difficulties, though she heard bits and pieces from servants or cousins. One day after Frank P. Glazier had died and not long before her grandmother would die, Henrietta Glazier sat down with Geraldine and the man she expected her to marry and told them the whole story. "It was like dragging something very hard and heavy out of her heart," the girl thought at the time.

"I don't talk about my grandfather's troubles," Geraldine Kraft says. "It was hushed over here in town and the people forgot the good that was done. But my grandparents were wonderful, kind, caring, lovable people and I would like to have people remember them that way."

She rests for a moment, embraced by memories 80 or more years in the distance, then sighs and says, "All this reminiscing is very, very tiring. And it's very emotional. I won't sleep tonight, thinking of all the people and places and happenings of so long ago."